Insuring Industrial
and Process Machinery

THE WORSHIPFUL COMPANY
OF INSURERS

CII

THE CHARTERED
INSURANCE
INSTITUTE

The Insurance Institute of London
gratefully acknowledges the assistance of
The Worshipful Company of Insurers and
The Chartered Insurance Institute
in the publication of this book.

THE
INSURANCE INSTITUTE
OF LONDON

Report of Research Study Group 237

Insuring Industrial and Process Machinery

Published by
The Insurance Institute of London

The contents of this report are not
intended to be a full and authoritative
statement of the law or practice
relating to any of the issues covered;
readers are recommended to take
appropriate professional advice upon
any issue which may affect them.

Statements and opinions in this report
represent the majority view of the
Advanced Study Group and are not
necessarily in accordance with those of
its individual members, their employers
or the Institute.

ISBN 0 900493 79 8

Printed by Cromwell Press Limited
Trowbridge, Wiltshire

The Insurance Institute of London
20 Aldermanbury, London EC2V 7HY

Telephone 020 7600 1343
Fax   020 7600 6857
E-mail   iil.london@cii.co.uk
Web Page www.iilondon.co.uk

Objectives

The objectives of the Insurance Institute of London are:

**"To raise the levels of professional knowledge
of those working in insurance in London, to
assist members in their career development
and to support and reinforce the role and
work of the CII."**

The Institute achieves its objectives through its lecture
and visits programmes, its journal and its advanced
studies scheme. With its 13,000 members, London is
by far the largest institute amongst the Chartered
Insurance Institute's 90 local and associated institutes.

Origins

The Insurance Institute of London was established on
18 June 1907 following the initiative of the president
of the Federation of Insurance Institutes of Great
Britain and Ireland, who was also general manager
of the Commercial Union.

In 1912 a Royal Charter was granted and the
Chartered Insurance Institute came into being.
Over the subsequent years the London Institute
handed over its library, museum, insurance courses
and membership administration responsibilities to
the CII and, in 1934, moved to the Insurance Hall,
20 Aldermanbury, which was specially built for
their combined purposes.

Advanced Studies

Advanced Studies have become a well established
and important part of the Insurance Institute of
London's activities. Under the guidance of the
Advanced Studies Committee, study groups are formed
to examine and report on new or emerging subjects
not covered by existing publications and which are
seen as being particularly important and relevant to
the insurance industry. These reports are highly
regarded and are sold world-wide. They are
acknowledged as providing a significant contribution
to insurance education and much knowledge and
experience can be gained from membership of a
study group.

Members of Advanced Study Group 237

Leader
Stephen Coward (Copenhagen Reinsurance Group)

Secretary
Ann Foss (Sunley Turriff Holdings Limited)

Pat Beckett BA, CEng, MIMechE, MInstNDT (Beckett Whelan)
Robert Glynn BSc Hons (Chem.Eng), ACII, Chartered Insurance Practitioner,
    MCIArb, Accredited Mediator (Marsh Limited)
John Hanson MA (Oxon) (Barlow Lyde & Gilbert)
Jason Harris BSc (Chubb Insurance Company of Europe)
Peter Kelly (AXA Global Risks UK)
Michael Quy (Willis Limited)
Joe Telford CEng, FIMarE (Crawford & Company)
Philip Veale (Aon Group)

A profile of each of the above members appears at Appendix 2

Contents

Chapter 4
Underwriting aspects — business interruption

Chapter 5
Loss prevention

Chapter 6
Scope of insurance cover

Chapter 7
Taking-over: putting recently erected machinery into use

Chapter 8
Assessment of maximum exposure

Chapter 9
Power generation

Chapter 10
Oil, gas and petrochemicals

Chapter 11
Pulp and paper plants

Chapter 12
Cement plants

Chapter 13
Mineral extraction and primary processing

Chapter 14
Iron and steel

Chapter 15
Integrated circuit manufacturing plants

Chapter 16
Other manufacturing industries

Chapter 17
Cross-industry topics

Chapter 18
Claims

Appendix 1
Power generation — risk areas and risk mitigation

Appendix 2
Member's profiles

Preface

The publication of this Study Report is the result of the lengthy and thorough deliberation of The Insurance Institute of London's Advanced Study Group 237 that has addressed the subject of 'Insuring Industrial and Process Machinery'. The Study Report tackles many facets that come under this heading and focuses on machinery and equipment used in an industrial or manufacturing environment. Its main subjects are the physical exposures, the treatment of risk and their potential impact on the industries which rely on the machinery used.

The Study Report does not deal with other branches of machinery usage and associated insurance, such as marine, aviation or aerospace. In the context of industrial applications of machinery and equipment, it covers a wide part of the production and manufacturing spectrum, ranging from large-scale power and energy generation plants through oil, gas and petrochemical industry processing, cement manufacture and electronics to light manufacturing industries.

It is the aim of the Study Report that it should be of value to a wide range of people, both inside and outside the insurance market, whether they already have a good grasp of the subject through past experience or are relative newcomers to the subject. The Study Report contains a blend of technical subjects — insurance, engineering and risk management — and therefore should be of interest to machinery users and operators, suppliers, maintenance engineers, risk managers and plant investors and those in the insurance industry. In places, the subject is complex and the use of technical engineering or chemical terms is unavoidable. However, it is hoped that process descriptions and their associated exposures are outlined in a simple style that is readily understandable and that the information given can be put to practical and pragmatic use.

Structure of the Study Report

This Study Report is structured to be useful to the general reader who has a broad interest in the subject and also to those whose interest is centred on one specific topic. The layout should allow the reader to navigate around the various topics with relative ease and find the specific area of interest without difficulty. While each chapter is an integral part of the whole, any one may be read in isolation and be a useful reference for the reader with narrower interests.

The first part of the Study Report (Chapters 1–8) deals with insurance and underwriting issues, including loss prevention; the next part (Chapters 9–16) concentrates on specific industries and their individual risk and exposure characteristics; and the concluding part deals with cross-industry topics (Chapter 17) and claims (Chapter 18).

To a limited degree, an element of repetition has been allowed from one chapter to another, the recurring topics of loss prevention, maintenance and critical risk exposures being the prime examples. For the reader of the entire report 'from cover to cover' this may be found mildly distracting, although it should also serve to reinforce the importance of the points being made.

The chapters addressing specific manufacturing and process industries describe the principal processes and major feedstocks involved in order to provide a basic understanding of the potential exposures that they might present. By explaining how things work, the critical areas and their associated risks can be evaluated and placed by the reader in a true and realistic context.

The key industries included are

- power production plants
- oil, gas and petrochemical plants
- pulp and paper plants
- cement plants
- mineral extraction and primary processing plants
- iron and steel plants
- integrated circuit manufacturing plants.

Chapter 16 deals with other manufacturing industries in summary format; this includes *inter alia* the smelting, printing, glass, sugar and textile industries, where the main emphasis is on their particular exposures.

Electricity — global, pan-industrial demand

The most comprehensively covered subject is power generation (Chapter 9).

The production of electric power is a worldwide subject and it will be of general interest to those whose main interests are in one of the other heavy manufacturing industries mentioned above. All industrial processes depend on electricity in order to function and all forms of mainstream generation are dealt with, together with their individual characteristics and exposures. Thus, Power generation probably contains some points of reference not only for those readers whose main interest is power production but also for those looking into industries that take power from a national grid.

Of course, many other industries generate their own private power through necessity or as an alternative to the national grid. This own-generating capability may range from the use of small diesel generator sets producing a few kilowatts of power to large-scale combined heat and power units using gas/steam turbines of more than 200 megawatts output.

By dealing with the different forms of electricity generation (*e.g.* hydroelectric, nuclear electric) that are found across the world, this chapter should offer useful information to a widely-spread international readership.

Issues critical to all industries

The chapter on power generation deals with those issues that are critical (to that particular industry and its insurers), many of which are also applicable to other heavy industrial processes. Examples are rotating machinery, transformers, pressure vessels and control panels, all of which can be found in many industries together with their attendant exposures. Likewise, the safety and maintenance practices in a power station may provide a useful reference for other industries. The content of Chapter 9 should therefore be found interesting to those operating outside the power industry itself.

Also focused on power generation, Appendix 1, 'Power generation — risk areas and risk mitigation', is a detailed chart showing specific areas of risk and suggested means of mitigation. Again, this information is likely to have a valid application to a wider industrial base and is therefore also recommended general reading.

Focus on machinery insurance

While this is the first time that an Advanced Study Group of The Insurance Institute of London has produced a Report specifically on the topic of insuring machinery, the published Reports of other ASGs address other interrelated property insurance subjects, notably that of ASG 208B on Construction Insurance (published November 1999).

This Study Report therefore concentrates on the particular exposures presented by machinery and its use in the industrial world. As such, it avoids dwelling on insurance subjects already addressed in other ASG Reports, or where there is already an abundance of written material of a broader base readily available from other sources, including the Chartered Insurance Institute.

Where a particular aspect or point concerns something specific or peculiar to machinery and equipment, this Study Report covers it in detail. Thus it does not, for example, deal with the basic principles of business interruption but concentrates on specific issues relating to business interruption following a machinery failure, which are potentially quite different to those following a building fire.

Acknowledgements

On behalf of The Insurance Institute of London, the members of Advanced Study Group 237 acknowledge with appreciation the support and assistance provided by

- Factory Mutual Insurance Company for its invaluable information in respect of modern clean room technology

- Blue Circle Industries PLC and The Rugby Cement Group PLC for invaluable information provided in respect of cement plants

- SCOR UK for hosting meetings in the early days and for providing some secretarial support

- Copenhagen Reinsurance for providing facilities for working sessions of the Group

- Aon Group for sponsoring the design for the front cover

- the various friends and colleagues who assisted with proof-reading and sampling

- R.W. Jordan, a former editor of *Lloyd's Log*, for his additional editorial work on behalf of the IIL in preparing this Study Report for publication.

1 Introduction

1.1 Machinery dependency in the business world

There are very few people involved in industry and commerce who are not working, in some way, with machinery or equipment and who are not reliant on this investment for the success of their business. Just as their workforce is required to perform to a high standard in order to succeed, the same is true of the performance and efficiency of their machinery and equipment upon which the business is similarly dependent.

Such a business would suffer direct and perhaps indirect financial losses in the event of damage to or failure of its machinery or equipment. Thus the importance of correct maintenance and service is well known to many users and there is a close link between loss prevention and an insurance policy that provides protection and security against the unexpected happening; this is a key area explored in this Study Report.

1.2 Technological change

In the modern world, with rapid and accelerating technological change, the development time from 'drawing board' to full-scale commercial production has shrunk considerably for many machines. At the same time, design parameters are becoming ever-more ambitious and novel, as industry at large strives for a greater competitive edge. Many new and relatively unknown materials and methods are now used and this trend will continue into the future, perhaps at an accelerating pace. Against this trend there is greater awareness of safety and health issues, whether driven by legislation or otherwise.

Each of these factors has a bearing on the subject matter of this Study Report. The human element remains an important factor as tasks are also becoming more and more demanding in the interests of efficiency and production targets. The relationship between these influences and the risk of machinery failure is also explored and developed in this Report.

1.3 Machinery damage and failures

The core subject of this Study Report is machinery failure and its effects. However, to think of this merely in terms of machinery breakdown insurance would be too narrow a concept, although insurance covering 'sudden and unforeseen damage' is a recurring theme.

'All risks' insurance is discussed as many of these policies intend to give some form of response in the event of a machinery failure alongside the traditional cover for fire, lightning, explosion, aircraft and allied perils. In some instances, the machinery failure risk is the target exposure (fire and environmental perils being less exposed) whereas in other cases it should realistically be considered as the secondary exposure. Where two different insurance policies ('fire/perils' and 'machinery') are in force, the interface between them is also considered in this Study Report.

1.4 Historical background

It is worth remembering the origins of machinery insurance and to contrast the exposures presented by the Industrial Revolution against those of the modern world.

The first specialist machinery insurance company was formed during the mid 1850s, at the time of the rapid mechanisation of the textile industry, the birth of the transport industry, the greater exploitation of rich mineral deposits of coal and iron ore, and, significantly, the use of steam power.

However, very serious problems were experienced with many early steam boiler explosions that resulted in loss of life and widespread damage to property.

A brief chronology shows that, in January 1855, 'The Association for the Prevention of Steam Explosion and for Effecting Economy in the Raising and Use of Steam' was founded.

Among the pioneers of this business there was strong disagreement as to whether it was desirable for the inspectors of steam boilers to supplement their services by also providing an insurance indemnity. Some leading Victorians saw a moral conflict in 'rewarding' those owners whose boilers suffered catastrophic failure, believing 'punishment' should be a more fitting response.

Robert Longridge argued in favour of providing insurance and resigned his membership of the Association over this issue. In January 1859, he founded 'The Steam Boiler Assurance Company', the first specialist machinery insurer, of which he was the Chief Engineer and General Manager.

In 1859, a registration system had been introduced for steam boilers on the same principles as those prescribed by Lloyd's for ships, with new boilers being inspected at the manufacturers' premises.

With a growing public concern in safety and accident prevention and with much of the new industries centred in north-west England, in 1869 the Association became 'The Manchester Steam Users' Association for the Prevention of Boiler Explosions and the Attainment of Economy in the Application of Steam'. This rather long-winded name was soon shortened to 'The Manchester Steam Users' Association'.

In 1878, 'The Engine Insurance Company' was formed to provide inspection and insurance of plant which fell outside the remit of the boiler company. A merger took place soon after and 'The Engine and Boiler Insurance Company Limited' was registered in the same year.

The passing of the first Factory and Workshops Act in 1901 was regarded as the Manchester Steam Users' crowning glory as it made the inspection of industrial boilers obligatory. This boosted the growth in the number of policyholders.

Towards the end of the nineteenth century, electric power began to grow as a means of providing motive power and at the same time the use of small gas engines was becoming more popular. In 1904, the words 'British' and 'Electrical' were added to the company's name and thus the 'British Engine Boiler and Electrical Insurance Company Limited' was established.

1.5 The modern world

One may contrast the exposures of the Industrial Revolution with those faced by modern industrialists and their insurers. The basic function of some machines may have changed very little but the rate of improvement — particularly in efficiency and, towards the end of the twentieth century, in 'environmental friendliness' — has continued apace.

The widespread reliance on the microprocessor in all industries represents a distinction between the past and the present. Its role is clearly seen in all walks of commercial life and in the financial sector and it also plays a vital role in manufacturing and process industries. The microprocessor industry itself continues to undergo rapid change in the search for greater efficiencies in capacity, speed and miniaturisation.

In terms of risk and insurance the potential problems associated with date recognition have been well publicised throughout the developed world. The computer programmers of the technological boom-period of the late 1970s and the 1980s saved memory space in their 'microchips' by shortening the year reference in a date to six two characters, *e.g.* 31 March 1999 would be expressed as 31/03/99. However, computers may fail to function correctly or close down altogether when the year is shown in this way, particularly when '2000' is shortened to '00'. Governments, regulators, industry groups and individual companies continue to take steps to upgrade systems to avoid the potentially serious problems that would otherwise result from widespread computer malfunction.

One of the guiding principles of insurance is that of fortuity. Events that are predicted to occur with certainty cannot be the subject of insurance indemnity. However, the consequences of the event may result in unexpected loss or damage and the resultant costs may be recoverable through insurance. The issue of correct data recognition by a computer or a computer-driven or controlled system provides an obvious example.

The demand for greater efficiency and integration in the next generation of mechanical systems is ever-increasing and financial pressures arise from the need to contain costs. New methods of selling machinery and financing its purchase are being devised and this Study Report shows how insurance has an increasingly important part to play in this refreshed market.

1.6 Future developments

This Study Report cannot predict the focus or direction of any particular industry nor the specific risk solutions that will be needed for future commercial success. However, it does address the trends that have been seen in recent years and shows how the insurance industry may be able to provide support for manufacturers, owners, operators and financiers of all forms of machinery.

Economics is one driving force for the future and insurance products are available to support development and operational risks in the most cost-effective way. Occasionally, these risks are better addressed in ways that have still to be developed, but the Study Report examines the driving forcesers within the insurance underwriting arena so that the reader may see how best to appreciate such risks in the future.

The interface between the development of new engineering products and the insurance industry is one of the most challenging and one that can easily affect the future market share and success of a product. This Study Report addresses the technicalities of each major industry so that the reader may draw such parallels as are reasonable, in order to help meet the challenges of the future.

2   Reasons to insure machinery

2.1   Introduction

The reasons for arranging insurance against the risks arising from industrial and process machinery may be obvious to the reader. In many respects they are no different from the reasons that private individuals take out insurance on their own personal property and possessions. In basic terms, it is a matter of transferring varying degrees of risk to another party — at a cost.

2.2   Capital expenditure

The high capital cost of machinery and its importance to the production processes heighten the influences that make insurance a viable solution to the risks faced by owners, shareholders, investors and customers of the business.

Another important influence is that of the banks that may be granting substantial loans to finance the business and the direct purchase of machinery. In this case they often require the security provided through insurance. Banks are generally risk averse and will encourage their borrowers to protect their respective interests, and insurance is likely to be an important component. Indeed, it may be a precondition to a loan being granted (or renewed) that adequate insurance is kept in force.

2.3   Budgeting; financing of the unexpected

An advantage offered by insurance is that it is provided a known cost, at least for the duration of the cover, which may typically be 12 months to 36 months.

This known cost can be built into the business's budget and corporate plans. This contrasts to the unknown and potentially high cost of carrying the risk entirely in the balance sheet. In extreme cases, these unknown costs could even cripple the business, either through the direct costs of repair or the loss of trade and customer base which ultimately could lead to insolvency. Insurance provides a stabilising factor for the finance officers, business planners and proprietors.

Through the independent security provided by insurance, funds can be made available quickly so that repairs are completed with the minimum of delay. This can be helpful in reducing any period of business interruption, which is vital for the future viability of any trading concern.

In considering the cost-effectiveness of insurance it should be noted that the premium cost is usually deductible from the taxable profits of the business.

In general terms, an alternative to insurance would be to build up a fund to deal with future events or accidents. Knowing what size the fund should be and what taxation implications arise are not questions easily answered.

Of course, the money in such a fund could not be used for other business development purposes, which could therefore have a poor effect on expansion plans and the like. To contain the amount of money set aside, a self-insured fund may be used to deal with 'routine' losses but with an insurance policy taken out for 'catastrophe' losses only.

A large corporation has the option of establishing a captive insurance company to handle its own risks, in part or in total. In certain 'offshore' legal and tax environments the captive can yield very attractive financial advantages.

2.4   Technical support

In addition to providing funds, insurers with a wide client base, international experience and contacts may be able to assist in expediting a repair in locating key components and mobilising repairers. Some insurers (and reinsurers) have established strong relationships with leading manufacturers and this can benefit the individual insured who may not be so well-connected in the commercial world. Industrial and process machinery insurers have their own technical experience to draw upon (partly because they handle the similar risks of many other insureds) and this can prove invaluable when determining the best course of action after a loss has been suffered.

This technical know-how from machinery insurers can also be invaluable with regard to loss prevention, again using the knowledge gained from a wider experience, including that learned from the past claims of other insureds.

2.5   Security

In a joint venture business, the individual partners will enjoy greater security from the independent protection provided by insurance. Customers of the business may also take comfort and increased confidence in the trading relationship, knowing that it is adequately insured.

When machinery is leased or is on hire, the owner will undoubtedly require a suitable level of financial security from the lessee or hirer. Insurance is typically the only acceptable security and effecting adequate insurance may therefore be an obligation under the contract.

3   Underwriting aspects — material damage

3.1   Introduction

The object of this chapter and the next is to highlight those areas of risk that are evaluated by professionals in the insurance industry when considering the insurance of machinery. The degree of evaluation will vary according to the type of machine or industry that is being assessed. In all cases, such an evaluation will be necessary in order to gain an accurate appreciation of the risk and this will allow appropriate premium, terms and conditions to be determined.

In both chapters, these areas are addressed under a variety of headings, allowing direct reference to a point of particular interest; this approach has led to a certain amount of unavoidable repetition as some topics overlap with others. This chapter deals primarily with physical loss or material damage whereas supplementary information and specific underwriting aspects relating to business interruption arising from machinery damage or failure are discussed in Chapter 4.

3.2   Key underwriting information

To begin the underwriting evaluation process, reliable information needs to be collected that is relevant to the particular physical risk. This information may be obtained through a proposal form completed by suitably authorised officers of the prospective insured, through a survey by the underwriter, or from a combination of the two. It will need to be periodically updated in the case of renewable insurance. Each risk characteristic will then need to be considered on its particular merits, depending upon the extent and scope of insurance cover in question.

Key underwriting information falls within the following broad categories, each of which is addressed in detail in this chapter:

- the nature of the industry and the particular business

- identification and situation of perils; location of risk

- description and type of machinery, its characteristics and the maintenance and repair arrangements

- extent of cover; sums insured and deductibles

- matching insurance requirements with the insurance available

- declaration of historical information and other material facts, including claims records, incidents not necessarily resulting in claims, previous insurances.

3.3   The industry and the insured business

3.3.1   The type of business

By their nature, certain businesses rely more heavily on machinery for their success whereas in others it is people who have thegreatest bearing on the result. The broad distiction is between 'industrial/manufacturing' and 'commercial/service' industries. Even within the latter sector, machinery and other equipment plays an important part in the 'production line' and in the age of information technology and modern communications all businesses have become reliant on these techniques to some extent to remain competitive.

However in the industrial/manufacturing sector, the vital role played by machinery is perhaps more obvious, although the selection, operation and maintenance influences are essentially dependent on human choices. Therefore, it is the combination of these factors that have a bearing on the success or otherwise of any business, whatever its nature.

3.3.2 Economic conditions; the financial health of the insured

Machinery insurers, like most commercial insurers, are likely to have been affected by adverse underwriting results stemming from distressed risk exposures and insureds who may be experiencing financial difficulties.

Prudent underwriters would be well advised to explore this area of risk hazard when considering new proposals (or at the time of renewal for existing business), depending on the economic climate of the territory concerned. In times of recession, there appears to be little doubt that there is a direct and negative relationship between recession and the frequency of fraudulent acts, particularly those involving arson and theft. Spurious claims pursued under insurance policies might prove to be a last resort attempt at a 'way out'.

Unfavourable economic conditions, lack of business confidence and difficult trading conditions are likely to mean machinery is retained longer. These conditions may discourage capital investment in new machinery until such time as the economic situation improves. The repair of old machinery, the availability of spare parts and which repairers are to carry out the work all need to be considered carefully by underwriters. Financial restrictions may enforce a saving of operational costs that could adversely affect general maintenance and the frequency of service intervals/turnarounds and thus potentially increase the risk of machinery failure.

3.4 Identification and situation of perils

3.4.1 The external environment

The location of machinery will influence the risk of loss or damage if items are kept exposed to the natural elements rather than housed under cover in a building. However, items kept under a single roof without adequate firebreaks could for example cause unexpected accumulation in values at risk without adequate fire detection and/or extinguishment systems being in place. Depending on the type of equipment and business occupancy, the heat and smoke generated by an outbreak of fire could cause as much damage to machinery through contamination and the like as would have been the direct effects of the fire itself.

Irrespective of the physical arrangements, certain elemental perils such as flood, wind, frost or water exposure will render the machinery vulnerable, particularly when at times weather patterns become erratic and unpredictable. Some locations may warrant a specific form of protection depending on the type of machinery being operated. The indirect effects of lightning during severe storm conditions has been known to damage sophisticated electronic machinery that has not been fitted with appropriate arresting equipment or is housed in buildings with inadequate electrical earthing arrangements.

Ideally, machinery of a general nature should be properly housed in buildings of standard construction formed of substantially non-combustible materials.

It is essential, particularly in the case of mobile or portable items of machinery, to assess the security arrangements to deter theft, malicious damage or attempt thereat, as highlighted later in this chapter.

3.4.2 Fire and allied perils

Machinery is exposed to damage from fire and allied perils in the same way as the premises in which it is housed and therefore the nature and extent of fire protection, detection systems and fire fighting facilities are all of utmost importance. Explosion, whether due to chemical reaction or to excessive pressure, can have catastrophic effects on the machinery and its surroundings.

Often, machinery is the source of the outbreak of fire through electrical faults, short circuits, fuel or lubricant leakage, abnormally high temperatures or rupture. Such a fire can spread to other parts of the premises and other machines through cable tunnels, conduits or ducting and this risk can be minimised by suitable seals and fire protections.

Boilers and other pressure vessels present an obvious exposure to explosion, including flue gas explosion and collapse.

Although perhaps less exposed than building structures, machines and their foundations are susceptible to earthquake hazards, where they are present, whether through direct damage or misalignment. This is particularly relevant to high speed rotating equipment.

All these risk exposures should be evaluated having regard to the protection provided, the standards of housekeeping, the operators' general attitude towards loss prevention and the anticipated frequency of incidents.

3.4.3 Theft

The concerns for safeguarding machinery from theft and related crime damage will be addressed by post-survey requirements and recommendations, part of which will be influenced by the underwriters of the main property and contents risk, as well as the machinery underwriters, if different.

Proprietary deterrents should be employed wherever possible and, where appropriate, mobile items should be immobilised. Spare parts stored by the operator should be given similar protection. Larger static machinery does not present the same risk characteristics and each risk should be assessed on individual merit.

It is the responsibility of the insured to safeguard its machinery adequately and to take reasonable precautions to prevent loss or damage as though it were uninsured. The insurance policy should not be taken as an excuse for inadequate care and control as a result of poor housekeeping and operating standards.

3.4.4 Security

Security measures are especially important if the insurance provides cover against theft, malicious damage or the acts of malicious persons. Due consideration must be given to machinery that is mobile and located outdoors, or static and situated inside buildings or working areas. Highly portable equipment can be particularly exposed and the growth of microprocessor-related theft is a good illustration. Indeed, in certain territories, electronic machinery or its 'cannibalised' components is a prime example of this problem and underwriters would be well-advised to introduce appropriate requirements for stringent housekeeping standards of safekeeping.

Clearly, different requirements need to be assessed to meet individual insured's requirements in the form of alarm systems, physical deterrents and barriers, immobilisation systems, warning signs, security patrols and the like.

3.4.5 Moral hazard

The primary object of insurance is to return the insured to the same financial position as it would have enjoyed had the insured incident not occurred. Insurance is a means of financial safeguard should the unforeseen occur; it does not compensate for inevitable occurrences.

Underwriters ought, when considering proposals and at other opportune times, to take into account the morality of individual insureds, including their working practices, housekeeping standards, workforce relationships and all other aspects of the business and the methods of management. These aspects will assist in the correct evaluation of risks and provide a better understanding of the business operation. Information obtained regarding previous incident history, loss experience and its causes will also assist in ascertaining how the insured's business operates.

3.4.6 Location of machinery

Depending on the scope of cover to be offered, consideration needs to be given to the location and environment in which the machinery to be insured is housed, *i.e.* within permanent premises or, being mobile or portable, at any of a variety of workplaces.

3.4.6.1 Machinery in permanent premises

Often, the property (fire) insurance arranged will relieve the machinery insurer (if different) of the fire and related perils exposure of machinery permanently located within a factory or other workplace but on many occasions an 'all risks' comprehensive form of cover is required.

A purpose-built environment presents a better prospect than where machinery is incorporated into a building that originally had other uses or had been designed for something else. Likewise, accessibility (including accessibility to carry out repair work), ease of maintenance, loading facilties, a clean atmosphere and optimum layout are all-important factors.

The physical characteristics of the exposure may be ascertained through a survey of the plant or by obtaining a fully completed questionnaire from the proposer, to allow the following risk factors to be assessed by the underwriter:

- the age of the building and its current condition

- the materials used in the construction of the building

- the number of floors, the siting of machinery and its imposed loadings

- the separation within the premises and the existence of fire breaks and their construction

- the suitability of buildings for business operations intended, taking into account types of processes, materials and products

- the standard of building maintenance and housekeeping and whether all obligations have been satisfied under current statutory regulations; *e.g.* in the United Kingdom, the examination of fixed installations for pressure systems and compliance with wiring regulations

- the on-site security arrangements

- the nature and standards of fire detection and protection.

The risk to machinery underwriters might well be affected by accidental extraneous damage brought about by poor housekeeping and cramped conditions, introducing the hazards of impact, collision, dropping and the like.

Certain machines will be supported by other dedicated machinery installed to assist their operation (as in the case of an overhead travelling crane loading a furnace) and this in itself can introduce extra hazards that should not be disregarded in the overall assessment.

Basement locations are often unsuitable for machinery without specific control features being in place. This type of environment may lead to water damage due to the 'tanking' effect in the event of accumulation of water in the building, rising water table levels, or backing-up of drains which may have become restricted or blocked altogether.

Where there is a concentration of electrical or electronic machinery in a building, the integrity of the weather protection and any roof-mounted water tanks also becomes significant.

3.4.6.2 **Portable or mobile machinery**

Machinery regarded as portable, so being capable of being moved around various worksites or other locations, presents an increased risk compared to a static item working at specified premises. The increased activity of loading operations, transportation and handling increase the accidental risk of impact and other external forms of damage and require a suitable adjustment to the premium. For items moved under their own motive power within the confines of the premises, or by road, collision impact and similar forms of risk become apparent. The insurer will need to decide whether all or part of the machinery is better suited to a cover under some form of motor insurance.

Similar items of machinery performing their normal function can present an entirely different risk perspective, depending on individual circumstances and location. A mobile crane working in a dockside environment, adjacent to the waterside, can be regarded as more hazardous and may suffer a greater degree of damage resulting from toppling than would a similar crane suffering the same type of accident on dry land. Static machinery located near a river or other watercourse where there is history or likelihood of flooding should be assessed thoroughly and underwritten on merit.

The problem of theft or the attempt thereat in some territories is a prime consideration when assessing mobile or static exposures. Items that are mobile or can be easily transported are more vulnerable and require stringent standards of protection to be employed to safeguard them. Insurers need to know the details of physical security deterrents and procedures in force, including where appropriate immobilisation once items are left unattended. Such problems not only affect site or industrial compounds. Office premises also become targets for organised or opportunist walk-in thieves to steal electronic equipment where there is a ready market for their disposal. There are many proprietary devices currently available to deter thieves and these should provide the minimum level of risk management, coupled with provision of a secure gated compound to house items when they are not in use.

Mobile machinery may also suffer the effects of being operated by a number of different operatives and, unless care is exercised, the items may become subject to neglect and/or abuse. The same unsatisfactory situation may also apply to any items taken on hire and the insured's attitude to proper plant management should feature in the overall risk assessment. Where machinery is not housed and is left exposed to the natural elements, the underwriters would expect the insured to take reasonable care to protect the plant from the effects of climatic conditions. If necessary, specific action may be called for to tailor the correct type, level and frequency of maintenance and overhaul to individual circumstances. Static machinery operating internally within a controlled environment is obviously not subject to the same degree of hazard. The exposure faced by the underwriter will ultimately be governed by the scope of cover provided by the machinery policy.

3.5   The machinery

3.5.1   Recognition

Whether individual machines or complete process plants are proposed for insurance, the underwriter should check, as far as possible, that the plant is of a standard, proven type with no prototype, experimental or untried features. For key items, operating either in a stand-alone basis or as part of a larger process, it is desirable to compare these with similar installations in terms of the reliability achieved, successful commercial operating hours completed and the record of failures and losses.

The function of a machine, if not obvious from its name, should be identified and the implications of the intended work application should be taken into account when assessing the exposure. Long operating periods and multiple shift patterns are likely to worsen the breakdown element of the risk and need to be handled accordingly. Similarly, machinery working automatically without supervision, especially outside normal working hours, may introduce hazards that, despite inbuilt controlling devices, potentially allow serious damage to occur.

The quality and experience of machine operatives should be satisfactory to eliminate as far as possible the results of human error. The manufacturer or supplier can have considerable input in this area if training programmes are made available to its customer's operatives and maintenance personnel. Good overall design features, easing the task of preventive maintenance, and a properly structured loss prevention programme instituted by the operator should not be underestimated when making an overall risk assessment.

Irrespective of the policy deductible, the insured should be aware that consumables and periodically replaceable parts are specifically excluded under most policies.

3.5.2   Origin and reliability

For lesser-known items of machinery with unknown records or where the manufacturer or country of origin is unusual, it is useful to conduct some specific research. Such items are likely to be incorporated within a process layout where their significance may not become apparent until a claim-related incident reveals some unexpected onerous features.

The following aspects, some of which are addressed more fully below, should therefore be ascertained:

● the identity of the manufacturer or supplier

● proven reliability

● acceptable build quality

● whether the chosen sum insured represents the true 'installed' cost of the machine

- confirmation that the machine has been handed-over without qualification from the installing contractors after successful commissioning, testing and acceptance trials, including sustained achievement of designed production capacity

- the availability of spares and repairers in the country of location

- the repairability of the machine and its components, to identify any potentially disproportionate claim costs if unit repair is not practicable or economic, *e.g.* sealed-life items

- the 'marking up' of the cost of replacement parts inconsistently in comparison with the total initial machine cost

- recourse under the terms of a supply warranty or guarantee

- the extent of repair improvisation using readily obtained 'off-the-shelf' components

- the anticipated life expectancy and operating efficiency commensurate with age and/or use if the machinery being proposed for insurance is at an age when more frequent failures might be expected.

Depending on the facts established, a site survey may be arranged by the underwriter or his appointed representative during which the implications of machine origin can be fully reported. In extreme cases the terms and conditions offered might be restricted or some limits introduced in the form of loss sharing or loss participation by the insured.

3.5.2.1 Manufacturers and suppliers

Unless the machinery to be insured is well known to all, it is important to establish the identity and origin of the manufacturer in order to assess the normal operational risk associated with the machinery and its intended application. The integrity of the manufacturer's build quality needs to be considered in order to check the operating reliability and performance reputation. The measure of 'after-sales' support provided could also impact on the risk and should therefore be investigated.

For new machinery, the period, scope and terms of the manufacturer's warranty are important, remembering that wide variations are possible. If the warranty covers both the supply of replacement parts and the associated labour costs necessary to remedy defects attributable to manufacture/installation, it is likely that the cost of insurance may qualify for a discount until such time as the warranty expires.

It is also important to establish whether the manufacturer provides initial operator training and also detailed procedural guidelines for subsequent operating and maintenance.

One should question the availability of both replacement spare parts and authorised repairers as a means of containing future potential claim costs. While the time factor in procurement may not prejudice the material damage underwriter, spares that are difficult to obtain may introduce disproportionate costs relative to the new machinery value, upon which the premium would have been based. If any doubt persists, enquiries should be made to determine the practicality of unit component repair or the existence of a service exchange facility. Similarly, in certain territories underwriters may be faced with the fact that, owing to a lack of skilled repairers, technical resources will have to be brought in to undertake repair work, thus incurring extra claim costs.

Proven characteristics and technical misgivings

The degree to which machines have 'built-in' safety tolerances can vary significantly. As a generalisation, it is true that machines from a past era were built to very robust standards; design and material tolerances were a feature and manufacturers carried out exhaustive works testing before putting their products on to the market. In modern times, with new materials, and demands for greater efficiency and improved margins, all within a more commercially competitive world, these tolerances have become comparatively slim and the development time, from design to commercial supply, far more compressed. On the other hand, finer tolerances in materials arises from greater understanding of their characteristics and behaviour.

New machinery proposed for insurance, having just commenced commercial operation, should have been satisfactorily tested to the contract specification and achieved an unqualified handover. Normally, the machine will be supported by a manufacturer's warranty for the first 12 months of into use, against which claims for inherent faults may be made. Often, during the initial operational phase of new machinery, the maintenance or defects liability section of an erection all risks policy will apply and may also provide relief (subject to its specific exceptions) against erection and or manufacturer's defects which cause damage.

The purchase of second-hand or refurbished machinery supplied by reputable agents may also be supported by a similar warranty, although normally for not more than three to six months, and it could be restricted to either parts or labour costs only.

In all cases, it is desirable to check for a satisfactory track record and the number of operating hours completed at specified production or output. At the proposal stage, specific confirmation should be sought from the insured that there are no known problems or existing defects, and in the case of certain machines, such as gas turbines, this should take into account the status of any technical upgrading or changes in technical specification. That having been said, a well-drafted policy would contain a condition to prevent claims being made for pre-existing damage or defects which were known to be present before cover commenced. Through such a declaration, the insurance proposer accepts the burden of proof that a subsequent claim is in fact due to a previously unknown defect.

Where history suggests that repetitive failures have occurred to the same or similar machinery, consideration should be given to the introduction of a series loss clause or specific exclusions. A series loss clause states that, after a certain number of claims from a common cause, the insurer will not be liable for subsequent events of the same type, as these events would no longer be regarded as unavoidable or unexpected. Alternatively, a greater measure of coinsurance with the operator, by way of a higher than normal deductible, may provide a solution. Where possible, a comparison of the experience with similar machines, in the same type of application and environment, should be made.

Material science has progressed significantly over the last fifty years to the extent that failure mechanisms such as fatigue, creep, stress corrosion cracking, hydrogen embrittlement, etc. are much better understood. Normally, these failure mechanisms are associated with certain materials subjected to specific environments, both physical and chemical. To ensure adequacy of operation, manufacturers should select the materials, design and manufacturing process that will result in a machine operating successfully in the chosen environment. Certain operating processes will be predisposed to known failures, *e.g.* those of boiler superheater manifolds to creep, nuclear calandria alloy tubes to hydride cracking, rotating machine components to fatigue, sour crude refinery components to hydrogen embrittlement, condenser tubes to stress corrosion cracking.

Expired working service life compared with normal expectancy should be considered, as should the manner in which claims are expected to be settled.

Particular maintenance attention coupled with more frequent service intervals might be the answer for machinery in salty, corrosive or sandy/dusty environments.

Full maintenance, both corrective and planned, is vital for reliable service and prevention of damage. Strict adherence to the implementation of preventive maintenance can significantly reduce failures and losses as in theory components would normally be replaced before the likelihood of damage occurring.

3.5.3 **Age**

Different types of machinery have varying normal life spans, depending upon their function, design, manufacture, configuration, utilisation, working environment and maintenance. It is essential to ascertain how an operator's business functions and the strategy for machinery repair, provision of spares, overhaul and general maintenance, regardless of age.

3.5.4 **Capacity and output characteristics**

The characteristics of the machinery and the demands placed upon it, either in the course of normal production or at peak periods of production, are important issues. Whether the capacity is met by one large machine with sufficient output for the demands of the business or by several smaller machines whose combined output is the equal is a complex choice made by industrialists.

A business which increases its size gradually over a period of time is likely to have either added additional machinery to increase throughput incrementally, carried out a 'de-bottlenecking' exercise or upgraded the older machinery. With suitable planning and investment, a brand-new business is more likely to have its capacity needs met from the beginning (with some 'spare capacity' to allow for future growth) and where choices between single and multiple machinery capacity can be taken more objectively.

It is apparent that the amount of work expected from a machine will have a bearing on its overall performance. Machines running in a uniform way, within their design capacity and with due time for correct servicing and maintenance, can be expected to be less likely to fail than those running 'flat out' or being overloaded.

The variable dependency and flexibility offered through these differences impact on the production achieved and will be especially important to business interruption underwriters (see Chapter 4).

3.5.5 **Process configuration**

The layout of the machinery is important, not only in terms of meeting the capacity demands but is also in terms of the degree of flexibility of normal working and abnormal working. If one machine is out of service, owing to either a planned shutdown or an unexpected event, there is a question of whether other machines can take over its work or that production will be disrupted. Inevitably, this can also have a bearing on the maintenance strategy. It is also an important point in relation to the business interruption risk discussed in Chapter 4.

Another factor present is the risk of a machine failing and possibly damaging other machines in the same vicinity. This is particularly important for high-speed machines that carry the risk of physical disruption or flying debris. A good illustration is the difference in damage potential which exists between turbine generators in the same power house, positioned with their spin-ning axes either 'in line' or 'in parallel', the latter presenting a greater threat of one damaging another.

3.5.6 Quality of operatives

A high proportion of losses that occur are due to human error, negligence or faulty work-manship. Experienced staff and managers should be aware of process technology weaknesses; critical items and any deficiencies should be known and kept under proper control. Properly-trained staff should be familiar with any peculiarities of individual machines and their associat-ed risks. Poorly trained or new staff have no such control over operating parameters of machinery and new staff need to become accustomed to their working environment and the operational methods.

In certain cases, only general recommendations from the machinery manufacturers are adhered to, which may well cause problems. The way a business organises itself with regard to their training programmes and the monitoring of operational machinery will assist the under-writer in assessing the possible areas for concern. The role and responsibilities of the risk man-ager and the level of his authority within the organisation are important factors.

3.5.7 Automatic machines and unattended working

Through technological development and the search for greater economy and efficiency, auto-matic devices and systems increasingly control the management and operation of machinery. Additionally, 'robotics' have been used to perform highly sophisticated and repetitive tasks in manufacturing industries for many years, with very low levels of human attendance.

Many machinery failures from the past can be attributed to 'human failure' and intelligent sys-tems with fail-safe programming may be seen as welcome progress. However, on the other hand, one may genuinely question whether this an adequate substitute for a well-qualified engineer, with good experience. The answer lies between the two, leaving the engineers and operators with the task of interpretation and reaction to a great deal of information made available through this new technology.

Underwriters will need to evaluate each of the following features:

- control monitoring
- performance monitoring
- quality of software and compatibility
- alarm signalling, cut-out devices
- shutdown/slow-down procedure
- management and supervisory controls, procedures, theoretical and practical training, and authority to act, *i.e.* to override the controls.

3.5.8 Maintenance and repair

The maintenance and repair policy of the operator will need to be assessed to ascertain whether it is based mainly on proactive measures or simply on reactive measures taken when the need arises. *Inter alia*, aspects to be considered are the management philosophy, legal requirements, scheduled programmes, controls, reporting arrangements and budgeting. This topic is discussed more fully in Chapter 5 'Loss prevention' and in the later chapters dealing with specific manufacturing industries.

A major consideration regarding the insurance of machinery is the facilities available to support the operator's repair and maintenance policy. Naturally, the type of machinery involved will influence the practicality of using in-house workshops and other facilities and the operator's own technical expertise or whether it is desirable or necessary to seek outside assistance from subcontractors or manufacturers. These decisions are often taken in consultation with machinery underwriters.

3. 5.8.1 **Maintenance contracts — preventive or remedial**

The correct level of maintenance appropriate to the machinery concerned is vital to ensure safe working, prevention of damage, maximum reliability and longevity of working life. If machinery is to be kept in optimum working order, the maintenance schedule must be properly structured, recorded and undertaken by suitably-trained personnel. In the event that adequate maintenance capability is not available within the insured's own workforce, all such work should be undertaken by the manufacturer or its agents or by independent experts approved by the manufacturer or supplier.

The scope of the maintenance and the proposed service-time intervals should not be less than that recommended by the manufacturer taking full account of the locality, environmental factors and type of work application in which the machinery is involved. The manufacturer's minimum recommended maintenance schedule will have been assessed on the basis of its total experience to date, including compliance with engineering changes or subsequently-issued engineering bulletins which provide fresh technical advice, comment and specification. Maintenance is broadly of two types: preventive and corrective.

The aim of preventative maintenance is to keep the machinery in good working order, achieving the highest possible level of reliability and performance. Machinery that is properly maintained is more likely to operate at maximum efficiency. The duration between the recommended overhaul cycles (as specified in the manufacturers' recommended operating procedures) must be observed at all times. Simple daily tasks also fall under this heading, such as cleaning and lubrication. Appropriate methods of diagnostic checking can be considered as part of normal operation and preventative maintenance plan and can be used to determine the condition of components, allowing adoption of a generalised philosophy of renewal rather than repair after an inevitable failure has occurred. The scope of relevant diagnostic checking will vary from machine to machine but can range from permanently installed devices to portable specialist monitoring equipment.

Preventative maintenance would also include the recommended inspection requirements for any machine influenced by its type of use and location as well as the obligation to satisfy any local statutory regulations in force.

Corrective maintenance includes the need for attention following unscheduled stoppages, failures, wear and tear or repairs. Such work is likely to be of a more serious nature and the maintenance programme will need to reflect the extent of in-house engineering capability and the formalised arrangements for employing independent specialists.

A comprehensive maintenance plan will provide greater accuracy in spares control and stock-handling, based upon the combined experience of predicted and proven operating history.

All aspects of maintenance work must be adequately logged and monitored for future attention. Risks involving the larger industrial plants, where maintenance teams overlap or shift working is the norm, require detailed monitoring as it is vital to record the status of any on-going maintenance work or work most recently undertaken.

3.5.8.2 **Spare parts**

Identification of whether or not an operator maintains a stock of spare parts and has arrangements in place as far as repair facilities are concerned will clearly show any underwriter how a business operation functions and will give an insight into possible loss scenarios.

It is quite clear that those businesses which maintain a reasonable stock of spares and have a facility available to perform repairs are a far better risk than those who have to seek external assistance. Not only will this affect the cost of individual claims but also the time elements involved could be crucial. Thus it is true that the existence of an insured's own workshop and an in-house repair capability will help minimise overall repair costs, even allowing for reasonable internal on-costs.

As already mentioned, the spare parts philosophy adopted by an operator will provide a strong indicator as to effectiveness of management. For example, it is usual in some multinationals to have registers of spares worldwide that may be called-off against any incident by individual group companies. This capability may have resulted from the strategic decision to standardise on a particular type of machinery and by using common suppliers of original equipment in order to allow a reduced spare inventory. Also, many industries may have entered into local mutual assistance protocols and this may include the facility to call against other operators' spares

The storage of certain spares may require special attention to ensure they are maintained in good condition and are therefore suitable for use when the need arises. Storage of spare turbine rotors requires special investigation of the storage arrangements, including the nature of the atmospheric or climatic controls and the turning programme in order to avoid warping.

3.5.8.3 **Disproportionate repair costs**

The considerations applicable to this area of the risk are similar to those stated in the previous section. However, such features are not restricted to manufacturing or supply aspects but can equally arise from shortcomings in the operator's own risk management and working practices.

Poor design or restricted access due to cramped conditions can hamper repair times and increase remedial costs. Lack of preventive maintenance and an ineffective loss prevention programme inevitably leads to escalation in repair time and cost.

Policy wordings which do not adequately express the intended basis of loss settlement when faced with factors of age, substantial expired working life and obsolescence are likely to lead to increased claim costs. Machinery that proves to be under-specified for the function intended may produce frequent failures. The extent of a supplier's 'mark-up' factor when replacement components have been required has been known to escalate costs beyond that of a complete replacement unit (*e.g.* for small electric motors within process machinery) and this can lead to disproportionate costs.

3.6   The insurance

3.6.1   Basis of cover

It will be appreciated that the scope and breadth of the insurance cover, as either sought by the insured or provided by the insurer, will have a very significance influence on the underwriting processes. This aspect is discussed in Chapter 6, 'Scope of insurance cover'.

The range of machinery to which the insurance is to apply will be taken into account, as will the question of a 'whole schedule' or 'selected items' approach. The level of deductible (that part of any claim that is retained by the insured) will have a bearing on price and the degree to which the risk at the lower end needs to be appraised.

The basic cover, or the cover that may be available for specific risks, may be modified, following the usual processes of commercial negotiation, by the introduction of special policy clauses and warranties in order to make the insurance acceptable to all parties.

3.6.2   Selected 'key items' or 'all plant' insurance

The insured has to decide whether to opt for an 'all plant and machinery' basis or to select only specific items to be insured. For operators of large plants or complex process installations, it is likely to be impracticable for every item of plant to be specified; where total machinery cover is required it would normally be acceptable for an inventory to be compiled specifying only key or critical items, leaving the remaining plant to be grouped into categories of similar types of plant. Information relating to the key items will need to be assessed in detail.

The overall machinery values will need to be calculated by the insured, if possible, reflecting a 'reinstatement as new' basis together with the individual values of the key items. The greater detail provided by such an analysis gives the underwriter the opportunity to be flexible in the manner in which the premium is calculated, irrespective of other terms and conditions imposed.

Some circumstances giving rise to selection may cause underwriters concern, but each case should be considered on merit. Some examples are

● deteriorating claims history or other recent technical problems that have influenced the decision to buy insurance

● unusual machinery or application

● ageing machinery

● the inevitable lack of spread in the risk and the inequitable premium fund generated which may be required to finance claim costs

● the effect and application of the deductible, especially when dealing with items of low value.

The effect of insuring a restricted range of key items and their respective sums insured may not result in a premium reduction as great as that anticipated, in comparison with that for insuring all machinery. The terms for the latter will reflect the fact that the balance of machinery presents a lower risk and will be rated at a comparatively lower level.

3.6.3   **New replacement value ('NRV')**

It is customary for the sum insured upon which the premium is based to be equal to the 'new replacement value' of the machinery to be covered. In the case of old or used machinery, this does not mean the original cost but a figure that would realistically represent the current purchase price of a new identical machine or, if unavailable a similar type performing the same function and achieving comparable output or capacity.

The value of the machinery, and therefore its sum insured, should additionally reflect all other costs associated with its installation and commissioning, wherever that may be in the world; *i.e.* it should fully represent the cost of a replacement machine 'as new' and ready for commercial operation. Such additional costs would include freight charges, customs duties, erection and commissioning costs, local taxes and the like, all of which may vary with time and place and should be reviewed from time to time to ensure the adequacy of the NRV. The installation of a single replacement machine into an existing factory might present a different task in comparison with the original work, and a contractor's current costs must be allowed for. Also, the possibly disproportionate cost of purchasing individual ancillary equipment or accessories must be considered, particularly if those items are subject to special import duties or other local taxes that differ from those applying to a complete machine which may have benefited from more generous tax treatment.

Special trade, quantity or promotional discounts are offered by some manufacturers, especially at the time of a new product launch or where they are breaking into new markets, and these should taken into account. Underwriters are unlikely to be able to take advantage of such discounts at the time of repair or replacement at some time in the future and they should be excluded from the NRV.

The onus is upon the insured to furnish valuation detail, particularly as model ranges can vary substantially in cost depending on build specification. It is in the insured's best interests to select values as accurately as possible to avoid the possible affects of underinsurance when faced with a claim.

Once established, the sum insured should be kept under regular review to ensure continued adequacy as relevant external factors could have an effect, *e.g.* inflation and the impact of currency fluctuations on imported items.

The principal reason for machinery underwriters preferring to calculate premiums geared to NRV (as opposed to written-down valuation, like many other classes of insurance) is that, broadly speaking, machinery insurance is not that of a catastrophe risk, where items are totally destroyed and the application of indemnity principles becomes relatively simple. Most machinery losses relate to partial damage where repairs can be effected; the insurer is thus faced with the current cost of spares and labour at the time of the repair rather than the historic significance of the original price, hence the need for continual updating of the sum insured. There are other solutions that can be explored to suit particular circumstances but these are usually tailored by mutual agreement to comply with the intention of the policy cover arranged. Apart from producing an equitable basis for determining a premium level, the NRV also allows underwriters to gauge the effectiveness of a suitable deductible.

3.6.4   **Obsolescence**

Machines that are obsolete, particularly after many years of use, may present a difficulty with regard to the availability of spares and specialist repair techniques. Replacement parts may need to be specially made or adapted which will result in disproportionately high costs.

However, well-maintained machines in good condition, although obsolete, remain insurable. The underwriter may wish to introduce a specific clause to restrict the claim settlement basis to the costs that would, theoretically, arise from replacing or repairing similar machinery which, together with its spares, is in current production and readily obtainable.

3.6.5 **Extensions to the basic cover**

Extensions to the basic cover may appear innocuous at the time of initial consideration but can prove to be financially onerous if itemised individually and aggregated with the basic sum insured. Their impact should not be treated lightly in terms of risk and total exposure. An insured would expect to be guided by its insurance adviser or intermediary but, as machinery insurance is a specialist class by its very nature, the insured's own risk management philosophy often governs the precise extent of the overall cover.

Typical extensions include

- removal of debris

- temporary repair costs

- protection against impending loss

- third party liability

- the insured's or third party surrounding property

- third party property in the insured's care, custody or control

- expediting expenses, *e.g.* express carriage, overtime working rates, etc.

- professional fees, *e.g.* those of consulting engineers

- capital additions

- automatic transits.

This list is not intended to be exhaustive and the precise cover may need to be individually tailored to suit the particular requirements of an insured. The importance of some of the typical extensions exemplified will vary depending upon the risk exposure, *e.g.* the structural failure of an overhead travelling crane would obviously present a different damage scenario compared with that of failure of a static machine.

Where extensions are provided, suitable sum insured limits should be negotiated to avoid leaving the extent of cover uncapped.

In the case of computers or similar data processing equipment, the extra cover required to provide wider protection is likely to become more sophisticated. For example, the problems of incompatible software or programs may need to be overcome when trying to replace equipment that has been lost or extensively damaged.

Where 'reinstatement as new' cover is provided and there exists a degree of catastrophe cover (as in the case of a boiler explosion affecting structures in the vicinity), extra cover will be required. A typical 'local authorities' clause will meet the additional costs of replacement or repair which are incurred for the sole purpose of complying with whatever building or other regulations are in force. Such additional costs would however not include any cost incurred to comply with any compliance notice previously served upon the insured prior to the occurrence of destruction or damage.

3.6.6 **Unexpired machinery warranty or guarantee; subrogation**

The existence of an unexpired valid machinery warranty or guarantee is of fundamental importance to the underwriter when assessing the level of premium required for insuring the machinery concerned. Faced with machine failure during the remaining warranty period, the insurer is likely to be able to pursue subrogation rights against the supplier.

The detail and scope of the warranty is worth individual scrutiny but, in its basic form, it should offer protection from those inherent faults in design, workmanship or materials for which the manufacturer is responsible. Although it is the right of the insurer to exercise this right of recourse, it is also in the best interests of the insured as a successful recovery would not only protect the valuable asset of a good claims record but would also benefit the insured directly by recovery of the amount of the deductible.

Once the warranty has expired, the underwriter is likely to withdraw the discount allowed enabling the premium to be adjusted to a normal level, often at the first renewal of the policy. Depending on the circumstances, the warranty should be checked to establish its attachment date and duration (whether in calendar time or after so many completed operational working hours) and to check that the manufacturer's responsibility is not restricted in scope during the latter part of the warranty period owing to the achievement of predetermined time or other milestones.

The operator must be aware that it must comply with the terms of the manufacturer's warranty, thereby preserving the position of the insurer and respecting the policy conditions, and should therefore remain mindful of obligations in respect of prescribed maintenance, adequate care or operation and the use of only proper factory-approved components and consumables (*e.g.* filters, lubricants and the like).

3.6.7 **Seasonal work, idle time and stand-by plant**

Certain businesses are of a seasonal nature and its machinery may only be operative for this specific period. Assessment of the varying risk factors and obtaining information regarding the non-usage of such machinery will assist in the application of underwriting parameters. The location of such machinery (*i.e.* in the open or within buildings) will influence the risk of loss or damage. A regular maintenance and start-up procedure is a positive underwriting factor.

The importance of stand-by items will depend upon the nature of the insured's business and the type of insurance required, but this will also have an effect on the insured's financial position.

Machinery lying idle must be properly protected from various perils and continuous monitoring and checking of the working mechanisms is important. The insured must take all necessary steps to maintain the machinery in good working order and to provide reasonable protection against outside influences.

3.6.8 **Working patterns**

It is important to assess the working patterns of the various items of machinery. Regular maintenance and checks of machinery are positive underwriting factors. Continuous operation or multi-shift working could indicate a regime with little time available to carry out routine maintenance and general overhaul when required. This needs to be identified and addressed to ensure that the integrity of the machinery is not compromised. Failures due to such problems could eventually lead to the insurer invoking the policy conditions that require all reasonable precautions to be taken to prevent accidents and safeguard the property to be insured. If there is any alteration or material change in the nature of the risk during the period of insurance, it must be notified to the insurer for approval and/or for action to be taken as required by the insurer.

In the case of certain large plants, such as chemical plants, it is not unusual to have long turn-around periods (*e.g.* one month within a two year period) during which a heavy maintenance schedule is undertaken.

The extent to which machinery is utilised will provide an underwriter with an insight as to how a business actually operates. Continuous operation of machinery must be scrutinised carefully and underwriters ought to be aware of the 'wait until it breaks down' type of operation.

Although long working periods can have a detrimental effect on machinery, the same can also be true if machines that are meant to operate in a steady state for long periods are stopped and started too often. The reason for this is that the machine will normally be under severe stress at the time of stopping and/or starting-up, too much of which can reduce its working life. Any 'shocking' (sudden changes in the normal operation of the machine) should be kept to a minimum.

3.6.9 Special risk features

When considering a proposal for machinery to be insured, it is important to obtain as much identifying detail as is realistically possible. When dealing with larger risks where an extensive machinery inventory has been compiled, the degree of detail required by the underwriter can be focused on the critical and most valuable items or those in respect of which previous experience has revealed the need for more prudent consideration. It is important to obtain authenticated details of previous operating experience, whether resulting in claims incidents or otherwise, and to compare other risks presenting similar exposures.

The reputation and reliability of machinery performance can be checked with industry sources and information gleaned on the latest evolution of the specification standard for the same family or model group. Known problem areas or identified repetitive failures may have prompted a machinery modification or upgrade to eliminate recurrence but this will not necessarily protect the underwriter when insuring the earlier generations of the same model groups.

Use and age factors need to be assessed and appropriate decisions taken, should the underwriter be of the opinion that the machinery being proposed for new insurance is beyond the expected best period of its normal service life.

Machinery adapted to work in a unique situation or configured to a use to which it has not been designed need greater technical consideration.

Fully automated machines working outside normal working hours can introduce a situation where operating faults can occur undetected, ultimately leading to a more serious failure, with other even more serious consequences if adjacent machinery or surrounding property is also affected.

Modern machinery will incorporate integral safety, warning and cut-out devices. However, these have been known to fail or to be inadequate, resulting in much higher rectification costs than might have arisen had the machine been manually attended at the time of the original problem. Sophisticated control systems operating within process machinery present 'computer' type risks within an industrial environment, and the exposure needs to be assessed accordingly.

Some machine users will source spares from different origins as part of good contingency planning, with the intention of maintaining an identical specification, but operational problems have been known to arise due to shortcomings at suppliers' or manufacturers' premises. Underwriters need to satisfy themselves of the total integrity of the complete machine and its dedicated pool of spares.

Underwriters should be alert to the prospect of disproportionate claims cost. It may not be viable to repair vital constituent parts of a machine (*e.g.* printed circuit boards) as the diagnostic cost of fault-finding alone would exceed the cost of a replacement unit. Such items, depending on their function, can be costly to replace in the event that repair is not possible; a mitigating solution would be for the insurer to seek a contribution from the manufacturer in the form of a service exchange credit.

As a last resort, the underwriter may wish to introduce specific or bespoke exclusions or to restrict the scope of cover, even to the extent of insistence on of a 'trouble-free' running period to eliminate anticipated early faults or 'teething' problems.

3.6.10   Proposals, surveys and site visits

The overall size and nature of a machinery risk will determine the preferred method of establishing or updating the desired underwriting information. In many instances, technical and commercial visits will be appropriate; in other cases, a written proposal form or questionnaire may be acceptable.

4 Underwriting aspects — business interruption

4.1 Introduction

This chapter addresses the subject of the interruption to business that may arise after damage to machinery, or whilst machinery is out of service due to loss or damage, which is typically insured under the various forms of material damage insurance, as discussed elsewhere in this Study Report.

Whereas material damage insurance is concerned with the physical effects and costs of loss or damage, business interruption is concerned with the financial consequences for the business, which are generally time-related. This additional financial exposure may be insured either under a combined material damage and business interruption policy (with separate sections, limits and the like) or under a separate policy covering 'loss of profits,' 'consequential loss,' 'business interruption' or some similarly-named concept. For our purposes, the term 'business interruption' will be used to refer to all these types of cover.

This chapter does not address the broad concepts, principles and practices of business interruption insurance, on which a great deal of general material already exists. Instead, it concentrates on the subject in relation to the risks associated with the use of and dependency on machinery in various industries. Similarly, it is assumed that the reader will already have a good basic understanding of accountancy and how to read a balance sheet, as it is in this domain that the financial consequences of an interruption to the business would be shown and quantified in the event of a loss.

4.2 Total loss compared with partial loss

An important aspect of business interruption underwriting is the degree to which the insured peril will affect the business and for what period of time. Some exposure perils will have a widespread effect on the physical risk, where the damage is difficult to contain. In other instances, the peril only causes localised physical damage although, as will be seen later, the effect on the business may be out of all proportion and much more serious. On the other hand, the business might not be affected at all. This variable impact on the business is shown in the case of catastrophe perils underwriting and, to a large extent, fire underwriting, where there tends to be a direct correlation between the material damage exposure and the corresponding terms of insurance and those applicable to the business interruption exposure.

In the case of operational machinery exposures, the damage is more likely to be localised or 'contained' in a physical context. Because it may have a different impact on the business, there is greater 'independence' in the terms of the business interruption insurance; they are not necessarily derived directly from the corresponding terms of the material damage insurance.

The assessment of the extent to which machinery loss or damage may be expected to interfere with the business is one of the keys to successful machinery business interruption insurance and its underwriting.

4.3 Basis of cover; the sum insured

The financial items insured under the business interruption policy, and therefore the basis on which claims are settled, will be determined by the nature of the business and the way in which the provision of its services or products are priced and charged for.

As the sums insured are of various types, their nature and proper definition is an important part of the policy. For example, the sum insured may represent gross profit, gross revenue, net profit plus standing (non-variable) expenses, the output cost of units, or capacity payments.

Whatever basis of settlement applies, it is important that the sum insured can be quantified using normal accounting practices; otherwise difficulties will arise in the event of a loss when endeavouring to measure the normal performance of the business against the actual situation as affected by the interruption caused by damage to machinery.

Likewise, the adequacy of the sum insured is of particular importance in business interruption insurance as under-insurance will usually result in the application of the average condition, in full or in part. Whereas most material damage insurance makes provision for automatic increases in the sum insured, this may not be the case with business interruption cover.

Traditionally, the sum insured is based on the estimated gross profit (or other chosen value) for the forthcoming year, which is then adjusted retrospectively once audited figures are available after that year has ended. A suitable return premium would be payable for any overstatement of the estimated sum, usually allowed on up to 50% of the sum insured to encourage the insured to select an adequate amount and therefore avoid under-insurance at the time of a loss.

As an alternative, some insurers offer policies with an increase provision in the sum insured which grants a degree of tolerance should the actual sum insured prove greater, at the time of loss, than the estimated figure, with a corresponding easement in the application of the average condition. Subsequently, the insured is required to make an annual declaration of the actual sum (*e.g.* the annual profit actually earned) to obtain a retrospective adjustment of the premium (either upwards or downwards) for the previous period of insurance. Normally, there is an upper limit, allowing a maximum automatic increase of 33%. On the other hand, a minimum retained premium level may apply in the event that there is a large shortfall in the declared figure.

4.4 Increased cost of working, additional expenditure and savings

Following an incident that is covered by the business interruption policy, the insurer will meet the cost of those increased business expenses incurred by the insured for the purpose of avoiding or diminishing the loss of insured profit or revenue that would otherwise have arisen during the indemnity period. These increased costs of working must represent a saving on the loss that would have otherwise arisen and should be incurred with the prior agreement of the insurer. Hiring-in temporary machinery, such as emergency generators, or buying-in partly-completed products or processed materials, are examples of increased costs that have been justified in mitigation of the overall claim. A further example could be the extra cost of expediting the repair of the physical damage to the machinery, provided that bringing it back into service sooner than normal achieves a reduction in the business interruption loss.

It should be noted that the basis of settlement would take into account any amount saved during the indemnity period in respect of expense items that may reduce or cease as a consequence of the interruption to business, *e.g.* variable business expenses such as electricity.

With some unusual repairs there are costs that are necessarily incurred that are not proportionate, being greater than the savings achieved. Specific policy extensions may provide for 'additional increased costs of working' which caters for this initial high expense. The sum insured is normally a specified amount, not linked to any indemnity period, and accordingly carries a monetary deductible. The reasoning behind the need for this extension should be documented so that future claims may be adjusted in line with the intentions of the extension.

4.5 The importance of particular machinery

When insuring against loss of profit or revenue and the like, the contribution the various insured machines make towards the business is of key importance. This contribution may be major at all times, perhaps seasonally variable, or, by contrast, little or none in isolation from other machines. Therefore, an assessment needs to be made of those machines on which the business is dependent in normal circumstances; this may be expressed in terms of the percentage importance to the business and, more particularly, to the profits of the business. This assessment will have a direct bearing on the premium level required for that risk.

This point is illustrated by the following simple examples, where different machinery business interruption exposure is clearly apparent. It would be appropriate for the premium in respect of Case A to be less than that for Case B.

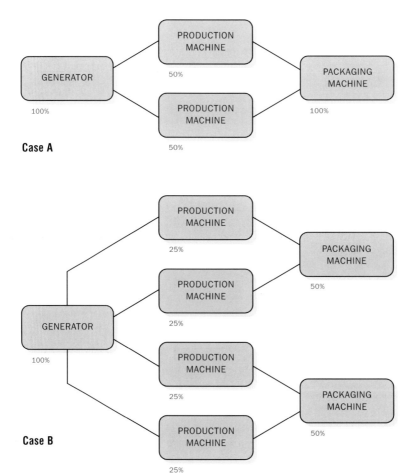

The importance of particular machinery, its contribution to the profits of the business and its effect on the underwriting of the insurance risk may be further illustrated by a further example. In Case C below, no single machine is 100% important to the business as a whole, as there are different 'product streams', and the importance of each machine to its stream is identified to establish its impact on the overall business and profit.

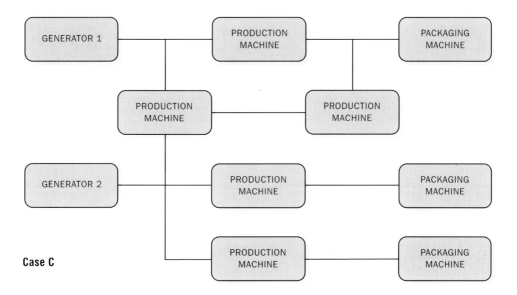

Case C

4.6 Machinery layout and separation

The proximity of one machine to others and their physical separation should be taken into account when considering the possibility of related damage. This is particularly important in the case of high speed rotating machines (*e.g.* turbines) or those operating under high pressure (*e.g.* steam boilers) where the spread of damage may span several individual machines. Fire perils presents a more obvious risk of widespread damage than may be immediately apparent from machinery breakdown.

4.7 Availability of spares and speedy repairs

Having identified *time* rather than *cost* as the prime consideration of the business interruption underwriter, the speed with which repairs can be commenced and completed is of great importance. One factor that will influence this is the availability of spare parts that are needed in the event of damage to a machine. These spares may be held by the machine operator, by a supplier (whether the original manufacturer or not), or by other users of the same machinery who may co-operate with 'spares pooling'.

If the process or equipment is a prototype or unique this will also influence the timescale for repair. In all cases, it is the speed with which spares may be made available where they are needed that is important. Mass-produced spares are likely to be more freely available, in minimum time, than would be expected in the case of custom-made parts.

Another factor is whether repairs can be carried out *in situ* or whether an entire machine or a component would have to be sent away for repairs, perhaps because of the size or nature of the repair. Obviously, it is likely that minor damage to simple machines can be readily repaired on site whereas major damage or damage to specialist machines may require off-site repairs.

Geographical considerations should be taken into account because transport arrangements, customs clearance, import controls etc can have an effect on the speed of availability and can create additional costs.

Having analysed the availability of spare parts to be used in a repair, the availability of qualified repairers similarly needs to be assessed. It would be no use having parts available without also having personnel competent to carry out the repair work. In some cases, both spares and the necessary repair facilities can be made available through mutual aid agreement. Once again, there is a geographical factor which needs to be taken into account. The location of the insured machinery, the origin of the machine and the proximity or locality of qualified repairers should be assessed, as these factors will have a bearing on the time involved in completing repairs. Obviously, the most favourable situation is where the insured has its own workshop and skilled engineering staff, with a comprehensive repair capability.

Another time factor concerns the accessibility of the item of machinery to be repaired. This may not be straightforward if, for example, there is need for an awkward or heavy lifting operation. This may call for the temporary removal of other property or the temporary demolition of walls and roofs and the hire of special apparatus and lifting appliances not normally available on the premises.

4.8 Surplus or reserve production capacity

A comparison should be made between the normal output levels of individual machines, or group of machines doing the same work, and the maximum safe levels (as stated by the manufacturer). Any surplus or unused capacity could be taken up in the event of localised damage. Allowance should be made for seasonal variations in business and the corresponding demands on machinery and the need to periodically shut down certain machines to carry out routine maintenance. Thus, the degree of surplus capacity can vary from time to time.

4.9 Parallel working and series-overlapping process plants

The machinery configuration and general plant layout may allow for alternative working or a degree of flexibility, which may be helpful in the event of damage to individual machines or groups of machines. The opportunities for this flexibility are illustrated in the various plant layouts shown in the cases illustrated at 4.5 above. It may be possible for undamaged machine output rates to be temporarily increased to take up some or all the workload of the damaged item. This may require some improvisation, for which any extra expense would be considered under the increased cost of working section of the policy.

4.10 Partly-finished products

In the case of manufacturing industries, the production process may be physically split into different phases, where one distinct process ends before another starts. An example might be the final stage of manufacture, the packaging process and the despatch arrangements.

If the business has some 'intermediate stocks' between these phases, these may be used to ease the effect of an interruption earlier in the production process. Obviously, these stocks would need to be built up again once normal production is resumed.

A similar reduction in the interruption may be achieved by transferring partly-finished products to other parts of the whole business, or to an outside company, for completion. Underwriters should also be aware of the impact of outside processing where this may itself be subject to a delay. For example, with dynamic metal markets, the value of the final product may significantly increase or decrease during this outside processing time. Equally, it may be possible to 'import' from external sources partly-completed products of the type normally made by the business, which can then be finished off downstream in the production process. This might allow delivery dates to be met, thus minimising the impact of a loss on customer relations and future trading.

Invariably, there will be extra expense with such solutions and this should be met by the policy, within the terms of the increased cost of working provisions.

There is a growing trend amongst high-efficiency modern industries for 'just-in-time' processes, whereby components enter the production line at the optimum moment and stockpiles are kept to an absolute minimum. It can be seen that a machinery failure would have a more immediate, and possibly more serious, effect on the production flow and a correspondingly adverse impact on the business, which may be forced to come to a complete standstill.

4.11   Stand-by plant

In some industries or businesses where continuous output or availability is vitally important, the plant may include stand-by items, which are not in normal service but are available for use in exceptional circumstances. These circumstances may arise during planned maintenance work to the primary machine, peak demand periods or in the event of damage to the primary machine. The diagram below illustrates one possibility.

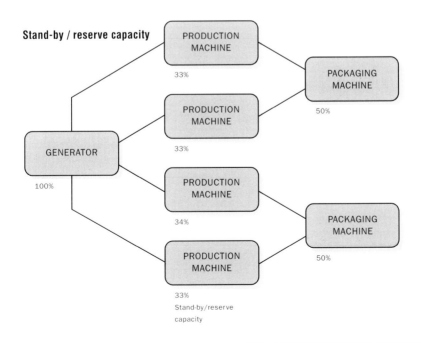

The maintenance standard and speed with which such stand-by machines may be brought into production service are an important consideration to the underwriter in assessing the benefits in terms of interruption exposure. Ideally, a stand-by machine should be readily available for immediate use at all times and this will require periodic start-ups and a suitable maintenance programme.

4.12   The customer/supplier extension; contractual obligations

Business interruption may arise through the failure of a supplier to deliver materials or through the inability of a customer to take delivery of the manufactured goods or services. Where this is due to damage to that supplier's or customer's own machinery and the cause is one that is covered under the insured's policy, the interruption may be insured as an extension to that policy. Suitable gross profit sums insured should be considered to reflect the percentage dependency of the insured business on the suppliers and/or customers concerned.

Normally, the incoming supply of feedstocks, materials, parts or products, or the delivery of these to customers, is governed by contractual agreements which, whether on the supply-side or the customer-side of the economic chain, can have an important effect on the business interruption risks. An insured may be faced with financial loss through the payment of contractual fines or penalties in the event of not being able to take deliveries from or make deliveries to contracting parties owing to an insured accident to his machinery.

An example of this exposure is the 'take or pay' agreement entered into by private power production companies with gas suppliers. In the event that a gas turbine is out of service, the gas normally consumed in the combustion process (which cannot be stored on site) cannot be taken and the gas supplier may invoke a penalty clause in the supply contract

However, such expenditure cannot be dealt with as a loss of gross profit under a standard business interruption policy, because it cannot be measured against a reduction in turnover, nor as an increase in the cost of working to avoid a comparative loss of turnover. The amount of the fine or penalty will vary from time to time, depending on the contracts in hand. The insurance of such losses can be dealt with by the inclusion of a separate financial item in the policy, with the sum insured equivalent to the estimated loss likely to be incurred according to the terms of the contract. Such items will attract a different rating approach to that of the main policy, as they are insured on a 'first loss' basis, which is a disproportionately 'harder' loss than that represented by the gross profit.

4.13   Failure of utility supply

Where the business is reliant on one or more incoming supplies of electricity, gas or water provided by public or private utility companies, an interruption to the supply will have an obvious and often immediate impact on the whole business. It is essential to know how dependable these supplies are at the customer end and what would happen in the event of a stoppage in the supply.

This exposure may be included in the insurance and it should be noted that the perils causing failure in the supply may be a wider range than those covered under the main operation of the machinery policy. Whereas direct damage to the machinery at the insured premises due to elemental perils may be excluded, the loss of overhead power lines due to high winds or heavy snowfall, causing an interruption to the supply of electricity, is an example of this wider approach.

The quality and reliability of the supply are extremely important. This aspect needs to be thoroughly investigated through enquiries into the history of the supply and the records kept by the supply authority, together with the experience of other similarly-placed customers. Fluctuations in the supply (whether it is electricity, gas or water) should be identified and evaluated in terms of impact on the insured business. Many machines require a supply maintained at a precise and constant level in order to function and perform correctly.

Even a short stoppage may have an impact on the business, especially where the shutdown and start-up of machinery involve complex procedures. This is particularly true of electricity which, unlike other sources of energy, cannot be 'stored' at the premises and where continuous operation is vital to the satisfactory completion of the manufacturing process, *e.g.* in the chemical and metal smelting industries.

If there is an alternative source of supply (perhaps from another business with supplies surplus to its own requirement), the period of supply interruption may be relatively short. In some industries, it is common to find an in-house electricity generation capacity and/or gas storage facility, which is available either as an alternative source or as a supplementary source at peak-demand periods. The reverse may also be true, *i.e.* the external supply is not generally used but it would be available, albeit at a penalty cost, in the event of unforeseen circumstances, *e.g.* when a generator operated by the machinery owner has failed.

Another important aspect in the supply of electricity arises where hazardous process machinery (*e.g.* in the chemical industry), which is usually driven by self-generated power, requires an alternative source of power. The provision of a stand-by power supply will help to guarantee a safe and orderly shutdown of the process in the event that the usual supply is unexpectedly lost. For this safeguard to be effective, the second (or reserve) source of power supply must be engaged automatically and without delay.

4.14 Disproportionate interruption losses

It has already been stated that the subject matter of business interruption insurance is 'time' rather than physical damage. It should be appreciated that relatively minor damage to a key part of the machinery may have a profound and disproportionate effect on the business. This occurs where the processes in the business experience a 'bottleneck'.

Less obvious sources of disproportionate business interruption losses arise where critical temperatures or pressures necessary for production efficiency or safety are lost by a short but unexpected period of machinery stoppage. Such exposures can be found in the chemical industry and in metal working processes that involve smelting.

Some machines are unable to operate below a certain minimum level of throughput. This may be due to safety considerations or simply because the machine cannot work at a low level of activity. In the energy field, this minimum level of operation (typically around 50% of the normal level) is known as the 'turn down ratio'.

It should also be remembered that some businesses (*e.g.* some fruit and vegetable processing and sugar refining) generate disproportionately higher amounts of profit or revenue during certain peak seasonal periods of the year. Damage to machinery at these critical times will lead to heavier losses than at other times.

The annual gross profit of private electricity generating companies often includes significant 'capacity payments' earned for generating those electricity supplies made available during certain periods, *e.g.* the winter months. Failure to supply the 'guaranteed' amounts of electricity during these months owing to machinery breakdown (or perhaps due a loss of primary fuel) would lead to a much greater profit or revenue loss than would normally be anticipated on a proportionate annual basis. The insurer ought to pay careful attention to the contractual supply agreement and the financial implications of failing to meet the obligations when assessing the terms for insurance. It may be recommended that the insurance of capacity payments should be dealt with by a separate item.

4.15 Alternative working possibilities

Most manufacturing industries can find alternative working possibilities to which the business may turn if an accident occurs. However, the viability of these alternatives will need to be evaluated in terms of their cost-effectiveness in the context of the business interruption that is being thereby avoided or minimised.

These alternative working possibilities are best identified at the outset and kept under constant review. This should form part of the loss prevention or contingency/disaster recovery planning undertaken by most well-managed businesses. Various solutions may exist within the business itself, by changing the way in which work is done and/or by hiring in temporary machinery, working overtime hours or turning to outside assistance to perform certain parts of the usual business functions.

The greater the possibilities in this context, the less the risk faced by the business and its insurers.

4.16 Indemnity, time-exclusion and franchise periods

The actual period during which the business is interrupted and during which the policy responds to the loss suffered is known as the 'indemnity period'. The policy should state whether this period commences on the date of the loss or damage or at the time that the business is first interrupted after the loss or damage. The difference is worth noting and some policies are ambiguous on this point.

The maximum indemnity period for which the insurer is liable is typically expressed as a number of months (*e.g.* 24) and the corresponding sum insured for that selected indemnity period will be specified.

With machinery insurance, unlike general fire insurance, there is a prospect of relatively unimportant but frequent interruptions arising. In order to avoid the costs of handling claims for these minor events under the insurance (which would erode the premium base and present an unduly high administration burden), a time exclusion or deductible is introduced.

Consistent with the approach to the indemnity period, the time exclusion will also either apply from the date of the machinery damage or the date on which the business is first interrupted as a consequence of the damage. The duration of the exclusion may be 3 – 14 days for light-to-medium industries and 14 – 90 days for heavy industries, including power generation. If the former approach is used, it may be that the time exclusion period has expired before the business is first interrupted

It should be noted that, even if the damage is repaired within the time exclusion period, indemnity might still be provided under the policy if the business interruption continues beyond the stated period. The financial consequences of the business interruption will continue to be covered until the business is returned to normal or at the expiry of the maximum indemnity period stated in the policy, whichever is the earlier.

For some types of business, policies with monetary deductible are available for the business interruption loss; the sum involved would be additional to any deductible applicable to the material damage insurance, combined deductibles being very rare.

In the case of public or private utility supply failures, the common approach is to apply a short franchise period rather than a time exclusion. This may be stated in minutes or hours; a short stoppage in supply for less than the stated franchise period would be excluded but, if the stoppage persists for more than that period, the entire resultant interruption to the business is covered.

4.17   Scope of cover

The scope of cover will depend on the needs of the business to be insured and the availability of cover from the insurance industry, at a realistic price. It is desirable that the perils covered under a material damage policy are the same as those under the business interruption policy; indeed, this may be a condition of the business interruption policy (the material damage insurance proviso or warranty). This helps to ensure that funds are available to finance repairs, an absence of which could lead to a lengthening of the interruption period.

A choice can often be made between insuring all machinery at the business (on a 'blanket' basis or under a listed schedule) or confining the cover to key selected items, which are likely to be those having an important contribution to the business and its profit.

4.18   Link to indemnifiable material damage loss

As previously stated, most business interruption insurance is coupled with an underlying material damage insurance. An indemnifiable event under the material damage policy is the trigger for the business interruption cover.

Whereas the cost of an event falling within the monetary deductible under the material damage policy would not be met by the insurer, if the same event resulted in an interruption beyond the time exclusion indemnity would then be provided by the business interruption insurer.

It may be considered desirable that material damage and business interruption covers are arranged with the same insurer, or group of insurers, in order to avoid a potential conflict in interest and differences in opinion as to the scope of indemnity. This would avoid disputes that can arise between cost and time factors, particularly when facing increased cost of working, temporary repair expenses and expediting costs.

Exceptions to this prerequisite for material damage insurance can be found in the case of manufacturers' warranties (to the extent that they stand in the place of machinery breakdown insurance) and some government-owned risks where financing concerns do not arise.

Machines that are newly installed may be required to complete a trouble free running period before they are accepted for inclusion under a business interruption policy, even though they are insured or guaranteed for material damage purposes.

4.19 Local authority or statutory inquiries

In certain circumstances, the degree to which a loss may be mitigated or the time to resume operations may be reduced can be significantly influenced by the involvement of statutory agencies. Authorities such as the Environmental Protection Agency, the Health and Safety Executive or a court-appointed expert may insist on action that will prevent speedy resumption of operations. This is likely to arise where injuries have been suffered or where there is either a perceived or continuing risk to public safety, including the risk of pollution.

4.20 Condition monitoring; planned shutdowns

Some material damage policies may not cover incidents arising as a result of machinery testing or whilst maintenance was being carried out. If such an incident occurred and the business interruption policy was only triggered following an indemnifiable material damage incident there would therefore be no cover. Moreover, if an incident occurred just prior to a planned shutdown, this is likely to be taken into account with regard to the time/loss quantum calculation. Underwriters should be aware of an operator's philosophy with regard to planned shutdowns, *i.e.* the nature, timing, duration of each.

Customers sometimes stipulate output- or performance-quality tests, and these may expose the machinery to onerous conditions. Failure under test usually suggests that the machine could not perform to the required standard; thus the customer has the option to cancel the contract or withhold payment. If the machinery is damaged, the policy will pay as if the original contract remained effective. Repeated advertising and marketing costs to secure a new contract after the repair would be an additional expense that could be included within an item for additional increased cost of working.

4.21 Deferred permanent repairs; temporary repairs

In the event that repairs to damaged machinery take a long time to complete, it may be possible and preferable to undertake temporary repairs, in a shorter time, thus minimising the interruption period. This will be considered when production or output is seasonal and the damage occurs during peak times. If it is desirable to undertake temporary repairs, the safety of such repairs cannot be overlooked and in this regard it may be necessary to obtain the support of the machine manufacturers.

The 'deferred' permanent repairs may then be completed subsequently at a more convenient time, when the down-time would have a less detrimental effect on the business. The aim is to reduce the overall interruption and, this being so, the costs of these temporary repairs may be agreed with the business interruption insurer as part of a reduction in the cost of the claim. Therefore, loss mitigation expenses may fall under the policy with the insurer's consent.

4.22 Demurrage charges

A demurrage charge made by a shipowner or charterer may be incurred by a machinery owner in the event that a ship's voyage is delayed as a result of the machinery owner being unable to relieve the ship of its cargo or to provide the ship with its cargo on time. It is a form of penalty for undue time spent in a port or docks.

Some businesses are more exposed to these charges than others and, if they are to be insured, they should be shown as subject to a separate sum insured as such charges would not form part of the usual business expense.

4.23   Denial of access

As with other forms of business interruption cover, a machinery insurance policy may cover denial of access to the business which results in the business being interrupted. The damage or incident causing the denial of access to the insured business may involve third party property (*e.g.* neighbouring premises or public roads) but, to be covered under the policy in question, the damage or incident should be caused by an insured peril. (*i.e.* damage to machinery) A collapsed crane blocking the access road would be an example of an indemnifiable denial of access incident, but only to the extent that it caused the insured business to be interrupted. More likely causes of denial of access, such as flood or fire damage to property in the vicinity, would be insurable under a property business interruption policy.

4.24   Prolongation of interruption by external events

Once the policy cover has been activated (*i.e.* an indemnifiable incident involving the insured machinery occurs), the insurer's exposure period and therefore the loss under the policy might be extended in certain circumstances.

For example, after a machine has suffered damage it is sent away to the repairers for work and is expected back in a short time. However, if it were then dropped and damaged more severely whilst at the repairer's premises, or damaged by a collision in transit, the prolonged business interruption loss would be covered by the policy. Unless stated otherwise, even if the 'secondary' subsequent damage is caused by a peril excluded by the policy (*e.g.* fire or marine losses), the prolonged period of interruption would be covered until expiry of the maximum indemnity period. In these circumstances, the business interruption insurer may have subrogation rights against the repairer with the possibility of recovery of an appropriate part of its outlay.

Another example arises where the prolongation is due to a strike at the repairer's premises or by suppliers of essential parts. The policy responds in the same manner as stated above and would continue to respond for the entire duration of the business interruption, until expiry of the maximum indemnity period.

A different situation arises where a machine is sent away for routine maintenance or overhaul work. If it is damaged in any of the above circumstances, the business interruption would not normally be covered unless the policy had been extended to include 'advance business interruption' which generally requires particular underwriting investigation and conditions. However, if the same machine was not returned on time and, owing to a separate indemnifiable incident at the insured's premises, there is a business interruption which the availability of that machine could otherwise have helped to avoid or minimise, the 'indirect' effects or business interruption would then be met under the policy.

4.25   Depreciation; capital allowances

Depreciation is a charge against the net profit of a business intended to enable the owner of machinery or other fixed assets to write-off its capital value over an agreed period of time, by putting aside enough funds to reinvest in new capital equipment once the existing item no longer has a useful life. The rate and basis of depreciation is governed by accounting principles, having regard to the nature of the business and the type of asset. For example, the owner may write down his machinery evenly at an annual rate of 7.5% of the original cost, which would mean that the machinery would be fully depreciated (to a balance sheet value of 'nil') after 13.3 years and, if it continued in use in the business, no further depreciation allowance would be charged against profits.

However, depreciation charges as such are not deductible from the taxable profits of the business. Instead, a special form of depreciation (at rates set by the tax authority) called capital allowances are set against the taxable net profit of the business. These allowances are often a combination of an initial allowance given in the year of the capital expenditure (which may be at an enhanced rate of anything up to 100% to promote capital investment) and an annual writing-down allowance (at a specified percentage rate on the reducing balance of expenditure after deducting all previous allowances). If an item is sold or scrapped, any difference between the proceeds of disposal and its then written-down value will normally give rise to a further taxable balancing charge or allowance.

For business interruption purposes, capital allowances rather than depreciation are considered. The following example shows the effect of availability of capital allowances on a business interruption claim:

Basic information relating to the business

	£
Annual turnover	40,000,000
Variable expenses	(7,500,000)
Gross profit	32,500,000
Fixed costs (excluding depreciation)	(21,500,000)
Capital allowances*	(4,500,000)
Taxable net profit	**£ 6,500,000**

Rate of tax = 40%
Indemnity period = 18 months
Time exclusion = 14 days

*6% of original cost of all fixed assets (£75,000,000); time to write-down to nil = $16^2/_3$ years.

Basic information relating to the loss and business interruption

- Machinery valued at £10,000,000 is totally destroyed, which halts production*
- Assets are 9 years old at the time of the loss
- Interruption period = 12 months.

Loss scenario

- As the machinery destroyed is 100% important, the business is brought to a standstill. No turnover is generated and the business suffers a net loss.
- The loss of machinery valued at £10,000,000 means that no further capital allowances can be claimed for tax purposes on these assets, although they will continue on the undamaged assets. However, the tax authority permits a balancing allowance on the destroyed machinery in the first year during which the business is interrupted, equivalent to the value of the balance of years remaining to write-down the destroyed machinery to zero multiplied by the capital allowance percentage rate multiplied by the tax rate.

Loss adjustment

To place the insured in the same financial position in respect of the 12 months of business interruption, the following settlement would be made:

	£
Fixed costs	26,000,000
Net profit	6,500,000
Gross claim	32,500,000
Deduction for time exclusion (14/365 days)	(1,246,600)
Deduction for tax value of capital allowances:	
Destroyed machinery	
(£10,000,000 x 6% x 7^{2}/$_{3}$ years x 40%)	(1,840,800)
Other assets	
(£6,500,000 x 6% x 40%)	(1,560,000)
Net settlement by insurer	£ 27,852,600

5   Loss prevention

5.1   Introduction

How would you walk across a busy road? This may appear a strange question to find under this heading and in the context of this Study Report. As a simple and practical example of 'loss prevention'. we should use our senses of sight and hearing, take the shortest distance and apply these with the experience of where it is safe and where it is hazardous, to ensure that the crossing is as safe as possible. Our individual personal approach to risk and the consequences of risk would be that we hope to manage risk and not just take risks. We can understand the benefit rationale for being careful when we cross the busy road, the techniques that ensure a safe crossing and the influences and factors that make the risk either reasonable or unacceptable.

In the context of industry, we would also wish to manage risk, including that relating to the operation of industrial and process machinery. The reasons for this will be diverse; however, in an increasingly competitive national and international business environment, successful financial performance is critical to survival. Risk management and loss prevention can assist in achieving this objective by maintaining high plant availability, efficiency and reliability and low insurance loss ratios.

However, loss prevention has the potential for both costing and saving money with the perception and reality of the benefit depending significantly on the viewpoint. For example, an insurer may only be concerned with the improvement of risk which directly affects the insurance contract, or an insured may only be interested in improving the operation as it affects the uninsured elements of the business. It is believed that to optimise the benefits of loss prevention it is necessary to adopt a proactive, team approach involving all the parties with a vested interest, so that an integrated and holistic plan can be pursued to their mutual benefit.

Loss prevention should be regarded as a practical activity but one that can involve a degree of human frailty, with poor behaviour patterns, errors and mistakes likely to occur. Even if analysis and modelling are utilised, the main emphasis should be on recognising that we live in a dynamic environment and that any theoretically based programme should be validated in the real world.

Effective risk management or loss prevention requires an enquiring approach: to challenge conventions, have vision, be analytical, imaginative and perceptive while endeavouring not to have 'mind-sets'. Consequently, wherever possible, practical examples of success or failure have been included to illustrate these points.

Conventional loss prevention strategy, irrespective of the application, requires risks to be identified, assigning a priority to each risk on the basis of perceived or measured severity and frequency impact. It is necessary to create a loss prevention action plan, in order that the results can be monitored against one or more measurable criteria, with a periodic review and correction phase. In addition to this well-established approach, it is suggested that the following fundamental concepts are also considered:

- The need to consider past loss experiences if we are not condemned to repeat them;
- The need to have the perception to identify those 'near misses' that could give rise to losses;
- The need to have the vision to understand the potential threat of future activities giving rise to losses.

Historically, the term 'loss prevention' has been taken to include all aspects of risk reduction, *i.e.* preventing the loss in the first place by hazard control and also reducing the loss and its frequency by minimising the severity and maximising the salvage or recovery potential. Loss prevention is, therefore, a complex subject with many inter related topics.

In the first instance, to simplify matters, an approach has been taken which assumes, for machinery insurance, that loss prevention can be categorised into five primary issues as follows:

- Machinery characteristics
- Physical devices
- Procedural methods
- Human factors
- Financial factors.

In the following sections, each of these subject areas is separately examined, with appropriate discrete topics identified. Recognition, understanding and analysis of these influences will enable an appropriate loss prevention strategy to be applied.

5.2 Machinery characteristics

Until recently, a renowned London hotel had steam boilers that were originally installed in the building in 1894. If these boilers are compared with, say, a modern gas turbine or computer-based control system, will the individual risks be the same and how could an effective loss prevention strategy be applied?

5.2.1 Age characteristics

We can consider machinery as having an 'age' characteristic, *i.e.* it may be classified as being prototype, proven or obsolete. Each of these classes of machinery will have attendant risks with the need to consider appropriate loss prevention.

In the case of prototype equipment, the design (including the materials selected, method of manufacture and prototype testing and modelling carried out) will significantly affect the degree of risk that remains, as will the availability of experienced operation and maintenance personnel. The questions that need to be addressed include:

- Do the design criteria accurately reflect the actual operating environment anticipated in service?
- Have materials been selected that will perform adequately under these conditions?
- Are the manufacturing techniques (*e.g.* welding) proven for complex structures where multi-site assembly takes place?
- How is consistency and interface quality maintained?
- How has the testing been carried out?
- How has operator and maintenance personnel competence been achieved?

Independent design-approval and inspection of pressure vessels in certain countries has been a mandatory requirement for a number of years and, increasingly, mechanical, electrical and consumer articles are subject to independent design, testing and certification controls. In some fields, such as in the design and approval of pressure vessels, the advent of computer-aided design systems have introduced their own risk factors. For example, a purchaser of a vessel, the nominated manufacturer and the independent design approval authority may all use the same computer-aided design programme. Hence, the integrity of the vessel is dependent on a single software program with a resulting high-risk exposure, unless strict validation of the program has been undertaken independently. If a prototype design is involved in this example, the computer modelling could well be flawed unless independent validation is carried out. This degree of care requires to be applied to any piece of equipment where modelling is utilised.

Clear design criteria also need to be stipulated and must relate to the anticipated operating conditions as closely as possible. An example is a cement plant pulse vessel of 2.5m diameter and some 20m height that suffered severe cracking through fatigue. On investigation, it was apparent that the designer had not been advised of the service condition of this vessel with regard to cyclic pressure loading (0–400psi every three seconds) and had only allowed for static design stresses. A potential catastrophic failure was fortunately averted through the vigilance of a plant operator. If the designer had been aware of the actual operating environment, allowances could have been made to reduce the risk of fatigue failure through more appropriate material selection and material thickness and improving the build quality with respect to reducing stress-raising crack-initiation sites.

In some cases, machines are now of such a size that full scale testing becomes very expensive. Prime examples are large capacity industrial gas and steam turbines. For example, for gas turbine generators in excess of 200MW it becomes expensive for original manufacturers to carry out extensive full-load testing. Limitations will include provision of gas fuel capacity sufficient for the facility, and local grid electrical demand or flexibility when long-term full load tests are being carried out.

As an alternative, manufacturers will use computer modelling to investigate and design components such as turbine blades, or use existing proven designs with scaled-up variants. In both approaches, significant assumptions are made and, for risks to be managed in these areas, the assumptions have to be identified and examined closely. Modelling may provide some degree of confidence but it is likely that only full-scale representative prototype testing will ensure results that can be validated.

For proven machinery (*i.e.* equipment that has been installed and running for a period of time to overcome the potential commissioning problems but remains within its design lifetime), risk exposure is more dependent upon intervention for condition monitoring and maintenance, suitable modifications and repairs, and, for certain plant, early planned remnant life assessment to ensure its continued safe operation.

Equipment assessed over its lifetime for unplanned shutdowns normally exhibits a 'bath tub' curve, with more incidents at the beginning and end of its life and fewer during the intervening period. There is also evidence that maintenance, modification or repair intervention in machines that are running normally can give rise to a higher subsequent breakdown incident rate. The human factors associated with this intervention normally give rise to problems, with inappropriate modification or repair methods, faulty assembly and poor housekeeping (leaving tools and equipment inside machines being one example. The associated risks and loss prevention strategies are included in later chapters in this Study Report; procedural methods can provide effective management.

The 'age' characteristic becomes more important for certain machinery that is subjected to high temperatures, cyclic loading or an aggressive environment. For each of these conditions, the time factor is critical to establishing when failure can be expected. At elevated temperatures such as those experienced by boilers, turbines and furnaces, a material response known as creep occurs; the material will deform, without an increase in load or stress, depending on time. In the case of fatigue resulting from cyclic loading, cracks will propagate at stress levels appreciably lower than the material characteristics would suggest and the final failure is dependent on the number of cycles and hence operating time.

Machines that typically experience fatigue failures include crushers and mills in cement plants and mining operations. These large rotating machines operate under severe conditions of varying load, both cyclic and in degree or in size, and some machines have changes of section where cracks will initiate more easily. Shafts for extrusion machines in the plastics industry will also be predisposed to this type of failure mechanism.

With aggressive environments, such as are found in chemical vessels and pumps, the time that the items are exposed to the chemicals is also critical. Even for proven plant, remnant life assessment will either be a mandatory requirement (*e.g.* for steam boilers in some countries) or a good practical loss prevention technique. The results of metallurgical investigations, non-destructive testing and modelling, such as those utilising fracture mechanics, can provide a basis on which to judge the further safe operation of the machinery.

The availability of original manufacturer's spares may become difficult to acquire where machinery is obsolete. This can lead to extended running periods without the correct spares and/or the use of partially repaired damaged parts, with the increased probability of failure through the time- and wear-related conditions of the machine or associated components. Makeshift spares may be made or non-original manufacturer's spares utilised with the attendant risk of inadequate material, heat treatment, geometry, etc. Care should be taken as to the pedigree of any spares introduced into the operation. This was not the case where an insured obtained locally the bottom-end bolts for a diesel engine. Although the geometry was identical to that set by the original equipment manufacturer, the quality of the material in terms of chemical and physical properties was not. After a short period of operation, the bolts failed, resulting in a catastrophic machine failure requiring extensive repairs including a new crankshaft, at a cost of some US$200,000 and loss of generating capacity for a period of six months.

Just as the machines may become obsolete, there is also an associated human factor where the original plant operators and maintenance personnel may retire without an adequate transition period for training new personnel. Experience has shown that for personnel to gain knowledge of a plant over an extended period of time is generally beneficial, provided that suitable management reviews are undertaken.

Increasingly, new and innovative repair techniques are being utilised, rather than replacing machines with the need to involve non-original equipment manufacturers. This provides equal or better repair reliability at an economic benefit but normally requires the insurer to be consulted and give prior approval.

Many of the 'age' related characteristics have been described above and concern either the original or continuing fitness for purpose, but there are other machinery characteristics that we should also consider.

5.2.2 **Application sensitivity**

Some machines can be regarded as independent in operation so, if they suffer a failure, the impact is limited to the machine itself. With the increasing use of computer technology in sensing, controlling and recording, the control systems become the brain and neural system of many plants. Where the control system fails, this not only affects the control system but will also lead to the malfunction or failure of the machinery and equipment that it controls. Therefore, it is necessary to identify the characteristics of the machine's potential for incapacitating other machinery or operations (which will be termed here as 'application sensitivity'), and then to formulate or introduce options for reducing the plant's resulting sensitivity.

An example of a machine that impacted on a number of other machines is a bank of batteries that provided an uninterruptible power supply ('UPS') to a number of control and management systems for a power station. In this incident, a hurricane was predicted to strike the area where the power station was located and the management took the difficult decision to de-energise the plant so that minimum damage would result if salt-laden spray and water came into contact with the equipment. Unfortunately, they forgot to isolate the UPS so that, when the hurricane struck, some of the systems were still energised and the salt-laden environment caused damage costing some US$250,000.

Application sensitivity becomes critical in the case of business interruption with not only the hardware (*i.e.* computers, cabling, air conditioning, etc.) but also the operating software being of importance. If dual independent systems are not available or believed to be cost effective, contingent recovery plans require creation and testing.

5.2.3 **Uniqueness**

Just as a machine's application sensitivity has been discussed above, it is necessary also to consider whether a machine is 'unique' or 'standard' as this will affect the ability to replace or repair it and return it to service in a reasonable period of time. Although this issue is allied to that of the characteristics of prototype plant, a unique piece of machinery may have an adequate service history and it is only in regard to its uniqueness that the risk exposure should be considered. By being unique, the available options for spares, maintenance and expertise are reduced and risk exposure can become significant.

5.2.4 **Size**

A machine's physical size is also an important characteristic to consider when reviewing risk and loss prevention. Once a large single-entity machine has been delivered to site, access may be difficult (depending on the site location) in the event of replacement or significant repair being required. For example,

- a low-quality road with severe gradients and fourteen tunnels approached a hydroelectric plant located in a mountainous remote area. The contingency plan called for heavy-load-capacity helicopters to be used in the event of repair or replacement of strategic machines;

- with modern large gas turbines, where the rotors weigh in excess of 100 tonnes, heavy lift aircraft are used for shipping to repair facilities, partly in response to the very large business interruption values at risk; *e.g.* in excess of US$250,000 per day;

- the position of the machine within a plant can be critical with regard to the provision of adequate 'laydown' space for maintenance purposes and the potential for surrounding property damage in the event of a catastrophic dynamic loss.

5.3 Physical devices

This term covers those devices that are intended to assist in reducing losses and are generally designed into the machinery to protect the machine, the safety of personnel, the product quality and/or the process or activity performance.

Such protection devices are critical to the loss prevention strategies adopted for machinery insurance. There have been many recorded instances where these devices have not operated correctly and caused a serious failure. Although the subsequent investigations have in most cases led to an improvement in loss prevention strategies, it is unlikely that a record has been made of the many instances where these devices have operated correctly and so saved life and property. Protection devices can be separated into:

- sensor or advisory monitors that advise and require further human intervention;

- those that may or may not have a perceived sensor element that will act automatically.

The types of parameter that these devices monitor include temperature, pressure, flow, content levels, speed, vibration, concentration, relative movement, etc. Even in the case of those devices that are self-acting without a perceived sensor (*e.g.* safety valves and bursting discs), indirect sensing of pressure is taking place, *i.e.* through spring characteristics or differential pressure loading in the case of the safety valve and material and geometry characteristics in the case of the bursting disc.

Are the physical devices appropriate for the type of service protection for which they are intended? As an example, consider a high-speed diesel engine operating at 900rpm, so that in one second the diesel engine will have completed 15 revolutions. If the lubricating oil for the engine fails, any sensor and trip mechanism will have a very limited time in which to act and so stop the engine before it suffers serious damage that is expensive to repair. Although the lubricating oil trip may operate as intended, by itself it may not provide effective protection owing to the speed of the machine. After an incident of this type, a high level oil reservoir tank was fitted which, in the event of the lubricating oil trip operating, allowed the engine to remain provided with sufficient lubricating oil until it had stopped. By providing inappropriate physical safety devices a false sense of security and protection can be created.

Where physical devices are provided, losses have occurred from operators disregarding the indications and messages provided, perhaps after experiencing many previous spurious warnings. These risk issues are primarily concerned with human factors and procedural methods of loss protection. Effective loss protection includes ensuring that good maintenance is carried out, implementing realistic failure simulations where possible, providing focused training of staff (*e.g.* not to disregard indicators, or to switch them off or accept alarms without investigation) and ensuring that trend records are acted upon.

The mimic diagram provides an example of the effect of such shortcomings. A mimic diagram is a display of processes or operations which schematically illustrates what is happening in a plant; it can provide basic information such as valve positions, levels, etc. Although increasingly superseded by computer control and monitoring systems, mimic diagrams are still widely used and experience in an international context has shown that the accuracy and operability of a system will generally depend on the type of operation involved, *e.g.* electrical utility, pulp and paper, cement production, petrochemical. For example, electrical utilities, petrochemical and utility operations within other process operations would be expected to have 80–100% operability through mimic diagrams, whereas wood preparation for pulp and paper and milling and grinding operations in mining and primary material processing would be expected to be 40–60% operable.

With sensor and display devices such as mimic diagrams operating correctly, the potential for a loss is reduced considerably, provided that operators are vigilant and trained to deal with the situations that arise. The above example illustrates the importance of the relationship between device and human operator and that maintenance of these devices is critical to ensure effective loss prevention. Continuing effective operation is important and can be significantly impaired, with a heightened probability of loss by inappropriate maintenance.

For example, in the case of bursting discs (which are used as a last resort for over pressure relief where hazardous or toxic substances are involved), the incorrect installation with regard to flow direction will prevent the operation of the disc at the desired pressure. With the disc installed in the incorrect position, disc rupturing could occur at between three and seven times overpressure, therefore putting the plant, personnel and public potentially at risk from catastrophic failure of vessels and piping and release of hazardous substances. The design of many devices will take account of the significance of correct installation and maintenance and ensure positive safety features that reduce the risk of incorrect fitting. For example, by supplying a bursting disc as an assembly mounting block and disc, correct installation is ensured provided that the block is fitted correctly in the first place; subsequent replacement of the disc will allow correct orientation for pressure by a series of keys and slots.

Many of these physical devices will be part of fail-safe systems or have designed or inherent redundancy characteristics which will provide back-up protection. However, from some of the examples already detailed, it can be appreciated that the benefit of many of the physical devices intended to provide protection can be reduced by inappropriate selection. It is important to recognise the relationship between device and human operator and also the significance of continuing effective maintenance.

5.4   Procedural methods

Many of the major industrial disasters (*e.g.* Flixborough, Bhopal, Mexico City, *Piper Alpha*, Phillips Petroleum, Arco Chemicals, Channel View, Guadalajara, the Taiwanese wafer plants) can be attributed in part to procedural failures. The risks associated with various procedural actions and the potential for loss prevention through the application of effective procedures can be categorised into three areas:

- Maintenance-related
- Operation-related
- Change-related.

5.4.1   Maintenance-related procedures

Machinery in operating plants may be subjected to various forms of maintenance and the relative effectiveness of these in preventing losses has been the subject of many detailed studies.

With 'breakdown maintenance', the machines are allowed to run until they fail and then are maintained. A disadvantage of this approach is that unplanned shutdowns occur with process interruption.

'Preventive and planned maintenance' involves the periodic servicing of equipment irrespective of the machine's need for intervention. Inspection and maintenance down time may be more frequent than necessary and the intervention itself may introduce further hazards that become risks and then losses.

'Predictive and condition based-maintenance' relies on monitoring of equipment and accurate record-keeping of results by the permanent staff and contractors involved such that the trend in deteriorating performance is noted and acted upon through planned shutdown before a failure occurs. The cost of the monitoring devices, surveillance and analysis may be regarded as a significant investment, with a great deal of reliance placed on appropriate timely human intervention. Regular testing and recalibration of monitoring devices is essential since their loss prevention effectiveness is only maintained while they are accurate.

Further maintenance strategies include 'reliability-centred maintenance', which focuses on the functionality of equipment to determine what preventive maintenance may be needed to improve the reliability and availability of equipment. This is risk-based maintenance, in which the emphasis of inspection and maintenance is moved away from low-risk machines, which may be inspected too frequently, to more frequent inspection and maintenance of high-risk machines.

For machinery having a high capital cost or which is strategically important to a process, 'condition monitoring' is widely used. Some of the techniques used include

- infrared thermography for detecting temperature differentials within plant such as switchgear or transformers, where it would indicate loose connections or deterioration of insulation, and in refractory-lined vessels where refractory deterioration may be detected early;

- *in situ* endwinding accelerometers that monitor the continuing integrity of the endwindings of electrical generators;

- testing of transformers by means of turns ratio testing, oil testing (measuring the dielectric strength, power factor, resistivity and water content), gas chromatography and capacitance testing and dissipation factor testing for the windings insulation.

For rotating machinery such as diesel engines, turbines and gearboxes, lubricating oil spectroscopy enables wear patterns to be monitored with minute debris particulates being identifiable. An increase in particulates may be the result of liners or bearings deteriorating.

The effective application of maintenance will assist in loss prevention. However, the factors that will significantly affect this are the adequacy of maintenance periods for the operating conditions and the availability of maintenance documentation and manuals, suitable tools, correct spares and trained staff.

Planning and recording of action is also crucial, as is illustrated by the following incident. A large electrical utility had invested in extensive periodic condition-monitoring of the turbine lubricating oil. The plant manager returned the reports to the individual power station for action; the reports from three periodic tests showed that there was a significant increase in lead present in the oil samples for one particular turbine, indicating potential severe deterioration of the bearings. The station staff had taken no action but, fortunately, action was taken after a risk-engineering audit which potentially saved a catastrophic turbine failure. If a failure had occurred, it would have involved minimum repair costs of around US$2m and interruption in the region of six to nine months. Periodic management reviews or audits will also ensure a consistent high performance level for maintenance staff.

The maintenance of stored spares should be actively pursued. Secure storage is required; the spares should be in a controlled environment with regard to temperature and humidity, retained in original protective packing and (in the case of sensitive electronic equipment) in a static-free environment. Large rotating equipment should have its shafts turned periodically to prevent rotor sag. These precautions will ensure that the spare will perform successfully, when fitted. Sufficient strategic spares need to be available to reduce business interruption exposure.

5.4.2 **Operation-related procedures**

With operation-related procedures, steady-state operation of equipment is likely to be less of a problem than when machines are being started, shut down or are suffering rapid process excursions. Procedures that enable staff to understand clearly the actions required and the expected results, together with effective personnel training, will assist in reducing operational losses involving machinery. Overloading or off-specification running of equipment should not be allowed or encouraged and there should be sufficient process and plant records to identify where potential problems can be expected. General housekeeping should be maintained at a high level to prevent inadvertent interference with operating equipment through ingestion of debris. Periodic independent statutory inspections can assist, as can management reviews and audits of actual operations. Detailed permit-to-work systems should also be created and implemented for certain activities such as working on isolated electrical or mechanical equipment, working at heights or in confined spaces, and for hot working such as in welding and gas cutting.

Significantly, all of these safety systems are likely to be flawed if independent review is omitted. For example, on a major transformer the unit was isolated to carry out a major inspection. A permit-to-work system was in place but not an interlock system. On isolating and de-energising the unit, the earth switch was closed. On completion of the inspection, the transformer was re-energised but the earth switch had not been reopened and consequently the transformer experienced overload until such time as the protection operated. In this case, the permit-to-work system was flawed in that the individual carrying out the work was also the person who signed-off the permit to say that it was in order for the transformer to return to service.

5.4.3   **Change-related procedures**

Where modifications are taking place, such as the expansion of a process plant or development of further generating capacity in an electrical utility, the tie-in of old and new systems need to be carefully planned and managed. Repairs should also be rigorously prepared for and executed. It is likely that some of this work may be undertaken by contractors who are unfamiliar with the plant and machinery and it is suggested that named individuals be made responsible and accountable for safe performance during these activities, with daily records being maintained. A plant which is either mothballed or lying silent poses significant exposure for loss through deterioration owing to environmental conditions and lack of maintenance; it should be just as carefully managed as an operating plant. Contingency plans and procedures should be available and tested, as far as is possible, for strategic machinery or supplies failure. Planning should include mutual aid agreements for rapid transfer of expertise, technology and machinery if necessary, sourcing of strategic spares and identification of appropriate repair facilities.

Quantitative risk assessment, including hazard analysis and operability studies, is being increasingly utilised to assist in loss prevention strategies. In relation to procedures, it is necessary to look for validation or harmony between those planned for and what is actually happening. Accurate records are vital; there should be a clear distribution and action responsibility detailed on any pro forma or report. Monitoring of machine condition is critical but of even more importance is establishing and analysing the ongoing trends of the data and taking appropriate action.

5.5   Human factors

As previously mentioned, human frailty exists and human factors and influences will affect all aspects of machinery insurance, from design and conceptual studies, through manufacture and assembly of machines and their control systems, to operation, repair, modification and maintenance of equipment. The problem is to reduce those risks associated with human factors that create a high potential for failure of machinery while still encouraging those human factors that contribute to operating machinery safely and reliably.

In many failure situations, the ensuing investigation will attribute the failure to a human error and identify an individual or individuals who are regarded as the cause of the failure. Occasionally the investigation will go beyond this stage and ask the question 'Why did the individual or individuals take the action which led to the failure?'. A rigorous examination and investigation is believed to be a more appropriate approach in terms of preventing the reoccurrence of the failure.

Most companies will state that their most valuable asset is their human resource. In regard to the influence that the human resource exerts over the safe and profitable operation of a business, this is undoubtedly true. There is a need for both the individual and the organisation to work in concert, so that an individual's contribution to the overall synergy of the operation is maximised. The next section examines the influence of human factors in terms of individual and organisational characteristics.

5.5.1 **Individuals' characteristics**

The selection of an individual to undertake a certain role must be carried out intelligently with regard not only to his existing experience and capacity but also to his potential future development.

Although the following example could just as well be regarded as an organisational matter, the experience or lack of experience of a senior operator of a gas turbine power station led to a major failure when he was charged to carry out a periodic water wash of the compressor. This operator had no experience of this procedure and was not provided with any guidance in terms of procedure documents. The simple action of forgetting to open a small valve resulted in reverse gas flow from the combustion area of the turbine to purge air service pipes.

Combustion gases in excess of 1200°C entered pipework designed for air at a maximum temperature of about 300°C. Failure of these pipes followed rapidly and molten material was projected through the hot gas path of the turbine. Any of the following important actions could have prevented this incident:

● identification of the profile of attributes that would assist in achieving the role objectives and its comparison with the candidate's characteristics;

● induction training on first joining a company or on transferring to a new role;

● periodic review and continuing training and updating of the individual's skill base and expertise.

5.5.2 **Organisational style**

The organisation style and structure will influence the safe and reliable operation of machinery, impacting on an individual's motivation and morale in striving to achieve good results. Worldwide maintenance and reliability management studies have indicated that the degree of effective reliability for best performance has come about through a management task model where planning and systems, central shops and stores services and maintenance engineering departments are available to support a work-execution group, with centralised control of maintenance policy and work priority determination.

Experience of machines operated in all types of territories and environments, some extreme or harsh, would suggest that the organisational characteristics could include those structural elements mentioned in the previous paragraph. However, it is believed that more significantly it is the organisation style in terms of leadership which is important. The ethos of a petrochemical plant was clearly illustrated when carrying out a risk-engineering audit when, as a test of the security of the main control room, the no-go area adjacent to the main process controls was crossed. The yellow line that demarcated this was to prevent unauthorised individuals interfering with controls. The senior operator physically removed the risk engineer to behind the no-go area — a successful test! The individuals at this plant were fiercely proud of their operation and the co-operative regime was led, encouraged and maintained by the plant manager's enthusiasm and commitment.

Organisational style with periodic reviews and action plans based on the whole operation, and not on discrete sections' interests, are found to be beneficial. Stewardship, ownership and the accountability of individuals contribute to this high-reliability performance.

Other factors that need to be considered are the possible presence of cultural influences, the involvement of expatriates or specialists, and a history of or predisposition to substance abuse. The staff age disposition which allows for a line of succession is also significant, as is the turnover of personnel. The personnel records and reviews will assist in the assessment of some of the human factor influences for any particular operation.

5.6   Financial influences

The cost of loss prevention has to be weighed against its benefits. The budget for expenditure on loss prevention will be a matter of interest not only to those directly involved in the day-to-day business of plant safety but also to those controlling the business's overall finances. The reporting lines between the 'safety manager' and the 'financial controller' may reveal the broad corporate attitude towards loss prevention and risk control.

With machinery insurance, there will be many influences that will be common to all forms of insurance, whether one is self-insuring, using a captive or effecting traditional market insurance. These will include financial optimisation, budgetary constraints and minimising risk costs.

5.6.1   The sum insured

Historically, there have been many instances the sum insured under the insurance policy has not matched the actual physical value. In the event of a claim, this can result in the indemnity payment being reduced in the same proportion as the under-insurance (the application of 'average') and can lead to dispute. Taking loss prevention in a wide context, to ensure that any valid claim is met in full, there is a very real need to ensure that an appropriate sum insured is declared. The accuracy of the various selected sums insured (as required under the insurance policy) depends on a number of factors, preferably supported by an independent valuation or review, and these should be reasonably current and representative of the present situation. Therefore, an independent valuation or review at periodic intervals will be an effective loss prevention technique in this area.

5.6.2   Taxes and duties

Allied to the need for accurate declared sums insured is the requirement to consider the influence of import duties on machinery requiring replacement or repair from outside the operating country. The terms of the insurance contract will be critical in determining whether import duties are an agreed inclusion in any claim settlement. Import duties internationally are dynamic, in relation not only to time but also to the type of business in which the equipment is being used, *e.g.* for a Government electrical utility or politically-strategic process plant, duty can vary from 0% to 100% or more of the original machine or spare value. As an example, a diesel engine crankshaft was being sourced from the USA with a free-on-board value of some £100,000. However, by the time the crankshaft had arrived on site at the final destination country, the cost to the insurer was some £200,000 once import duty had been taken into account.

A similar situation can arise if an irrecoverable domestic tax or excise duty is levied on the purchase or use of particular goods or services. Here again, the policy should be explicit in terms of the extent of insured indemnity.

5.6.3   **Warranties and support agreements**

On many new operating plants, the original equipment manufacturer ('OEM') will provide warranties and guarantees and these may give some financial support in the event of any failure and loss. However, their effectiveness will depend significantly on the financial and business pedigree of the OEM, the relationship between the operating company and the OEM and the extent of the warranty in terms of the time and scope of protection. In general terms, these factors will also apply to any other related insurance policies such as engineering, construction, property, all risks, etc. This additional financial protection may help or hinder in the overall or specific loss prevention strategy. It is necessary to know of their existence and the scope of cover. Additionally, the expertise and experience of the OEM should be considered so that it can be approached to provide assistance.

5.6.4   **Production sensitivity and profit contribution**

With regard to business interruption, the cost of repair of a piece of failed machinery is in itself likely to be small when compared with the overall cost of interruption to the business. A number of factors will significantly influence the financial exposure or loss in the event of a machine's failure. For example, there may be duplicated equipment or streams for processing a particular product, there may be a strong or weak interdependency between products for a site's effective operation and there could well be a disproportionate profit contribution from a minor-volume product. Experience has shown that, for financial loss prevention, an effective approach to analysing the real exposure to loss is by starting from an analysis of the derivation of the profit of an operation in terms of product and volume, then regressing through the process to identify the machines and operations that contribute to or impact on the various products. In petrochemical plants, this analysis can produce results which show the complex interrelationship with processes and intermediate products.

Specific services such as electricity, fuel or water may also have a major impact on the whole site rather than on just a particular operation. Experience has shown that the provision of electricity is especially critical, with the adequacy of transformer or generating capacity being particularly important. One illustrative incident involved a step-down transformer that had two different low voltage outputs. Although in total the capacity of the two transformer windings provided a 100% standby capacity, owing to the process demands being weighted towards one of the voltages, the process could not operate at 100% production capacity in the event of one output winding failing.

5.6.5   **Seasonal influences**

Seasonal processing, such as found in the sugar industry, will provide either a long or a short time-window for repairs in the event of machinery breaking-down without affecting production. Many industries will operate with a periodic annual shutdown for maintenance and development projects, while others have adopted a strategy of continuous operation.

5.6.6   **Dynamic commodity prices**

Internationally, the availability and price of most products are very dynamic. This is particularly so in the case of sales of electricity where, in some countries, the price will change every 30 minutes. This not only leads to difficulties in estimating potential financial exposures and possible loss prevention techniques but also, in the event of a valid claim, will require a substantial amount of analysis to estimate the quantum of loss.

5.6.7 **Acquisition of 'hard' currency**

Within some countries, the acquisition of 'hard' currency is difficult. This can lead to a delay in providing funds for repairs and replacement machinery that can significantly increase the business interruption exposure. Contingent arrangements will include having external funds available or mutual aid agreements with other external organisations and even to the agreement of the insurer to fund certain plant or machinery.

5.6.8 **Stocking of spare parts**

For any equipment that fails, the operating company's philosophy on stocking spares will be critical, as will the repair facilities available locally and internationally and the lead time to replace critical components or machines. Strategic spares are likely to be expensive in simple investment terms from a company's perspective but, with some lead times for particular machines being in the region of 15 to 18 months, the business interruption exposure can be seen to be substantial.

5.7 Summary and conclusions

Loss prevention in the context of machinery insurance can be seen to be a complex subject covering many fields of interest, including behavioural science, diverse engineering disciplines, material science, international finance and markets, and commercial accounting.

With this degree of complexity, it is essential that a structured approach be taken with a need to identify and analyse risks before creating loss prevention strategies. A single loss prevention action may enable a wide range of risks to be addressed, as in the case of improved man management, or there may be a need to create a focused loss prevention plan which specifically targets a particular machine or process, as in condition monitoring.

The application and implementation of an intelligent loss prevention philosophy can be an effective investment — a small outlay with a significant return.

6   Scope of insurance cover

6.1   Fire cover

Practically all property owners face a potential exposure to damage caused by fire. Many owners of property also face additional exposure to damage caused by lightning, explosion and aircraft. Owners of industrial and process machinery are no exception and the practice of arranging fire material damage insurance dates back to the origins of the insurance industry. Fundamental insurance against the perils of fire, lightning, explosion and aircraft (often abbreviated to 'FLEXA') does not require any further explanation at this point.

In many instances, additional exposures are also present and cover for extended perils (typically storm, tempest, windstorm, flood and impact by vehicles) forms the basis of many property insurance policies. Likewise, theft or attempt thereat may be included where required.

In some geographical locations, the property may also be exposed to damage by certain natural hazards such as earthquake or volcanic eruption or that due to riot, strike and civil commotion and these perils can also be specifically included in the policy.

The above outlines the basis of fire and specified perils insurance. Provided the physical loss or damage that is suffered is due to one or more of these stated perils, then the policy indemnifies the owner by paying for repairs or reinstating the property. Of course, some exclusions apply and there are certain policy conditions that need to be respected by the insured owner; one of the more important relates to the adequacy of the sum insured and the fact that it must represent the full replacement value to avoid penalty in the event of a claim.

6.1.1   Underinsurance: the average condition

If, at the time of a claim, it is found that the sum insured had been understated, the insurer is entitled to apply an 'average' condition (provided of course that this condition appears in the policy). In these circumstances, the basis of settlement of the claim (*i.e.* the amount recoverable) would be the same proportion of the loss as the sum insured bears to the true actual value of the property, even where the damage is partial and has a value below the sum insured. This is illustrated in the following simple example:

- replacement value at risk   £100,000
- sum insured   £75,000
- amount of loss   £20,000
- amount recoverable under policy = (£75,000/£100,000 x £20,000) =   £15,000

There are variations to the average condition to permit a degree of underinsurance without penalty. They may allow a margin of discrepancy of, say, 20%, which is useful in times of rising inflation. To similar effect, the policy may include a capital additions clause, which makes provision for automatic increases in the sum insured, useful where the actual schedule of property insured may vary during the period of insurance.

Where the values insured are understated and there is no provision for the application of average, it may be contended that the risk has been misrepresented (*i.e.* material facts were not disclosed) to insurers. If in these circumstances it is shown that the understated value is material to the acceptance of the risk, the insurer may be entitled to avoid the policy.

A policy arranged with a limit of indemnity (as distinct from a sum insured) or on a 'first loss' basis may not have an average condition nor any of the protections against underinsurance described above.

6.2 'All risks' cover

A wider form of protection may be found in policies that provide cover on an 'all risks' basis. Whereas a specified perils policy will state those perils that trigger the operative clause, an 'all risks' policy takes a broader approach. It will respond to loss or damage from any cause not otherwise specifically excluded elsewhere in the policy.

A typical operative clause would read

'Subject to the exclusions, conditions and limitations contained herein, this policy insures the property of the insured and the property of others, which is under their care custody or control and for which they are legally liable, against all risks of direct physical loss or damage occurring during the period of insurance.'

A key difference in this approach that should be noted is the importance of the policy exclusions. The onus rests with the insurer to prove that a policy exclusion applies after the property has been 'lost or damaged from any cause'. In many instances, this may prove difficult to apply in practice.

In the context of buildings and other objects of a static nature, the exposure to damage comes from external factors and the forces of nature, despite the design and build specification. Apart from the built-in structural strength of static property and buildings, fire detection, fire prevention, lightning conductors and security devices all play important parts in avoiding or reducing these exposures.

The same exposures are faced by owners of industrial and process machinery which can also suffer damage from these same external causes, but being dynamic objects of property there are additional exposures to consider. In basic terms, the machines may suffer damage, which may be severe in some cases owing to internal forces or failures.

In practice, this additional exposure and the associated risks make the approach to machinery insurance and the scope of cover quite distinct from general property insurance. The following policy extracts would typically appear where this operational exposure is not covered by the insurance.

'Damage shall mean accidental loss or destruction of or damage to the Property Insured.

Property Insured shall include ... buildings including lifts heating air conditioning and all other installed plant ...

Excluded Causes: This cover does not include:

Damage caused by or consisting of ... (1) latent defect, ... its own faulty or defective design or materials; ... (2) bursting of a boiler, economiser or vessel, machine or apparatus in which internal pressure is due to steam only and belonging to or under the control of the Insured.

Damage consisting of ... (3) joint leakage failure of welds cracking fracturing collapse or overheating of boilers economisers superheaters pressure vessels or any range of steam and feed piping in connection therewith; (4) mechanical or electrical breakdown or derangement of the particular machine apparatus or equipment in which such breakdown or derangement originates.

but this shall not exclude ... such Damage not otherwise excluded which itself results from a Defined Peril or from any other accidental loss destruction or damage; ... subsequent Damage which itself results from a cause not otherwise excluded; ... the amount of the deductible.'

It can be seen that, whilst machinery breakdown is excluded, some degree of resultant damage is provided by the policy by suitable qualification of the exclusion. This is clear from the opening words of the two exclusions given as examples above where 'consisting of' is taken to be a narrower exclusion term than 'caused by or consisting of'.

6.3   Sudden and unforeseen damage; machinery breakdown cover

Cover for these operational causes may be found in a traditional machinery breakdown policy, in which the terms electrical and mechanical breakdown are defined, or (more commonly today) the policy cover will refer to 'sudden and unforeseen' damage. Such a policy would typically provide

'Sudden and unforeseen damage which necessitates immediate repair or replacement before the machine can resume normal working ...'.

The main exclusions would be

- 'fire, lightning, explosion, aircraft, water damage, flood, subsidence of buildings, earthquake, riot, strike and civil commotion (*i.e.* fire and specified perils);
- normal wear, tear, or gradual deterioration, corrosion;
- periodical replaceable parts, filters, tyres, hoses, etc.;
- known (or which ought to have been known) faults present at the commencement of the policy;
- the amount of the deductible.'

The following are examples of the types of cause of damage to machinery that would be covered under this policy.

- faulty or defective material, design, construction or installation

- faulty maintenance, maladjustment, misalignment, poor calibration

- failure of safety or protective devices

- faulty operation, lack of skill in use, malicious acts

- defective lubrication, overheating, abnormal stress, molecular fatigue, centrifugal force, lack of boiler feedwater

- failure of insulation, short circuits, electrical arching, excessive electrical pressure, including indirect effects of lightning

- storm damage, frost, impact, collision, flying debris, dropping or falling

- entry of foreign bodies.

While this is not an exhaustive list, it serves to show that this policy covers accidents to machines from both internal and external causes.

6.4 Boiler explosion cover

The approach to explosion risks is worth comment, in particular with regard to industrial boilers and other steam pressure vessels.

As outlined in Chapter 1, the earliest forms of specialist machinery insurance originated from the use of steam boilers during the Industrial Revolution. This development followed some disastrous accidents, and many fatalities, caused by pressure vessel explosions. This poor experience led to early forms of machinery loss prevention and an insurance against the heavy cost of these explosions developed. In considering explosion risks, it is important to differentiate between the various forms of explosion.

Chemical explosion and the explosion that can be associated with the ignition of gases is traditionally the domain of fire insurers. Fire damage often ensues with such explosions, through the escape of highly inflammable and combustible materials and/or through the very high temperatures that are generated.

In contrast, fire insurers often exclude pressure (physical) explosion (or collapse/implosion), as can arise in steam boilers and associated pressure vessels, in a similar manner to their exclusion of machinery breakdown. This type of explosion is caused by a pressure build-up of steam (or other gas or liquids) which ruptures, tears or dangerously distorts the vessel, without there being any chemical reaction. The common causes of such major failures are the same as those leading to less serious breakdowns in other types of machinery, *e.g.* mechanical failure, lack of maintenance or operator error.

Insurance cover against internal failures of boiler plant where no explosion occurs is provided under a machinery breakdown policy. An example would be damage to the tubes in a steam boiler which would require repairs before the boiler could resume normal working. On those rare occasions where an explosion does occur, it is likely to be due to internal failure and/or operator error, coupled with an associated failure of safety devices or early warning systems.

Logically, this type of explosion risk can be regarded as being an extension of machinery breakdown insurance. This is reinforced by the practice of linking the insurance cover against boiler explosion with independent periodic inspection services, required by law in most developed countries. Boiler explosion/collapse insurance may be provided under a separate policy or included under a machinery breakdown cover.

At a slight variance with the above distinction between the two forms of explosion, boiler flue gas explosion is considered as a normal extension to the boiler explosion policy.

In some insurance markets, it has become quite commonplace for fire insurers not to make a distinction between chemical explosion and pressure explosion in their policies and, in so doing, they include the latter within their cover. Of course, this approach will not only vary from one insurer to another but will depend considerably on the nature of the boiler risk in question, particularly for those industries where large steam generating plants dominate the overall exposure; *see* Chapter 9, 'Power generation' and Chapter 11, 'Pulp and paper plants'.

A further point of clarification is required in respect of turbine disruption or where the turbine casing bursts, owing to the high level of internal forces within these high-speed and high-pressure machines. These risks are part of the standard cover under a machinery breakdown policy.

6.5 Package or combined covers

Package policies that contain two sections of cover (*i.e.* fire/specified perils and machinery breakdown) have grown in popularity in recent years and offer an attraction to the machinery owner and insurer alike. One benefit is to reduce doubts over which policy might apply or which policies should contribute to any given event. With certain claims, the proximate cause may be difficult to determine and the event may even fall between two policies. This can present problems when different insurers issue those policies. From the machinery owner's point of view, the package policy approach leaves the burden of resisting a claim on the grounds of proximate cause entirely with the one insurer. However, package policies require skilled drafting as otherwise some ambiguity can remain.

A dual-section combined cover may have individual exclusions, conditions, sub-limits and deductibles applicable to each section.

A further broadening of the insurance of machinery is to provide an 'all risks' policy, which does not specifically exclude nor make any distinction in respect of machinery breakdown or operational causes. Even where this is the apparent approach, some exclusions may have an impact in the event of a claim, *e.g.* that of damage caused by or consisting of latent defect, faulty design or materials, which is often a feature of such policies. It will be remembered that this exclusion does not appear in a 'sudden and unforeseen' machinery breakdown policy and the intention of the all risks policy may be unclear.

Whereas some all risks policies have absolute exclusions in respect of defects, other policies intend to limit the application of the exclusion, by using suitable qualifying words, to the defective machine immediately affected. In some instances, the exclusion applies only to the defective component within a machine, thereby providing some measure of cover for 'resultant damage' to other non-defective property otherwise insured under the policy.

As indicated, the extent of these exclusions and the approach towards defective machinery, and/or resultant or consequential damage, lies at the heart of many insurance disputes. This is likely to be compounded in the case of partial damage to a machine, which is often the case with machinery failures where total losses are uncommon.

Additional difficulties may be encountered when considering business interruption insurance and the apportionment of the interruption loss in respect of partially indemnifiable material damage claims.

Although the nature of the machinery itself and the industry in which it is used are important considerations, there are clear benefits in having all available insurance cover under one policy, provided of course that the overall cover is wide enough and that the packaged insurance product is sustainable from the insurer's viewpoint and therefore remains available in the long term.

6.6   Basis of material damage claims settlement

Classically, machinery policies are written on an indemnity basis and so undertake to restore the insured to the same position after the loss as he was in immediately prior to the loss. This restoration is subject to the application of the policy deductible (or excess) and any limits of indemnity and, if applicable, the average condition referred to earlier.

Where a machine is either an actual total loss or a constructive total loss (*i.e.* where repairs are uneconomic), some deduction may also be made for depreciation. However, the cost of repairs (*i.e.* the cost of new parts and the labour to supply and fit them) is normally met in full. In some instances, an allowance for 'betterment' may be negotiated between the insurer and the insured.

Property fire policies are accustomed to dealing with total losses and most provide 'reinstatement as new' cover. Such cover may apply under machinery policies (although not perhaps to older machines) and, while there may be an element of betterment involved in the claim settlement, the replacement machine would be more or less equal in size, capacity and functionality to the machine that had been written off.

The policy may be extended to include the expenses of debris removal and compliance with local authority conditions, which might add to the overall settlement figure.

6.7   Summary of cover for material damage

Material damage insurance in respect of industrial and process machinery may take one of the following forms or, where appropriate, a combination of two such forms:

● Fire and named or specified perils

● Sudden and unforeseen damage or machinery breakdown

● All risks, excluding machinery breakdown

● All risks, including machinery breakdown under a sub-section or clauses

● All risks, without a machinery breakdown exclusion

Regardless of what form the insurance takes, the wording of the entire policy or policies should be studied and understood to ensure that the overall cover is sufficient in the unfortunate event of a claim having to be made. Where more than one policy (or section of cover) is involved, unnecessary overlaps or unintentional gaps in cover should be eliminated.

6.8   Business interruption cover

A defined form of physical loss or damage will trigger a business interruption policy. The scope of cover (*i.e.* the nature of the accident that triggers the policy) should therefore be considered in the same way as for the material damage risks already described above.

The plant owner could choose just to insure the business interruption risk following fire, lightning, explosion and aircraft damage, whereas he may have an all risks policy in force for the material damage risks. The reasons for this approach may be that he can afford to self-insure the risks from the relatively minor exposures to, say, water damage or machinery breakdown but the business could not survive a major fire without the protection afforded by insurance. Moreover, to save premium costs, the owner may choose to insure only items of machinery that are vital to the continued running of the business, whereas the material damage policy may be on a blanket schedule basis.

Where business interruption risks are to be insured, it is very likely that there will be a material damage warranty in the policy. This means that a valid material damage policy should be in force and that a valid claim thereunder would be the trigger for indemnity under the business interruption policy. One important reason for this requirement is to ensure compliance with the policy condition that the insured machinery is maintained in good order (including undergoing statutory inspections where applicable). A second reason is to ensure that, in the event of damage, independent funds are available under the material damage policy to meet the costs of repairs; any lack of funds to finance repairs in a timely manner would otherwise extend the interruption period and so increase the business interruption loss.

There are two common exceptions to the requirement for a material damage warranty. The first is in respect of material damage claims that would be covered but which fall within the policy deductible and nevertheless cause an indemnifiable business interruption. The business interruption policy would respond in this case subject to its own terms and conditions. The second exception is where a manufacturer's warranty (rather than the owners' material damage policy) responds to the costs of repair or replacement parts. It is unlikely that the manufacturer's liability will extend to cover the machinery owner's business interruption losses.

6.8.1   Basis of business interruption claims settlement

Once the indemnifiable loss or damage to machinery has triggered the business interruption policy the basis of the loss of profit settlement will be on either

- the 'difference basis', *i.e.* gross profit (which is turnover less those specified working expenses which diminish with a reduction in the business activity); or

- the 'addition basis', *i.e.* net profit plus standing charges (being those fixed costs which do not diminish with reduced business activity).

Normally, there will be a time exclusion, expressed as the number of days of business interruption which have to be exceeded before the policy responds. In some policies, the time exclusion (and therefore the indemnity period) commences on the date of the accident whereas in other policies it may not commence until the business is first interrupted. Once the time exclusion period is exceeded, the policy will continue to pay until the business is no longer interrupted or the indemnity period is exhausted, whichever happens sooner.

A standard policy will also respond to increased costs of working expenses, provided these are incurred with the agreement of the insurer and the additional expense is less than the loss of profit that has been thereby avoided or reduced.

Some manufacturing businesses are insured on a straightforward 'loss of output' basis. This approach is suitable where the manufacturing process, expenses and normal output are all regular and achieved evenly over time with little fluctuation.

The difference basis is the most common approach to machinery business interruption and the relevant terms are defined below.

6.8.1.1 **Gross profit**

The generally accepted definition is the difference between turnover and all specified working expenses, expressed as the amount by which the sum of the turnover and the closing stock shall exceed the sum of the opening stock and the specified working expenses. The opening and closing stocks are to be valued in accordance with the insured's normal accounting methods with due provision being made for depreciation.

6.8.1.2 **Turnover**

Turnover is defined as 'the money (less discounts allowed) paid or payable to the insured for goods sold and delivered and for services rendered in course of the business at the premises'. This definition is of central importance because turnover is the gauge of business activity. It refers to 'the business' to make it clear that the indemnity provided by the policy relates only to the business stated in the schedule to the policy; thought should therefore be given to ensuring that this embraces the whole of the insured's activity.

6.8.1.3 **Specified working expenses**

These are the uninsured working expenses, *i.e.* those expenses that will diminish as the activity of the business diminishes. Examples of such expenses are raw materials, power, packaging, carriage and freight.

It is important that any alteration to these expenses should be ascertained to ensure that the cover meets the needs of the particular business involved. If the specified working expenses shown include any working expenses which will continue during the interruption period, the insured will not be entitled to a complete indemnity.

6.8.1.4 **Rate of gross profit**

This is defined as 'the rate of gross profit earned on the turnover during the financial year immediately before the date of the accident'. The insured's last financial year results are used as the basis in order to obtain the most up-to-date annual profit ratio for the business.

6.8.1.5 **Standard turnover**

The standard turnover is defined as 'the turnover during the period in the twelve months immediately before the date of the accident which corresponds with the indemnity period' (*i.e.* the annual turnover up to the date of the particular accident which gives rise to the claim for indemnity). By comparing this standard turnover with that achieved during the indemnity period one can establish the reduction in turnover experienced after the accident.

6.8.2 **Extensions to business interruption cover**

The business interruption policy may be extended to include the additional cover explained below.

6.8.2.1 **Denial of access**

Under this extension, the policy responds where access to the business premises is physically prevented by a specified type of damage or accident to other property (*e.g.* buildings, access roads, etc.) in close proximity, which thereby interrupts the insured business.

6.8.2.2 **Suppliers' and/or customers' damage**

If the insured's supplier or customer suffers damage, as specifically defined in the policy, at its own premises, it may not be able to fulfil its obligations to supply or take materials, component parts, or completed products. Where this causes the insured business to be interrupted, the insured's policy will respond under this extension.

6.8.2.3 **Accidental failure of utility supplies**

Where there is an accidental failure in a supply of electricity, gas or water before the intake point at the insured premises (*e.g.* the feeder end) which interrupts the business, the policy will respond under this extension. Having regard to their normal reliability standards, such failures of utility supplies would usually be subject to a short franchise period rather than the usual time exclusion. Typically, any interruption in supply of less than 30 minutes would not be covered but the entire period of resultant business interruption lasting more than this 30 minutes would be covered.

6.9 Specimen policies

It is beyond the scope of this Study Report to include specimen policy wordings from a range of insurers or reinsurers world-wide. Each insurer has developed its own style and form of wording, which can vary quite appreciably from one to another. Equally, some markets favour one style over another and this difference is clearly seen between European and US policy forms and terminology.

Whenever a machinery policy wording is being considered or compared, it should be read in its entirety in order to ensure that it suits the purpose for which the insurance is being effected.

7 Taking-over: putting recently-erected machinery into use

7.1 Introduction

The specialised area of construction and erection insurance is the subject of a previous Advanced Study Report of The Insurance Institute of London (ASG 208B: *Construction Insurance*) which addresses matters such as risks arising during the erection and the testing and commissioning and maintenance and defects liability phases under a construction contract. That Report deals with the allocation of risk between the contractor(s) and the purchaser/ owner (sometimes known as the 'employer'), whose individual responsibilities are normally defined in the contract, including the obligations to arrange various forms of first party and third party insurance. In simple terms, in most industrial projects the contractor is responsible for 'care of the works' throughout the erection phase and until the satisfactory completion of testing and commissioning. Suitable 'contractors' all risks' ('CAR') or 'erection all risks' ('EAR') insurance is effected accordingly.

For industrial manufacturing plants generally, the construction contract will specify at what time, and under what conditions, responsibility for the completed project will be transferred from the contractor(s) to the purchaser. Normally (except for oil and gas plants) this will be after the completion of a specified period of operational testing and commissioning. The issue of a taking-over certificate (sometimes called a 'certificate of practical completion') by or on behalf of the purchaser (or its engineer) to the contractor usually marks the satisfactory completion of the operational period; from that point, the purchaser becomes the true owner.

In contrast to this arrangement, it is important to note that, with oil and gas projects, it is common for the purchaser/owner to assume responsibility for the erected plant prior to testing and commissioning, which will be carried out under his full control and direction. Should the plant not perform to the standard expected, difficulties may arise as to where responsibility lies for the remedial works, and in turn which policy of insurance should respond.

At the point of taking-over (sometimes referred to as the 'hand-over'), the need to arrange 'permanent insurance', including that relating to the machinery itself, is assumed by the new owner. However, there will normally be a residual responsibility (and sometimes an insurance) 'to make good defects' and to repair any resultant damage; this remains with the contractor during the defects liability or maintenance period, typically stated in the contract as being 12 or 24 months from the date of practical completion. Normally, the contractor is also responsible under the terms of the construction contract for damage to the completed works caused by him while back on site for the purposes of fulfilling his obligations thereunder. Insurance against this responsibility is known as visits maintenance cover.

It can be seen that the first year or two of the permanent insurance (often known as the 'operational insurance') runs concurrently with the maintenance cover under the construction policy. If a claim is met under the permanent cover during this period, it can, depending on the cause, lead to a subrogation action and a recovery against the contractor and his insurers.

7.2 Partial taking-over

Difficulties might arise where there is a partial taking-over, or a qualified taking-over due to technical or operational problems. Part of the project would still be at risk to the contractor whilst the balance would have passed to the owner who would wish to operate the plant commercially, paying due regard to the taking-over position. In high-value and complex risks such as oil refineries, one common reason for encountering this difficulty is where a plant is mechanically complete but is unable to achieve design specifications once tested. In other words, the plant cannot reach the desired temperatures, pressures or output levels, the reasons for which might be any of the following:

● Insufficient feedstock available.

● Problems at the customer-side of the supply chain which means that the product, if produced in full or in part, would have nowhere to go.

● Fault(s) or defect(s) in the design, specification, materials or workmanship relating to the erection of the plant.

● Damage has occurred in another part of the plant.

7.3   CAR/EAR insurance

This situation presents 'off-cover, on-cover' difficulties for the respective insurers of the CAR/EAR risks and the 'permanent' machinery risks, who, between them, may struggle to dovetail the two. Not the least of the problem lies in the fact that two policies will have different insured parties, with differing interests, and differences in scope of cover. Further difficulties can arise with the interpretation and application of the construction contract, to which insurers are not party and over which they have little or no influence.

7.4   Permanent insurance

Permanent machinery insurers (as opposed to CAR/EAR insurers) are not insuring the erection phase nor are they primarily concerned with the risks to be borne by contractors. They will usually expect the machinery that is to be protected by their policies to have undergone 'full and satisfactory' testing and commissioning before becoming exposed under their policies.

7.5   Testing and commissioning phases

As already indicated, the machinery constituting the contract works is normally held at the contractor's risk during the testing and commissioning phases of the project. As a result of particular difficulties in the oil, gas and petrochemical industry, insurers involved in that sector frequently incorporate strict conditions and/or exclusions to remove the testing and commissioning exposure from their cover.

In other sectors, testing and commissioning is not perceived as such a problem and, if an exclusion is included in the permanent insurance policy, it commonly tends to be more generalised and to some extent will depend on the scope of cover provided in respect of the machinery. For example, it is quite common to include a testing and commissioning exclusion under a fire and named perils section of a property policy that covers boiler and machinery. However, it is quite usual for 'all risks' policies to cover machinery without specifically excluding testing and commissioning. However, it should be noted that some insurers might contend successfully that the status of the machinery in respect of testing and commissioning is a material fact that should be disclosed, regardless of policy conditions. In any event, other policy exclusions may be relevant to an operational failure that would limit the cover, *e.g.* defects in material workmanship or design.

It is particularly difficult to draft a testing and commissioning exclusion clause that is relevant to all machinery covered by a global policy. It is quite possible that such a policy covers everything from highly-specialised technical processing to simple 'turnkey' operations. In those circumstances, it is unrealistic to expect the testing and commissioning clause to be specific to the extent that is usually expected in the oil, gas and petrochemical industry. Thus, if a testing and commissioning exclusion is incorporated it again tends to be of a general nature.

7.6   Policy exclusions

In regard to taking-over, the policy exclusion relating to defects is important. Alternatively, a right of subrogation would arise against contractors in the event that the permanent policy might respond to a loss which turns out to be the 'contractor's responsibility'.

Oil and gas insurers may express their intentions through a specific exclusion, *e.g.* '... this policy does not cover destruction or damage to property in course of construction or erection, dismantling or undergoing testing or commissioning, including mechanical, performance testing, and any business interruption resulting therefrom.'

The policy may further state that: '... acceptance of property hereon is subject to satisfactory completion of the following procedures.

1. Mechanical testing;
2. Testing and commissioning;
3. Performance testing conforming to 100% design criteria as specified in the building contract;
4. Official acceptance by the insured following formal taking-over certificate procedures (it being understood that no equipment faults or snagging-list items affecting the operational integrity of the plant are outstanding).'

Ideally, the taking-over position should be 'clean-cut' and this should be mirrored by the cover provided under the CAR/EAR policy as otherwise some gaps in insurance cover may arise (*e.g.* owing to non-compliance with points 1 to 4 above), making the dovetailing between two insurance policies difficult to achieve.

7.7   Solving taking-over problems

The sooner taking-over problems are identified, even when arising unexpectedly during the performance testing, the better the prospects of finding a solution are likely to be. The solution may be found in any of the following.

●   Agree a special extension to the CAR/EAR policy until compliance is achieved.

●   Obtain the special agreement of the machinery insurer to accept the project in full. It may be possible to demonstrate that the testing/commissioning completed so far has in fact fully proved the critical machinery to a level that is acceptable to the insurer for the purpose of providing the insurance.

●   Obtain agreement from the machinery insurer to accept the part of the project which is unaffected by the taking-over problem and which has been fully tested or which does not need testing/commissioning, leaving the remainder of the plant at risk under the CAR/EAR insurance until the problem is resolved.

● Obtain agreement from the machinery insurer to accept the risk on the basis of restricted cover or terms. This may mean that the insurance would only meet claims from the affected machines if, for instance, they are operated at lower temperatures, pressures or outputs than originally intended in their design, thereby introducing an extra level of safety.

In all cases, clear communication between interested parties will be necessary and any special agreement or exclusion will need to be carefully drafted to reflect the intention of the parties to the insurance contract. In so far as they relate to the permanent operational insurance, these intentions may not always start off or end up as the same as the intentions of those protected under the construction contract.

8 | Assessment of maximum exposure

8.1 Introduction

This chapter is likely to attract the interest of the insurance provider rather than the buyer. Consideration of assessment of the maximum exposure presented by a given risk does not impact directly on the premium level, terms or conditions but has more to do with the structure employed to spread the risk exposure and maximise insurance acceptance capacity.

It is not the intention to comment here in detail on the need and use of such assessments, since this subject is covered in considerable length by the existing Report of Advanced Study Group 236: *Estimated Maximum Loss Assessments: London Market Practice*, published in September 1995. The main objectives of that ASG were to

● carry out an appraisal of London market insurance and reinsurance practice with respect to the evaluation and usage of estimated maximum loss property damage and business interruption

● create a statement of recommended practice for the future

● recommend points of action which might be necessary to facilitate the adoption of the recommended practice as a London market norm.

The Report of ASG 236 is directed towards a general readership (albeit one assumed to have a working knowledge of the subject, which has widespread application throughout the insurance industry), whereas the intention here is to provide some background information and to concentrate on those particular issues that are relevant to machinery exposures.

Most industrial risks present some forms of property material damage and business interruption exposure that are assessed principally on the levels of fire protection, physical separation and fire-fighting facilities that are present. Where relevant, the likelihood of natural catastrophe may come into the reckoning and this applies to the buildings and other structures as much as it does to the machinery that they house.

The more specific exposures affecting machinery, whether static, mobile or sited in the open, is the focus of attention in this chapter. History has shown that insurance of machinery is not so prone to catastrophic incidents and therefore the factors influencing a maximum loss assessment may not be so obvious. Equally, the trend of loss types which are suffered by machinery insurers does not tend to follow the typical pattern of general property risks.

8.2 The purpose of assessing maximum loss exposure

In order to calculate a premium for a particular risk, the underwriter should obtain an accurate impression of the overall nature of the risk and the individual hazards involved. Once in possession of the various facts, the underwriter will assess the risk and calculate the appropriate terms and conditions accordingly.

It then remains for the underwriter to determine what share or part of the risk he wishes to accept. This will be determined by his appetite for risk, the capacity available to him to accept such risks and the maximum loss assessment of the given risk.

The insurer seeks to establish how a significant claim occurrence that may be expected would impact on his business. The assessment of the loss that is in mind should include both the direct material damage costs and, if insured, the resultant business interruption costs.

Insurers have to decide on how large a share of a risk they wish to carry within their gross underwriting capacity, including an amount for retention in their own net account. They assess not only its degree of hazard (which has a bearing on the total loss to be expected in the course of the period of insurance) but also the estimated likely maximum amount of any one single loss that may occur. This information, together with the insurer's appetite and financial ability to assume risk, will enable the insurer to decide upon a suitable reinsurance programme.

When a co-insurer (or reinsurer) is offered a following share in a risk it will ask for details of the leading insurer's maximum loss assessment. Then, relying on that being a correct evaluation and having regard to the overall desirability of the risk, a suitable percentage of the risk is accepted after taking account of their own financial capacity and other know risk commitments.

Although statistically based, most assessments are personal estimates which, although taking account of prevailing experience and circumstances, depend on the judgement of the underwriter concerned. It is quite normal for two individual underwriters who are assessing the same risk independently to arrive at different results. This shows that the assessment itself can be highly subjective exercise.

8.3   Historical development

It was not much before 1900, at a time of increasing world industrial development, that insurers began to make net retentions (*i.e.* amounts retained for their own account prior to the application of reinsurance) and reinsurance acceptances on the basis of the maximum loss assessment. The practice evolved from that of fire insurers.

In the early days, insurers' net retention and reinsurance was decided on the basis of the total sum insured per location. As these values increased, insurers found that, on average, their loss ratios were good, enabling not only rates to be reduced but also the retained part of the risk (after reinsurance) to be increased without threatening their liquidity and capital. They did this by fixing their retention per location on the basis of the highest sum insured per building, *i.e.* the main or target risk.

Results generally remained favourable and insurers looked for further suitable ways of raising their net retained premiums. Claims statistics were evaluated and locations inspected with a view to dividing their main or target risk into fire sections. Firewalls were built in accordance with strict building regulations to ensure the prevention of fire spreading to neighbouring sections. Insurers therefore determined their retention on the basis of the highest sum insured per fire section.

As a further development, in some cases insurers decided that a total loss of the fire section with the highest value was unlikely, allowing a further increase in risk retention. However, experience subsequently showed that it was potentially dangerous to accept business on this basis because, all too often, fires did spread to adjacent sections, thereby doubling losses or increasing them to even higher amounts. Therefore, insurers had to tread with greater caution when using this approach, which led directly to the analytical approach adopted today.

8.4   Terms used to express maximum loss

A number of terms are used to express the various types of maximum loss in the period of insurance that might arise in relation to insured property through an insured peril. The most frequently used are

- MPL   =   maximum possible (or probable) loss
- PML   =   possible maximum loss
- MFL   =   maximum foreseeable loss
- MAS   =   maximum amount subject
- EML   =   estimated maximum loss.

If abbreviations are used (as is normal practice), confusion may arise, *e.g.* with MPL, which can refer to either 'possible' or 'probable' loss. In that case, 'possible' means something that may be capable of being true under the present interpretation or in some circumstances (in other words, feasible but less than likely); whereas 'probable' means something that may be reasonably expected to happen, but not necessarily so ('reasonably' having the sense of 'soundly judged as' or 'sensibly' or 'judged to be appropriate or suitable to the circumstances or purpose as'). It should be appreciated that an MPL assessment truly depicts a probable situation but the circumstances taken into account at the time of assessment might not necessarily hold true at the time when the expected event actually occurs.

The word 'foreseeable' in 'maximum foreseeable loss' appears to be less firm than 'possible' and it does not contain the element of sound judgement implied in the word 'probable'.

'Maximum amount subject' originated in the United States and is considered to reflect an extremely pessimistic assessment.

The meaning of the term 'estimated maximum loss' is open to wide interpretation; the Reinsurance Offices Association introduced this term in 1974 in an effort to avoid the use of the letter 'P' in the abbreviation given it is capable of more than one meaning. The apparent intention is that EML and MPL mean the same.

A working party of the International Machinery Insurers Association made the attempt to find some guidelines for MPL evaluation, producing the following definition:

> 'The MPL is an estimate of the maximum loss which could be sustained by the Insurers as a result of any one occurrence considered by the underwriter to be within the realms of probability. This ignores such coincidence and catastrophes as may be possibilities but which remain highly improbable'.

The definition rules out the consideration of accidents that could only occur when a number of highly unfavourable circumstances coincide. If a turbine disrupts, some damage to an adjacent set is a probability but that the original failure should lead to a disruption of the neighbouring unit is possible but not probable.

8.5   Distinguishing between 'possible' and 'probable' loss

An accurate and reasoned MPL assessment is as vital and important an underwriting feature as risk appreciation and pitching acceptable terms and conditions themselves. Prudent MPL assessments should be conservative and one way to approach the calculation would be to assume initially the insured value will be totally exposed and then adjust down to a lower figure justified by the existence of specific loss reducing features.

Maximum probable loss

The maximum probable loss is an estimate of the maximum loss that could be sustained by the insurers as a result of any one occurrence considered by the underwriter to be within the realms of probability. This ignores such coincidences and catastrophes that are possibilities but which remain highly improbable.

As seen from the above, the difference between possible maximum loss and maximum probable loss is substantial.

Insurers who are underwriting business on a pure possible maximum loss basis will be exposing less of their real capacity and as a consequence may pass on to other insurers (or reinsurers) unnecessary amounts of risk and the related premium with it, thereby prejudicing their net operating ratio.

The resultant amount is usually expressed as a monetary amount although it is not uncommon to show it as a percentage of the limit of indemnity. However, as policy limits may take different forms, *e.g.* full value sum insured, any one accident limit or first loss limit, the use of percentages can be misleading. Ideally, percentage amounts should only be used in the context of the full value sum insured.

Possible maximum loss

The possible maximum loss is estimated by the degree to which the insured subject would in the light of all feasible circumstances and factors be affected by a major accident caused by an insured peril. It results when a number of unfavourable considerations occur at the same time.

8.6   The insurer's subjective view

As already stated, an underwriter should be both conservative and realistic in the assessment and not leave too wide a margin between a probability and a possibility. The amount and frequency of losses that have occurred in the past need to be considered. The estimate is primarily based on facts within the insurer's own experience or from other independent experts. Naturally this will depend upon the underwriter's own judgement of the type machinery, its physical location, the perils to be insured, and upon the knowledge and experience gained through insuring comparable risks.

No hard-and-fast rules can be laid down when making appropriate estimates. Only the ultimate claims experience will show whether the estimates were on average correct.

Therefore it can be seen that the calculation of a risk MPL is a subjective exercise, which depends heavily on the experience of the underwriter. However, in certain circumstances independent sources of information can be used, such as computer programmes and loss modelling or simulation to help calculated specific exposures, *e.g.* vapour cloud explosion for a petrochemical risk.

Risk quotations and acceptances are often based on provisional information that needs to be confirmed and validated later, *i.e.* through surveys or enquiries. All too often risk information is difficult to obtain from a single source, especially where the insured comprises numerous operating companies and at various sites, all potentially aggregating in a single loss scenario.

Many physical risk characteristics or factors need to be taken into account in the assessment as illustrated in the list below. This list is not intended to be exhaustive but shows the diversity of aspects to be considered.

- Spread of risk and the likelihood of a single loss affecting more than one machine given the physical separations in relation to the scope of cover provided by the policy, *e.g.* fire or turbine bursting.

- The type of materials being treated or processed undertaken is likely to influence the risk.

- The extensive use of automation, robotics, central computing facilities, central warehousing, the dependence on public utilities and the universal use of 'just in time' concepts have led to significantly lower inventory levels both in terms of raw materials, components and parts, as well as in finished products. Buffer stocks at each end of the process may have little margin and there will therefore be no short-term 'comfort factor' available in the event of loss or damage. In effect, the margins of safety in time and alternate working methods have been reduced. The impact on business interruption losses could be dramatic.

- Even when escaping the direct effects of fire, modern machinery can be severely damaged as a result of subsequent heat, smoke or soot contamination. Current restoration techniques available can reduce claim costs if applied quickly but it may be prudent to ignore this possible benefit within the MPL assessment.

- When risks are located in certain territories concern may arise over

  - possible escalation of the sum insured in times of high inflation

  - the potential of fluctuating currency exchange rates

  - local taxation levies, import duties and issues that could delay repair or prolong any stoppage period

  - the availability of spare parts and repairers having the required skill to undertake such repairs.

Accurate assessment of an MPL needs to be reflective of the scope of policy cover. Clauses or extensions permitted within a policy wording that themselves do not appear onerous could feature in a worst case scenario, such as

- extension clauses without financial limit or simply geared to an available percentage of the total sum insured without maximum limitation. An example would be the costly removal of debris, after serious damage away from the site to a designated suitable place.

- the effect of a typical capital additions clause allowing additional machinery at an existing location to be included, within limits, without prior notification having to be agreed.

- the claims settlement basis being subject to a 'reinstatement as new' condition.

Inner loss limits or sub-limits that fall within the assessment should be regarded as fully exposed. The existence of such a limit may offer the underwriter the prospect to write a greater share of the risk but this should be considered against the potential disproportionate exposure represented by the first part of any claim.

Specific configuration of plant and equipment could introduce special hazards such as the turbine and generator on a single shared shaft. Items of machinery within a process layout may not present a serious material damage loss but where their function is critical to the overall production the resultant business interruption costs could be unexpectedly high.

Lead time for replacement of critical plant and machinery needs to be assessed and should allow for the possibility of the loss being aggravated as a consequence of incompatible technology.

8.7 Practical applications

The assessment of MPL should be based on individual circumstances. Each risk needs to be considered on its own merits. Good housekeeping, for example, could justify a reduced assessment. As a rule, overly optimistic assessments should be avoided as they can lead to disastrous results and in extreme cases might threaten the solvency of the insurer. However, if the MPL is overestimated, it might then be difficult to place 100% of the insurance of large risks such as high value power stations or chemical plants.

8.7.1 Material damage risks

Material damage risks are based upon the percentage of the total sum insured or a percentage of the sum insured on the key item, *i.e.* the item with the highest value as a maximum probable loss unless there is some special hazard that exposes other items within the plant to simultaneous damage.

Other aspects which require consideration are

● nature of items, *e.g.* prototype

● type of materials utilised

● manufacturer's/operating history

● site facilities (if local repair impractical, heavy transport costs could be incurred)

● inter-damage possibilities

● manufacturers' guarantees in force

● difficulty of access to machine for repair or removal

● transit requirements

● accumulation with consequential loss covers

8.7.2 **Business interruption risks**

Business interruption risks are expressed as a percentage of the estimated annual gross profit/revenue sum insured. In considering business interruption risks, factors to take into account should be

- age/machine specification

- extent of cover requirements/perils

- percentage importance of machines to production

- indemnity period (may be greater than 12 months)

- excess period

- normal working hours

- repair and spare facilities (both in-house and external, bearing in mind locality)

- housekeeping standards

- stand-by and other alternative working arrangements

- business of a seasonal nature

- accumulation with material damage covers or conflict between time and cost

- buffer stocks

- alternative working possibilities.

8.7.3 **Computer risks**

The assessment of computer risks is based on a percentage of the hardware plus software and estimated gross profit/revenue/increased cost of working (ICOW) sums insured and reinstatement of data (ROD), which is usually insured on a first loss limit basis.

In assessing computer risks, consideration being given to

- highest value any one location

- spread of risk

- restriction of perils

- working conditions

- security arrangements

- information on back-up facilities

- percentage effect of annual gross profit (AGP) or annual gross revenue (AGR) relative to the computer operations

- existing disaster contingency plans or other alternative methods of working, *e.g.* hot start facility

- indemnity period

- excess levels

- dependence upon telecommunications/data links

- attractiveness of hardware/components to thieves.

9 Power generation

9.1 Introduction

As populations, gross national product and personal incomes increase so does the desire for electrical energy. This demand can be met by several different approaches, all of which have some common characteristics. All power generation systems rely on the conversion of one form of energy into mechanical energy, which is in turn converted into electrical energy.

All of the available processes have an inherent demand on the use of machinery and therefore present risks of which the insurance industry must be cognisant and attempt to evaluate.

The means from which mechanical energy is produced, characterises the type of plant:

● Steam turbine units in which steam, produced by a variety of processes, drives a turbine that is linked to an electrical generator.

● Gas turbines in which gases produced by fuel combustion directly drive a turbine and generator. These may be run individually or run in combination with a steam turbine.

● Diesel units, which rely on a conventional reciprocating internal-combustion engine to drive a generator.

● Hydroelectric units, which exploit the potential and kinetic energy stored in a watercourse by using it to drive a water turbine linked to an electrical generator.

Other technologies including wind turbines, and solar and geothermal units are less commonly seen but are still noteworthy.

It should be borne in mind that the power generation industry has always been and continues to be a rapidly evolving business. The manner in which electricity is now traded causes plants, both old and new, potentially to operate in a manner not considered at the original design and specification stage. It is important that these factors are understood and the implications of such changes are fully recognised.

9.2 History and development

Demand for energy has been a powerful stimulant for the development of new and more efficient conversion techniques.

Around 3000 BC the first wind power was harnessed to drive sailing vessels. The same force has been utilised to drive windmills from 500 AD up to the present day.

The energy to be derived from moving water has been used throughout the second millennium.

It was, however, not until the late eighteenth century that thermal energy was used to generate mechanical movement. Ultimately this led to the use of this technology to drive electrical generators but this did not occur on an industrial scale until the second half of the 1800s.

Since that time, the development of power generation technology has been dramatic with units growing larger, efficiencies increasing with machinery and control systems becoming infinitely more complicated. The increasing use of the gas turbine as the prime mover in power utilities has further evolved the industry and its insurance related risks.

Future technical developments will undoubtedly be as dramatic as those in recent times as materials are developed which allow unit power and efficiencies to be economically further enhanced. In addition, the environmental pressures placed upon the power industry, as a whole will become a more significant motivator, stimulating increased development in alternative, clean and renewable technologies. Availability of 'fuels', including changing weather patterns in the case of hydroelectric power, will inevitably modify preferred generating technology.

Developments do however produce significant changes in both the values at risk and risk assessment factors. Therefore the insurance sector needs to keep pace with the high-tech advances made by the scientific and manufacturing industries.

Political and sociological influences already experienced are likely to become ever more significant and these include world-wide electricity demand increasing, availability of power to remote areas, privatisation the operations of generation and distribution and integration of electrical generation as part of other industrial activities.

As new types of erection contract such as build, operate and transfer, project funding and ownership evolve, insurers must understand the impact that these changes might have on their policies. For example, energy and equipment suppliers may well have equity stakes in a plant and therefore seek protection under site insurance covers.

9.3   Processes

The processes are presented in terms of a basic description of the technologies employed in electricity generation such as boiler/steam turbine, gas turbine, hydroelectric power, etc.

However, there are several characteristics and functions that are common to all power plants. These areas are described in the following sections with the more unique aspects of specific generating technologies addressed subsequently according to plant type.

9.3.1   Control systems

Installations are controlled by dedicated computers, which are normally located in a central control room, specially programmed to manage the process. Increasingly they are connected to a data-processing system. The control programs manage the constant monitoring of the main operations and critical parameters as well as interlocks such as turbine vibration, lubrication systems, boiler firing, steam pressures, water levels and the speed of rotating equipment.

Plant control may be so sophisticated that an operator may simply press one button to initiate all start up procedures. Recent development in control systems is moving towards less use of specialised distributed control system (DCS) control systems and more use of standard widely available open platform systems similar to those used in PC networks.

The numbers of personnel located within the control regime is reducing, with increased reliance being placed on automated systems. In some cases control rooms are unmanned with staff on site carrying radios and visiting the control room at regular intervals. Alarms have also become increasingly sophisticated with both those resulting in an audible alarm only and those leading to automatic plant shutdown being installed. As control room manning levels are reduced so the need for fixed fire protection in this historically unprotected area increases.

9.3.2   **Water treatment**

All plants which operate with boiler and steam processes or have water-cooled plants require the ability to produce high purity water without the presence of undesirable contaminants. Natural water from the local supply is seldom suitable since it often contains impurities. This problem is accentuated as water is heated and vaporised since impurities become less soluble as temperatures rise. This can result in the build up of solid deposits on heating and cooling elements, which in turn reduces the efficiency of the heat transfer process. Ultimately it can lead to overheating and potential failure of the component, *e.g.* a boiler tube. In addition, insoluble salts will collect at the lowest point of any vessel or boiler and can introduce circulation and efficiency problems.

Proper water treatment and chemistry control can result in important benefits:

● Minimal waterside deposits.

● Limited corrosion rates thus extending component lifetimes.

● Prevention of carry over of water and impurities in the steam that reduces damage to downstream plant.

With larger industrial boilers and turbines, demineralisation or evaporative distillation is desirable. The evaporative process is relatively simple with make-up water heated in a heat exchanger, vaporised and condensed elsewhere as purified water. In demineralisation plants the ion exchange process is used to chemically create pure water. The cation and anions associated with the impurities are exchanged for hydrogen and hydroxide ions. The exchange resin can be regenerated after a defined amount of use to renew their exchange capabilities. Other technologies utilised to generate purified water include reverse osmosis and ultrafiltration.

Having produced 'pure' make-up water it is also important to continually monitor the process water condition and maintain an optimum composition

Plants must be sized appropriately so that they can supply all generating units at maximum load, ideally with some degree of redundancy. In a gas turbine facility where the units require steam or water injections to achieve environmental emission limits or increase mass flow, there is a larger demand placed on the demineralisation plant. This because it is not possible to recirculate purified water used for steam or water injection purposes since it is incorporated into the combustion process and lost to atmosphere with exhaust gases.

The correct and efficient operation of the water treatment/demineralisation plant in a facility is critical to its long-term operation. Single treatment plants often feed multiple boilers and can therefore cause the entire plant to shut down in the event of failure.

9.3.3   **Electrical systems**

All plant discussed in this chapter has the production of electricity as a primary objective. To this end the electrical systems which ensure that this occurs, are in simplistic terms identical across all plant types. The manner in which the rotation of the generator is achieved causes the diversity of the plant types.

9.3.3.1   **Generator**

In simplistic form the synchronous generator (or alternator) generates electricity by rotating a magnetic field (rotor) inside a coil of wire (stator). This field rotation induces voltage into the surrounding stator.

Alternators driven by gas or steam turbines are driven at high speeds (usually 1800 or 3600rpm in the United States, where the frequency is 60Hz and 1500 or 3000rpm for 50Hz countries). With these high-speed machines there are several advantages.

Total alternator power is proportional to the product of rotor speed and rotor size and therefore high-speed units can have smaller rotors. Such units are usually installed horizontally and may be up to 1600MVA (approximately 1600MW) in size. Generators release heat as they operate and must therefore be cooled. Most high speed, large output units are hydrogen cooled because it has better heat absorption characteristics than air. Smaller units are mostly air-cooled. In addition, liquid cooling may be used (de-ionised water) to cool parts of the generator.

In different power applications, primarily hydroelectric, low speed alternators are used. This lower speed necessitates that a larger unit is required for the same output as a high-speed alternator.

Typically, a water turbine rotating at 360rpm would be limited by size to an output of around 120MVA. Alternators of this size are usually mounted vertically, directly above the turbine, although some older installations and those using Pelton wheel turbines may be horizontally mounted. Again, cooling of the generator is required and this is usually air, water or a combination of both.

All generators, as already described, have a rotating magnetic field inside the stator. This field is produced by electromagnets since permanent magnets will not produce enough flux for industrial applications. This presents the problem of producing this 'excitation' field on a spinning rotor. Slip rings with physically touching brushes may be used or a brushless induction system.

Certain units, particularly some gas turbines and pumped storage hydroelectric units utilise the generator in more than one mode. In the former case, the generator can act as a motor to start the unit or in the latter case, as a pump for driving water back to an upper reservoir.

Generators feed their output via a circuit breaker (an open or closed switch) to bus bars which in turn lead to a transformer which feeds the transmission system. Either on one side or both sides of the generator transformer there will be circuit breakers which enable isolation from the system for maintenance purposes, in the event of a failure or for cross connection of plant.

9.3.3.2   **Transformer**

Transformers perform the essential role of stepping up and down line voltages and are critical to the operation of a power plant. They are relatively sensitive plant items that warrant careful maintenance. Properly designed and with good care they have a significant lifetime.

Transformers are characterised by their capacity or rating, quantified in MVA, and the voltages at which they operate. The larger generator transformers are usually within liquid filled (dielectric) tanks, which contain the core and windings. The dielectric fluid provides the unit insulation. The immersed magnetic core is surrounded by the windings both primary (incoming) and secondary (outgoing).

The dielectric liquid can itself present problems. The three main types of fluid are

- mineral oils: low cost but can represent a fire hazard

- silicone oils: less flammable but higher cost.

- halogenated dilectric: non-flammable synthetic fluid without PCBs and non-toxic, used to replace askarels.

It should be specifically noted that older installations might still have askarel-filled transformers. These liquids are polychlorinated biphenyls (PCBs) and present some unique problems. They are extremely resistant to bio-degradation and are toxic.

The dielectric fluid also provides a means of cooling the unit as it circulates by either naturally or forced means through a cooling system or heat exchanger.

Some smaller units are described as dry transformers. Such units perform the same duty but the windings are air-cooled. They have a greater fire resistance than liquid-filled units.

Transformers may be found throughout a power distribution system and may be located both inside and outside buildings. In the case of a hydroelectric plant, this may well be underground. The location has a bearing on the ability to extinguish fire and the knock on effect one transformer might have on an adjacent unit. Separation and fire protections are important issues as well as access for repairs, ease of removal or replacement.

9.3.3.3   Switchgear, electrical annexes and relays

The entire plant is heavily reliant upon switchgear and relays throughout the plant for control purposes, monitoring purposes, protective purposes, etc. It typically consists of panels, switches and circuit breakers.

Several different types of high voltage switchgear are used and either air, vacuum, oil or gas (sulphur hexafluoride, SF_6) will provide the insulating medium. The more effective the insulator, the smaller the breaker can be. There are also benefits in terms of fire hazard when SF_6 is used in place of mineral oil, particularly with regard to installations within a turbine hall or underground.

9.3.3.4   Emergency power

Emergency power equipment provides back-up to both AC and DC systems and may include both batteries and emergency generators.

Emergency battery banks generally provide DC power for control systems and emergency equipment usually with the primary objective of allowing a complete and safe shut down of plant. Batteries provide short-term power to a few critical systems. Battery rooms present their own safety hazards with the potential accumulation of explosive hydrogen.

Back up generators respond to provide longer-term power. Again, they rarely allow the functioning of all systems but will operate lighting and control systems and possibly provide a 'black start' capability.

9.4   Generating plant units

The most common type of unit in use today is the steam boiler and turbine unit. These units consist of a fired boiler that produces steam which is piped to a steam turbine, and which in turn rotates a generator to generate electricity.

A power plant that utilises this technology uses heat from burning fuels such as coal, gas oil and more recently waste and other biomass products to produce electricity.

The diagram below gives the basic schematic for a typical steam boiler thermal plant.

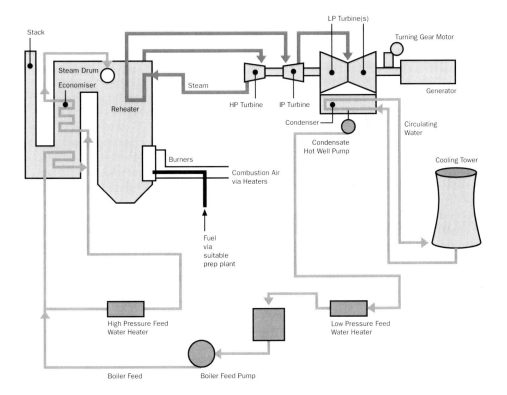

The plant has four fundamental components namely, the boiler (steam generator), the turbine, the generator and the condenser.

The optimisation of the efficiency of the process is essential for the competitive production of electricity. This helps to explain the complexity of the plant with reheaters, superheaters, feed water heaters, etc. A modern plant of this type is approximately 35% efficient.

9.4.1   Boilers

Boilers have a number of names within the power generation industry such as steam generators, heat recovery steam generators (HRSGs) (see also 9.7.1) and can vary enormously in size and configuration. Most large power station boilers are custom made for each location.

The boilers primary function is to transfer heat from an input source, usually burning fuel, into the boiler water to generate steam. Boilers generally have a loop system that consists of an unheated downcomer that feeds cooler water to the base of the boiler and a riser in the heated area that allows water and steam to circulate.

Small boilers (< 20 te/hour steam production) typically produce saturated steam at around 15 to 18 bar and would generally not be found as primary boilers in power generation facilities. Medium size boilers (20 to 140 te/hour steam production) generally have working pressures up to 120 bar. These boilers, which may produce superheated steam, are generally naturally circulated (as feed water is heated so it becomes less dense and rises which induces flow). These boilers are usually manufactured at a supplier's production facility and then shipped as a packaged unit to the customer's premises. Large boilers (>140 te/hour steam) are field erected at the customers premises and might produce steam at 200 bar and 550°C. These may be natural or forced circulation. Forced circulation boilers operate with a high-pressure pump actively pumping water around the boiler. Such boilers often have superheaters and reheaters, which improve the unit efficiencies. To give an impression of scale, a large boiler might contain 500 km of tubing and be 50 m in height.

In a natural circulation boiler the total circulation rate is dependent upon four factors, the height of the boiler, the operating pressure, the heat-input rate and the free flow areas of the components. In a forced circulation boiler a mechanical pump is added and the pressure differential that is produced across the pump controls the water and steam flow through the boiler. A boiler may have up to 40 burners arranged in one or more of the furnace walls.

The efficiency of a boiler in terms of energy conversion is increased as the steam temperature and pressure increase. Hence, steam should be produced at the highest practical temperatures and pressures. The maximum temperatures of superheated steam, limited by the corrosion and mechanical characteristics of the materials used is in the order of 580°C. Materials are available to operate at higher temperatures but at present, economics do not justify their use.

The diagram opposite shows a typical configuration for a water wall tube boiler. The term water wall describes the arrangement of adjacent boiler tubes lining the external walls of the boiler, which absorb a large amount of the boiler energy.

As process water is continually recycled around the boiler/turbine/condenser loop, so there are small losses of water and/or steam. This results in the concentration of any impurities remaining in the system to increase. Hence boilers have a 'blowdown' system which may operate continuously or periodically or in an emergency situation. This allows water at the base of the boiler, where impurity concentrations are highest, to be drawn off and be replaced with fresher make up water. Some utilities have found that periodic high flow rate blowdown is effective in reducing the rate of boiler corrosion.

The diagram opposite shows air heaters, which increase the unit efficiency by harnessing the residual heat in flue gases and transferring it to incoming combustion air. Air heaters in a boiler are either recuperative or regenerative.

In a recuperative air heater, heat is transferred continuously through a stationary, solid heat transfer surface, such as tubes or plates. These units function with very little contamination or leakage between the two streams.

In a regenerative air heater, heat is transferred indirectly as a heat transfer material is alternately exposed to hot and cold flows. Owing to their rotary action, these units have a tendency to exhibit leakage between the two gas flows. The rotary air heater is the most common type of regenerative heater and relies upon a slowly spinning rotor packed with heat transfer material.

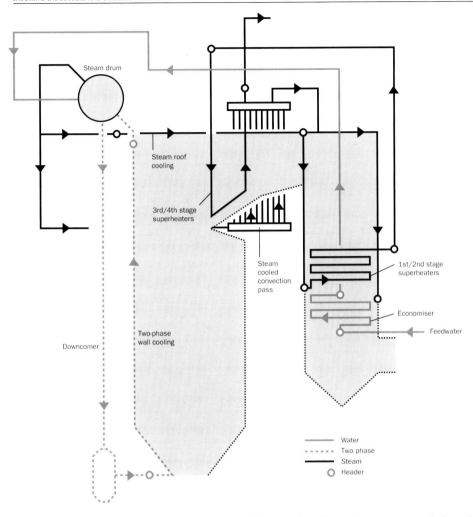

Steam drum

Steam roof
cooling

3rd/4th stage
superheaters

Steam
cooled
convection
pass

1st/2nd stage
superheaters

Economiser

Feedwater

Two-phase
wall cooling

Downcomer

———— Water
- - - - - Two phase
———— Steam
○ Header

Gases pass axially over this rotor with one half exposed to hot exhaust gases and the other 180° section exposed to incoming cold air. Hot gas and cold air travel in opposite directions. As the rotor spins, typically at 1-3rpm, so the heated sections move into the path of the cold air and lift its temperature. The rotary air heaters are susceptible to fire as unburned fuel tends to collect on the hot heat transfer surfaces and once ignited is fanned by the incoming air. Cleanliness is therefore essential and it is desirable that isolation dampers are fitted.

A boiler may well have a very long lifetime if well maintained and therefore component access and ease of replacement must be considered at the early design stages.

9.4.1.1 **Fuels and combustion**

The primary fuel selected for a boiler has a significant impact on boiler design and configuration. When fossil, biomass and by-product fuels are burnt, widely differing steps must be taken to cope with fuel handling and preparation, combustion, fouling of heat transfer surfaces, corrosion of material and emissions control. For example, gas fired units have minimal need for fuel storage and handling, only a small furnace is required for combustion and the heat transfer surface can be more closely spaced due to the lower ash deposition. Corrosion is not usually a significant problem and environmental controls are primarily for NOx produced in combustion.

Solid fuels such as coal with a larger level of non-combustible ash result in far more complex systems. Extensive fuel handling plant, a larger furnace, more widely spaced heat transfer surfaces, special cleaning equipment to reduce erosion and corrosion, more extensive environmental equipment and a means to transfer and dispose of boiler ash, may be required.

The fuel and its physical state have a bearing on the performance of a boiler and present a variety of different risks. The economics of fuel price, the availability and reliability of the fuel supply and, increasingly, its environmental characteristics, are all factors that influence fuel choice.

The most common fuels by far utilised in today's power plants are fossil fuels, *i.e.*, coal, fuel oil and natural gas. All fuels have in themselves, inherent risks such as spontaneous combustion and dust explosions for coal, tank fires for liquid fuels and vapour cloud explosion for gases. Boilers may be configured to burn more than one fuel.

The fuel and boiler burner systems must be closely integrated to work well together and minimise the likelihood of an unwanted event. Start up sequences should be well defined and during start-up, and in the event of a misfire, a full purge cycle must take place prior to further attempts at ignition.

9.4.2   Coal

By a large margin, coal is the most common solid fuel used in electricity generation plants but other materials such as wood, waste, and other biomass products are also used. Coal may be stored at a power plant without mixing if it meets the plant specification. Alternatively, it may be blended on site with, for example, a low sulphur coal to help reduce environmental emissions. All stockpiles must be managed to avoid spontaneous heating and combustion. The combustion process falls into one of three categories.

9.4.2.1   Mechanical stokers

In a moving grate system, an endless chain grate conveyor carries the fuel across the furnace area with combustion air being blown through the charge from below. As the fuel residue passes out of the furnace the waste clinker and ash is dumped into a pit. This boiler type is found in older coal fired stations and some modern waste to energy and biomass plants. The most common system is a spreader stoker in which crushed coal is fed at a controlled rate on to a set of rapidly revolving paddles that throw the material up on to the perforated furnace grate.

Primary combustion air is introduced below the grate and secondary from above. The coal fines burn while in the air and the coarser coal material burns on the grate. They have the advantage that they can operate with a variety of fuel grades and special fuel sizing, other than crushing, is not required.

9.4.2.2   Pulverised fuel

In a boiler burning pulverised coal, as the name suggests, the fuel is ground to a very fine powder, with a grain size usually less than $75\mu m$ in diameter, prior to injection into the furnace area. Fuel is carried from the pulverising plant to the burners by the primary combustion air and injected into the boiler. The pulverising plant consists of raw fuel storage system, a number of pulverising mills, which grind down the fuel and in some cases a storage system for fuel prior to introduction into the burners. Only large units can economically employ this technology due to the high capital cost of the pulverisers and their auxiliaries. This type of combustion generates a large amount of fly ash and bottom ash.

9.4.2.3   Fluidised bed

The fluidised bed boiler is not a common configuration for coal combustion. Crushed coal and residual ash are basically fluidised by the combustion air that blows from nozzles at the base of the combustion bed. In a fluidised bed boiler, there are three ingredients. These are crushed coal (crushed to a diameter of approximately 6–7mm), combustion air and an inert fluidised bed material, *e.g.* ash.

Turbulence in the fluidised bed, produced by the blown air, provides good mixing of the coal, the air and the hot inert material. This results in very rapid combustion. Fluidised bed combustion has a number of advantages for burning solid fuel to generate steam, which include fuel flexibility and reduced emissions. Long residence times ensure that fuel is efficiently burned at much lower temperatures (bed temperatures usually 820–870°C) compared with the conventional combustion process. Since fuel preparation is also not as onerous as pulverising plant, fuel preparation plant costs and operating costs are lower. A fluidised bed boiler may, however, be more susceptible to erosion and corrosion from the moving bed and higher gas/particle velocity.

A number of fuels can also be derived from coal. Coke oven gas is liberated as coal is coked in an oven. This may well contain a number of impurities that may deposit on burner and boiler surfaces. Gases such as hydrogen sulphide may be present and this can be removed by scrubbing.

Blast furnace gas discharged at a steel mill is often used in a boiler for steam generation (see Chapter 14, 'Iron and steel plants'). This gas also often deposits corrosive substances to boiler surfaces and provisions for cleaning must be made.

9.4.3   Gas

Gas is burned in certain power plant boilers where a suitable and reliable supply can be obtained. Gas burning furnaces produce little or no ash and are therefore less harmful to the environment.

9.4.4   Heavy fuel oil

Most oil-fired furnaces produce little or no ash. However, very heavy fuel oils do result in coking up and therefore require regular cleaning. They rely on the atomisation of fuel at the burner, which is accomplished using the flow of combustion air in conjunction with a pressurised fuel supply. The fuel must first be heated to ensure that it exhibits the correct viscosity and combustion characteristics.

Fuel oil presents an additional storage risk. It requires fixed tanks which are bunded (walled) to contain a large tank spill — usually a minimum of 110% of the largest tank volume. Additional fire protection and detection is also required on these storage facilities.

9.4.5   Oil emulsions

In recent years the discovery of large amounts of heavy hydrocarbon and bitumen in Venezuela has led to the development of bitumen oil emulsions and their sale as a power plant fuel. These liquid fuels consist of very small droplets of oil dispersed in water. A chemical is added to help maintain the emulsion. These fuels are an alternative to fuel oil but cause the same environmental concerns and can produce corrosive compounds on combustion.

9.4.6   **Waste and biomass**

Already popular in certain territories, with increasing interest in others, these fuels include materials such as wood, chicken litter, straw, domestic waste, recycling sludges, hazardous waste, peat and tyres. With biomass and waste fuels, they are most often burnt in a fluidised bed or moving grate system (or similar system with spreader stokers).

Throughout the United States, Europe and Japan, municipal solid waste (MSW) is used to fire plants. This fuel is the combination of residential and commercial waste which otherwise would have been sent to a landfill. It may be burnt as received, called mass burning or processed to a uniform size and consistencies to produce refuse derived fuel (RDF). In both the RDF and mass burn configurations the lower furnace area is continually changing from an oxidising to a reducing atmosphere which can rapidly accelerate corrosion. Therefore typically some form of corrosion protection is required. Corrosion resistant steel and alloy materials can be used in manufacture or for coating purposes, although they can be expensive to buy and install.

Bagasse is the dry pulp remaining after juice has been extracted from sugar cane and is often used to fire boilers at a sugar refinery. There are a number of exposures that can cause or contribute to loss. Cutter blades from the sugar cane cutters can fail and be carried into the boiler; the chain grate can become congealed, overheat and then distort; and the furfural released during the digestion process has the potential to exacerbate the effects of fire and explosion because of its high calorific value. See also Chapter 16, 'Other manufacturing industries' (16.7 Sugar refining).

9.4.7   **Boiler operations**

In correctly operating a boiler, certain interlocks and systems should be in place. These include:

- purge interlocks requiring a specified air flow for a specified time before the fuel valve can be opened;

- flame detectors on each burner connected to an alarm and interlocked to shut off the fuel supply in the event of loss of flame;

- shut off fuel on failure of the forced or induced draft fan;

- shut off fuel in the case of low fuel pressure (and low steam or air pressure when used in atomisers);
- shut off fuel oil supply in the event of low oil temperature;

- shut off gas supply to burners in the event of excessive fuel pressure.

Several procedures help ensure the safe and reliable operation of gas and oil fired combustion systems; examples are

- to never allow oil or gas to accumulate anywhere other than in a tank or lines that form part of the fuel delivery system;

- to ensure that at start up, shut down and low load operation, the minimum purge rate air flow should not be less than 25% of the full load air flow;

- to ensure that a spark producing device or lighted flame must be in use before admission of any fuel into the boiler. This must be correctly positioned and provide a permanent flame until the burner flame is self sustaining;

● to ensure that a positive air flow though the burners, boiler and up the stack is maintained at all times;

● to ensure that adequate fuel pressure for correct burner operation is maintained at all times.

● to ensure that where steam is used in atomisers, the steam pressure is maintained at the atomiser.

Investigations into boiler explosions have shown that the conditions leading to an explosion often exist for some considerable time before the event. With adequate monitoring and awareness corrective actions can be taken to mitigate the event.

9.4.8 **The environment**

Protection of the environment is an increasingly important aspect of power generation and the choice of fuel used. The capital cost of installing environmental protection plant must be built into new projects as well as the increased operational costs during plant lifetime.

The most common means of treatment of flue gases from boilers is through a flue gas desulphurisation (FGD) unit and the electrostatic precipitator, particularly for coal-fired boilers.

In the FGD process, sulphurous oxides, predominantly SO_2 with some SO_3, are removed from boiler exhaust gases. A number of techniques are available to achieve this and the choice depends upon the opportunities to freely obtain reactants and disposal of waste by-products. Both wet and dry systems are available using regenerative and non-regenerative processes.

The electrostatic precipitator is used to remove a large proportion of the fly ash from flue gases. The amount of particulate matter depends on the fuel type and the combustion process. The electrostatic precipitator relies upon electrically charging the dust particles in the gases and attracting them to an oppositely charged plate called the collector. When the plates are agitated, the dust falls into hoppers below. This operation is difficult to optimise since it is influenced by the particle size and type. However, if well run, it can remove up to 99% of the particulate.

Electrostatic precipitators have been the cause of fires and explosions. Most susceptible are plants that switch from coal to oil and back again. Coal dust can become ignited by the high potential on the precipitator electrodes and an explosion can result. Poor maintenance and operating practice are generally the causes of such events.

9.5 Steam turbines

The steam turbine is at the heart of the thermal power station. Fundamentally, a shaft (rotor), carrying blades is caused to rotate by the flow and expansion of high-pressure steam. The rotor turns within a casing, with a stator containing fixed blades, usually at 3000rpm for a 50Hz machine and 3600rpm for a 60Hz unit at full load.

Steam is passed through orifices or nozzles and directed to impinge or flow across blades, which results in shaft rotation. A casing surrounds the whole unit to confine the steam. Valves are used to control the steam flow to the nozzles. These valves are in turn connected to a governor and emergency shutdown. Normally a number of rows (stages) of blades may exist to improve the unit's efficiency. The larger the turbine, the greater the number of stages. Each stage consists of a row of stationary blades/nozzles to direct the steam on to a row of moving blades. The stationary blades form what is termed a diaphragm and the rotating set a wheel or disc.

Steam turbines take advantage of the fact that as steam expands or reduces in pressure through a nozzle it accelerates and forms a high-speed jet. As the steam expands passing through a stage, its volume will increase. To accommodate this and ensure that the unit functions, blade length and size necessarily increases in each successive stage.

Blades are attached to disks that are mounted on a shaft. Smaller units may have the shaft and discs machined from a single forged component. Larger units are more generally constructed with blades attached to discs that are heat shrunk and keyed or welded on to a machined forged shaft.

Shafts can be solid or hollow (bored) depending on their age and size. A bored rotor has obvious weight and access advantages for inspection purposes.

A turbine rotor spins within a casing which confines the steam as well as providing a locating structure for the stationary nozzles in the diaphragms. Casings must be designed to contain the design steam pressures and the reaction forces of operation and to accommodate the thermal expansion associated with temperature changes. Most power station turbine casings split horizontally to allow access for maintenance. Since the shaft passes through the casing, seals are required to reduce steam leakage. Stepped labyrinth gland seals are found on larger units. Steam that leaks is usually fed to the condenser or perhaps a lower pressure turbine stage. Clearances between fixed and rotating parts are very small to reduce leakage and improve efficiency.

At the turbine inlet, steam enters via a stop valve and a steam chest. Governing valves in the steam chest control the flow of steam into the nozzle chamber of the first stage and hence the unit's speed and load.

At the exhaust end of a steam turbine the steam passes to the condenser or to another part of the plant (reheater, external pipework, etc.). Certain projects utilise steam for town heating systems.

In larger units, the turbine rotor shaft sits on relatively soft metal journal bearings that rely on high-pressure lubrication oil. Smaller units use ball/roller bearings. These bearings help to ensure that the shaft rotates in a consistent evenly balanced position with minimal vibration. A thrust bearing is mounted at one end of the shaft and is responsible for absorbing axial loading as well as maintaining the axial shaft position. This bearing is particularly important since it helps to prevent the rotating parts from making physical contact with the stationary components (diaphragms, nozzles, etc.).

Steam turbines come in an infinitely variable range of sizes from 0.75kW to 1600MW.

In power station applications, the steam turbine may be split into two or more sections. With such a configuration, steam can first be fed through the high-pressure section, passed to a boiler reheater to lift its temperature again, prior to expansion through a medium then low-pressure section.

All turbines may be classed as single casing, tandem compound or cross compound. Smaller multistage turbines are usually constructed with the shaft and all stages contained within a single casing whereas in larger units, typical of industrial power plant applications, this becomes less practical. The unit may be split into anything up to six or eight casings on separate shafts, which then may or may not be bolted together in line. When in line, they are known as a tandem compound arrangement and when independent of one another, cross compound. Cross compound machines operate on more than one shaft which does give an inherent protection from catastrophic breakdown loss since the turbines are not physically joined.

Often the term 'double flow' is used to describe a low or intermediate pressure turbine. This indicates that steam flow travels through the turbine in two equal and opposite directions and is accomplished by the mounting of two identical turbines on one shaft within one casing but in opposite orientations. This dramatically reduces the resultant axial thrust forces on the rotor shaft and thrust bearing.

9.6   Cooling systems

As has already been indicated, steam is very often exhausted from a low-pressure turbine into a condenser. Condensers and cooling towers are key equipment in the power plants circulating water system, which provide a once through or closed loop cooling system. Once through, systems take water from a natural source such as a lake, the sea or a river, pass it through the condenser as cooling medium and return it at a higher temperature back to its original source. A closed loop system relies on the recirculation of water from the condenser to a cooling tower that reduces its temperature prior to re-entering the condenser. In both systems, the pure water used in the boiler and turbine is isolated from the cooling water.

9.6.1   Closed loop configuration

A closed loop system allows turbine exhaust to be condensed into water using cooling water. Most condensers are surface condensers with bundles of tubes conveying cooling water. Steam is exhausted from the turbine and condenses as it passes over the cooled tube bundles. A vacuum is created in the condenser to increase plant efficiency. The condensate passes to a hotwell where the water is pumped back to the boiler. The heated cooling water is pumped to a cooling tower to reduce its temperature prior to circulation again through the condenser.

Cooling towers can be wet, dry or a combination of the two. Wet towers, the most commonly seen, may be either natural draft or mechanical draft. The mechanical draft units may have forced or induced draft and may have water moving in a counter-flow direction to the air or across the airflow. Most towers have combustible components, usually the wooden fill material but more recently plastic is being used for fill purposes, fan stacks and blades. In both cases the fire risks should be recognised.

Dry cooling towers, which have become more popular, generate no plume but are significantly less thermally efficient than wet cooling units. The combination wet/dry unit is a compromise between the two options above. Water to be cooled travels first through the dry section of the unit and then the wet and a less significant plume than that in the wet unit should be produced.

9.7   Gas turbines

In view of its growing importance, application and risk characteristics, the gas turbine is comprehensively addressed in Chapter 17. Here the gas turbine is discussed as a means of driving an electrical generator.

The gas turbine can be coupled to a generator and its mechanical energy used in a similar way to a steam turbine, *i.e.* to rotate a generator rotor.

Simple 'open-cycle' gas turbines have historically been lower in efficiency than conventional coal-fired units and the smaller units used for peaking or black start duty. They have the advantages of rapid installation, lower capital cost and lower manning levels than conventional thermal plant. They also have the ability to generate very rapidly from standstill to full load. Open-cycle gas turbines have provided generation for peak and base loads in areas where fuel efficiency was not the primary concern.

9.7.1 Combined-cycle power units

More recently the introduction of the combined-cycle gas turbine (CCGT) has improved both efficiencies (55–60%) and power outputs. The advantages listed above are maintained in this configuration and this class of station is being developed in many locations around the world. It has relatively low capital cost and is capable of generating a good level of return on investment in many markets.

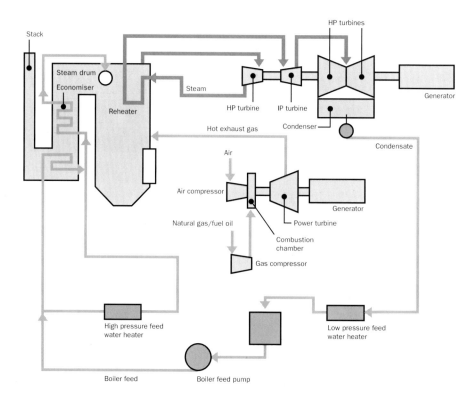

The diagram (above) shows a typical CCGT unit with one gas turbine and one steam turbine. In the (simple) open-cycle configuration, no use is made of the hot gases exhausted from the turbine whereas the combined-cycle unit harnesses this heat energy in a heat recovery steam generator (HRSG). In this 'boiler' the water is heated by the exhaust gases and the steam generated fed to a steam turbine which generates additional electricity. During construction of a CCGT in an area with an urgent requirement for electricity, the gas turbine(s) may be initially commissioned to run as an open-cycle unit before completion of the project as a combined-cycle station.

The HRSGs can, as the illustration suggests, be fitted with optional auxiliary burners. These can be installed to help steam generation at peak loads or to allow steam production independently of the gas turbine.

Typically, each gas turbine and each steam turbine has its own generator although single shaft designs are in operation. A modern 650-700MW plant may have two large gas turbines (200–250MW each), both feeding steam to a single steam turbine. A number of the latest plants have a gas turbine and steam turbine on a common shaft both driving one generator. There may or may not be a clutch between the steam and gas turbine.

Again, the availability of a large volume gas supply or liquid fuel is crucial to the siting of the plant. Many gas turbines used in power plant applications are dual fired (natural gas and fuel oil) to accommodate fuel supply interruptions although usually one fuel will dominate.

Gas turbines typically rotate at high speed between 3000 and 15,000rpm, although some aero-derivative engines may be higher, and may or may not have a gearbox between the turbine and the generator to reduce speed to the required revolutions per minute (rpm).

Some plants have additional 'hardware' fitted to introduce operational flexibility such as bypass stacks installed between the gas turbine and the HRSG which allow the plant the option to be configured in either an open cycle or combined cycle mode. This allows a CCGT station to run in the open-cycle configuration in the event of a problem with the HRSG or steam turbine. In many cases, however, the bypass stacks are installed for start-up only and the adverse economics of running in open cycle would not make it an attractive proposition.

As the operating regime of a plant moves further away from base load, so the efficiency of the more frequent start ups and shut downs become more important. Dampers may be fitted around the HRSG which close on shutdown to maintain as much heat in the boiler as possible. This reduces the energy and time required at the next start.

Manning levels in modern gas turbine plant are generally very low. The control systems are complex and extensive and require minimal operator intervention. All start-ups, shutdowns and operational transitions are usually fully sequenced and automated with a single input required from a plant operator. Emergency alarms and trips are also automated with the plant shutting itself down in the event of unwanted events such as excessive vibration.

9.8   Hydroelectric power plant

The harnessing of the potential and kinetic energy of water takes place in a hydroelectric power plant. Such plants can be located in the natural course of a river (run of river) with minimal water storage capability or storage plants with a dam or similar structure which is used to create a reservoir of water to be fed through the power plant as and when needed. This water flow may follow the original river route or be diverted through man-made tunnels and shafts to turbine areas, sometimes constructed deep in mountains.

Due to the need of a hydro plant to control and in some cases divert the natural flow of water, extensive civil works are often associated with a hydroelectric plant. Hydroelectric plants and their machinery are very often designed specifically for the site and this makes many aspects unique. The stream flow rates are taken into account when designing the units. The hydrostatic head of water and its flow rate at the plant determines the nature and the type of turbine employed.

The diagram below gives a simplified configuration.

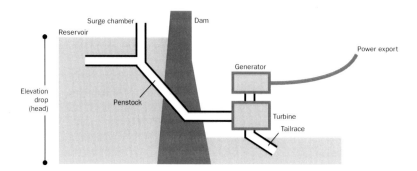

It should be noted that stations might be arranged in schemes with a significant number of plants, *i.e.*, up to 15 or 20 on the same river. In some cases, a catastrophic dam failure in the upper portion of the river may well adversely affect downstream dams and facilities.

Each component of a hydroelectric plant is briefly described below.

9.8.1 Dams

The dam is used to hold back water in order to create artificial head or to increase the amount of water stored. A number of different types of dam can be used and the most common categories are introduced below. Dams may be constructed in close proximity to the generation plant or in some cases some considerable distance away. The topography and therefore plant design are unique to each plant.

An earthen dam may be constructed out of sand, gravel or rock with an impermeable core or surface coating. Dams constructed in this manner rely on their mass to retain the water behind them rather than transferring forces to their abutments, as would an arch dam.

An arch dam relies upon horizontal thrust from the sides of a valley, the abutments, to keep it in place. It therefore has to be built on sound bedrock and, as the name suggests, is curved in an upstream direction. Arch dams can be constructed from concrete, stone or brick, concrete being the most common.

A gravity arch dam is simply a construction which is a combination of both types described above.

The buttress dam, normally constructed from concrete, stone or brick, usually has a straight rather than curved crest and relies on buttress supports on the downstream side of the dam to support the structure.

9.8.2 Water intake

The various elements of the water intake system are set out below.

9.8.2.1 Trash racks

Trash racks are a series of parallel bars, typically 6–7cm apart, which are designed to allow the passing of water but not objects that could cause damage to the turbine unit, such as wood and large ice blocks. These racks must be regularly cleared.

9.8.2.2 Intake gate (head gate)

The intake gate allows the penstock to be shut off, drained and following this the whole unit including the shafts can be inspected in a dry state. It should be noted that one intake gate and penstock might feed a number of units.

9.8.2.3 Penstock

The penstock is the pipe through which water is passed to the turbine units. It may be positioned above ground as a steel pipe or below ground, in some cases simply as an open rock tunnel.

9.8.2.4 Surge tank

The surge tank is important because it allows safe shutdown of the units, particularly in stations with high heads. A surge tank usually consists of a pressurised air chamber above the lower end of a penstock. It is designed to absorb the kinetic energy of the water in the penstock in the event that the turbines are shut down rapidly. The worst case is when a number of units fed from a common penstock are tripped or shut down at the same time. Without a surge tank or chamber the turbines would probably be destroyed.

9.8.2.5 Rock traps

A rock trap is usually found in open penstocks just before the turbine hall. It is simply a sump in the penstock into which any loose debris and rocks will fall instead of travelling through the turbine unit.

9.8.2.6 Main turbine inlet valve

Some units are fitted with a large valve, usually a butterfly or ball valve, which can be open and closed to isolate the pressurised penstock from the units. These valves can provide an emergency shut down capability and may be used in conjunction with the wicket gates at start-up and shutdown.

The wicket gates consist of a number of hydraulically actuated vanes, which control the flow of water through the runner. They act as the main control for governing purposes. They are susceptible to foreign object damage but should fail safe in the closed position.

9.8.2.7 Tailrace and gate

The tailrace is the exit path for water which has passed through the turbine runner, and as it is returned to its natural course. In order to inspect some units in a dewatered condition, a tailrace gate must be closed downstream of the runner.

9.8.3 Water turbines

A number of different turbines are used to generate power from flowing water. Selection normally depends on the on the head of water available, as described below.

9.8.3.1 Pelton turbines

Usually installed where hydrostatic heads are high, typically those plants in higher mountain areas. The Pelton turbine is rotated by 'jets' of water that strikes buckets on the turbine runner circumference. The water is released from a number of nozzles positioned around the unit.

This has the advantage that the unit itself can be run at part load with a number of valves open and a number closed. These units have no wicket gates since the nozzles are opened and closed (usually a needle valve) to control water flow. Hydrostatic head in Pelton applications usually exceeds 300m.

9.8.3.2 **Francis turbines**

Francis turbine units are often found in moderate head (30–300m), moderate flow regimes. The unit relies upon water flowing through wicket gates and entering the unit in a radial direction and exiting axially to the tailrace. The configuration of the blades in these units causes them to act as rotating nozzles.

9.8.3.3 **Kaplan turbines**

The Kaplan unit is used in high flow, low head (30m or less) environments, often encountered in run of river plants in the lower reaches of the watercourse. The impeller may have fixed pitch blades but often has variable pitch blades that are adjusted to regulate loads and optimise the use of the available flow. Kaplan units may be arranged vertically or horizontally.

The generator itself is usually positioned out of the water flow in its own enclosure. In some less common configurations the unit and generator are positioned together within the water flow in a 'bulb'. This is more common in very low head conditions (approximately 6m).

9.8.4 **Pumped storage**

Hydroelectric units generally rely on the head of water to drive a generator to generate electricity. However, where topographical and economic constraints allow, pumped storage units may be installed. The purpose of such a plant is to provide cost effective electricity at times of peak demand. Water is allowed through the units in a conventional manner as demanded and then pumped back to the upper reservoir at times of low demand and cheaper electricity, usually at night.

The turbines and generators themselves are usually reversed, the generator becoming a motor and the turbine becoming a water pump or in some cases a separate pumping mechanism may exist. These units rely on the economics of the power markets to be viable.

9.9 Diesel units

The diesel installation is very widespread. It is found both as base load generating plant as well as stand-by equipment on other plants. Commercial generating plant is frequently found in isolated communities, often islands, or used for small combined heat and power units that use the exhaust gases to heat community water.

A small diesel alternator set can be installed very rapidly and requires no special site conditions. For these reasons, despite a high cost ratio per kW/hr, many such generators have been installed in order to meet short-term energy requirements.

9.10 Other technologies

9.10.1 Wind turbines

The kinetic power in wind is without doubt the energy source with the longest history of use by man. The increase in the cost of fossil fuels, the absence of direct pollution associated with the use of wind-power and also technical improvements have now provided a new lease of life for its use in the production of electricity.

Experimental plants are under construction with levels of output of up to 10MW although units between 300kW and 1.5MW are most common. This type of plant presents no particular difficulties from the point of view of the general principle: a propeller fixed at the top of a mast is connected up to an alternator.

In order to obtain a high level of capacity and efficiency large installations are often required. Most commonly, a group of 300 to 600kW units are installed in a 'wind farm'. In some instances larger units up to 3MW output are used. A unit of this size would have a rotor mounted some 95m above the ground with blade lengths in the order of 50m. Maximum output might be obtained with a wind speed of no more than 12m/sec. Above this speed, the propeller has to be 'feathered' in order to avoid over speed and breakdown.

Wind turbine blades can be highly stressed and therefore material selection and build quality are crucial to reliable operation.

The alternator is generally connected to the turbine by means of a gearbox. In the event that conditions create the need to stop the unit (*e.g.* maintenance, breakdown) brakes, usually hydraulic, are applied to the shaft.

9.10.2 Solar units

The production of electricity in large quantities by means of solar radiation is dependent on the use of thermodynamic conversion. The principle of such a plant is that several hundred movable mirrors are positioned at ground level and directed to capture the sun's rays, these mirrors either being self-orientated or controlled by means of a computer.

The rays are reflected and concentrated on a boiler situated at the top of a tower with a storage system allowing the flow of heat to be regulated. The stored heat may then be converted into electricity by means of a boiler and steam turbine with outputs ranging from a few hundred kilowatts up to 10MW. These plants have a high capital cost with a large plant (approximately 2MW) requiring 200 heliostats (mirror assemblies), over an area of 10,000 square metres, which focus on a boiler 100m in the air. The solar flow is targeted on a receiver containing a heat-absorbing fluid (typically a mixture of nitrate and potassium nitrate) circulating in metal tubes feeding a boiler.

9.10.3 Geothermal power plants

The heat given off by the earth's core or geothermal energy has been in use as a source of hot water in the thermal baths for centuries. Several plants have been constructed to harness this energy and generate electricity. Only at locations such as California, Japan, and Italy, where underground heat readily comes to the surface, can this occur.

Two classes of geothermal energy are normally distinguished according to the temperature of the water or steam produced, high energy geothermal power, with temperatures above 50°C and low temperature geothermal power

With high-energy geothermal power, it is possible to transfer the steam directly to a turbo-alternator for the generation of electricity, normally on a cost-effective basis. Unfortunately such sites are only to be found along the lines of faults in the earth's crust, particularly in those countries bordering the Pacific Ocean.

Low temperature geothermal power is dependant on the much more frequent occurrence of water-bearing beds situated between 1500 and 3000m, with temperatures between 50 and 90°C.

It is possible to transform this energy into electricity by means of a turbine using a special fluid that vaporises at low temperature, ammonia for example. However, it is far better adapted to use for industrial or domestic heating purposes.

Geothermal power is among the most demanding service application of steam turbines. Impurities in the steam together with its wetness make the operating regime hostile. Impurities such as hydrogen sulphide, carbon dioxide and various silica, iron, calcium, sodium and potassium compounds exist and may give rise to a corrosive environment with solids being deposited on unit components. In the future, more contaminated-liquid-dominated systems will probably be exploited and this will represent a more arduous operation with new plants being designed with the environment in mind.

9.10.4 Coal gasification plants

Coal gasification is a process that converts coal into a gas through partial oxidation. The process allows a number of undesirable coal components such as sulphur and ash, to be removed.

If coal is subjected to heating in the presence of air but with less air than normal combustion, a gaseous reaction take place and less heat is given off. Products such as hydrogen, carbon monoxide and methane are produced. When the oxygen level is adjusted such that heat and gaseous fuels are produced, gasification is said to be occurring.

Impurities in the raw gas produced by the gasification process such as hydrogen sulphide and carbon dioxide must be treated to remove acidic impurities.

Commercial generation of electricity using coal gasification is not common. Conventional technologies are much simpler and cheaper. However, as the push to reduce environmental emissions continues, this technology may well become more widespread. The integrated gasification combined cycle (IGCC) relies upon a high degree of component integration in order to be efficient.

9.11 Nuclear power

Nuclear power plants differ from conventional thermal power stations in respect of the means by which steam is raised to drive the turbines. Energy in the form of heat generated by the splitting of the atoms of the heavy metals, plutonium and uranium, is used to heat water to produce steam which is then converted in a conventional manner to mechanical energy via a steam turbine. The nuclear reactor vessel is where the decay of fissile fuel (plutonium or uranium) takes place and this is contained in the so-called 'nuclear island'. The remainder of the plant is known as the 'conventional island'.

The principal components of the 'nuclear island' (the steam generating system of a nuclear power plant) are the reactor, the circulation system and the steam generator (except in the case of boiling water reactors). The reactor is a steel or prestressed concrete pressure vessel, which contains the nuclear fuel assemblies and the control rods. An important feature of the reactor is the substantial steel/concrete shield and water that is necessary to prevent external exposure to neutrons and radiation given off by the nuclear reaction and the fission products. The steam generator transfers the heat from the reactor coolant to the water in the secondary circuit from which steam is generated. Pumps and gas coolers circulate liquid coolants by blowers.

The components of the 'conventional island' are basically the same as those to be found in any other thermal power plant, plus some specific equipment whose functions are peculiar to the nuclear station, *e.g.* reactor control systems, air purification systems.

The type of fuel determines the choice of the 'moderator' of neutrons, which maintain the self-sustaining chain reaction, and the choice of liquid coolant, which permits the transfer of the heat, released in the reactor by the process of nuclear fission. The reaction process is controlled by a system of cadmium or boron rods that are moved inside the reactor vessel. Their function is the controlled absorption of neutrons whereby the rate of reaction and therefore energy produced is governed.

It is by the different methods of cooling the plant that the different types of nuclear stations are commonly recognised and the following two types represent approximately 90% of installed nuclear capacity around the world.

9.11.1 Pressurised water reactor (PWR)

The PWR is the most widely used system throughout the world. The coolant is ordinary water under very high pressure, which prevents it from boiling. When heated as a result of the fission process, it passes to a heat exchanger where it is used to boil water flowing in a secondary circuit. It also acts as the moderator. The fuel is typically enriched uranium oxide in pellet form, large numbers of which are fitted into zirconium tubes that are resistant to corrosion, to form rods running the length of the reactor core. The rods are arranged into groups of fuel assemblies. The gaps between the rods are relatively small, as water is a powerful moderator.

Due to the high pressure of the coolant, the pressure containment vessel has to be made in very thick steel, housed in a concrete shield, as are the heat exchangers, because the water from the core is radioactive. Control rods are clusters of silver-indium cadmium alloy rods moving in the fuel assemblies in spaces where fuel rods have been omitted. The purpose of these, apart from reactor shutdown, is to change the output level to match power demand.

9.11.2 Boiling water reactor (BWR)

In the BWR system the fuel is enriched uranium and the moderator and coolant are both light water. The water is not pressurised and is allowed to boil in the reactor, with the steam passing from the top of the reactor direct to the turbine.

A BWR does not have a heat exchanger and the reactor pressure containment vessel has to withstand lower pressures than a PWR and so is built with thinner walls. In effect, the reactor acts as a recirculation boiler with steam separators and dryers positioned in the top section of the vessel. The recirculation flow of water from the turbine condenser is normally achieved with jet pumps situated around the reactor core, which are driven by small external pumps.

Fission control is achieved by rods inserted hydraulically between the fuel assemblies from below the core and also by variation of the recirculation flow rate. The steam fed to the turbine obviously has some radioactivity although generally 'short lived'. Maintenance procedures must take account of this.

9.11.3 Advanced gas-cooled reactor

The advanced gas-cooled reactor uses ceramic uranium dioxide as fuel, canned in stainless steel that increases its potential energy. The moderator is graphite and the coolant is carbon dioxide gas.

9.11.4 Heavy water reactor

The heavy water reactor uses natural uranium as fuel and heavy water (deuterium) as the moderator and also the coolant. There are two types within this group, one which uses a pressure vessel and the other which uses pressure tubes.

9.11.5 Fast breeder reactor

The fast breeder reactor is physically small in size but is capable of producing vast quantities of heat. The fuel used is either enriched (in fissile atoms) uranium or plutonium but there is no moderator which means that the neutrons are not slowed down during the process. They have a small proportion of absorbent materials in the core and so few neutrons are wasted in the process. Efficiency is further enhanced by the blanket of depleted uranium placed around the core to absorb the escaping neutrons and in turn converts it to a greater amount of plutonium than that being consumed in the reaction, which gives it the name 'breeder'.

9.11.6 Basic definitions of nuclear reaction

The following basic definitions will provide an elementary understanding of the processes involved in power generation through nuclear reaction and some terminology used which is useful in appreciating some of the particular exposures presented by this sector of the industry.

9.11.7 Nuclear fission

Nuclear fission is the splitting of the nucleus of an atom into parts. If nuclear fission is conducted in a reactor, the fissile material in a nuclear fuel is fissioned by means of neutrons. This provides fission products, which carry the thermal energy and an average of 2.5 neutrons. Some of these neutrons escape from the core, while the fertile material absorbs others, and thus produces additional fissile material. More neutrons are lost due to absorption by structural materials, the moderator, coolant and fissionable products. The remaining neutrons are then available for maintaining the chain reaction.

9.11.8 Contamination

Contamination is the tainting of the surface of an object by radioactive substances.

9.11.9 Criticality

Criticality is the state where sufficient quantity of fissile material is assembled in the right shape and concentration for a sustained chain reaction to take place

9.11.10 Coolant

The coolant is a suitable liquid or gaseous substance that serves to transport heat from the reactor so that the heat can be used. Light water, heavy water, helium and possibly sodium are suitable coolants.

9.11.11   Nuclear energy

Nuclear energy is the energy generated in nuclear conversion processes (fission, fusion, and radioactive decomposition). The most important method of generating nuclear energy today is the fission of nuclear fuels by neutrons in the reactor.

9.11.12   Nuclear fuel

Nuclear fuel is a mixture of fissile and fertile materials in suitable chemical form such as in the form of a metal, oxide, carbide or silicide.

9.11.13   Reactor control

The reactor control is a system serving for the short-term or long-term control of reactor output, and which utilises substances with a particular ability to absorb neutrons, such as cadmium or boron.

9.11.14   Special risks

The risks and associated insurance solutions arising from nuclear power plants stand them apart from other forms of generation. Concerning insurance, they call for special treatment due to the potential catastrophic nature of the exposure in terms of damage to property and more particularly, damage to the environment. This high level exposure is beyond the 'capacity' of the conventional direct commercial insurance markets and traditional reinsurance markets and this has lead to the emergence of national nuclear pools whose sole function is to accept these nuclear risks. The risks accepted by these pools are excluded by insurance policies provided in the commercial insurance market, where most insurance policies (and reinsurance contracts) contain a 'nuclear energy risks exclusion clause' which defines what constitutes a nuclear risk and what is covered/not covered by the particular insurance.

While a serious accident at any power station can have a detrimental impact on the environment and present a danger to public safety, this is especially true in the case of nuclear plants. In fact even a relatively minor incident could lead to enormous hazards to the public due to exposure to radioactive contamination. The catastrophic incidents at Three Mile Island and Chernobyl led to widespread damage, injury and loss of life, both immediate and progressive and raised the political debate and heightened public awareness as to the acceptability and the whole future of nuclear energy. The clean up costs and time required to decontaminate the areas physically affected by the release radioactive contaminants can be expected to be huge.

Therefore, the whole question of plant safety takes on its own dimension in the context of nuclear power and industry standards, set by government legislation and controls, reflect this unique situation. The most stringent rules and restrictions will govern access to the site of a nuclear power station. These restrictions could affect the freedom of insurers to investigate risks and any subsequent losses.

Equally, these safety concerns will have an enormous bearing on maintenance and plant shutdowns that require the most stringent planning and must be co-ordinated to extremely high standards. Moreover, the finite useful working life and/or safe working life and/or changing political attitudes towards nuclear power generators and the closing down or 'decommissioning' of a station, also presents health and safety issues.

9.12 Critical areas

There are a number of areas of potential exposure, which are common to all power generation plants and these generic concerns are described below.

9.12.1 Vibration

A characteristic of all rotating plant and particularly relevant to power plants. Plant resonates at various critical frequencies during start up, running and shut down which may lead to elevated vibration. Other factors such as wear and tear, alignment, balancing, turbulence and cavitation may increase vibration levels. Vibration, which induces fluctuating stress into plant, may be due to one or more of unbalance, bent shaft, misalignment, bearing wear or miscentering, looseness, gear noise, foundation problems, resonance and parts failure.

The profile of vibration in terms of frequency, amplitude and phase can be measured and analysed. The cause of a particular vibration can then normally be identified as the profile is related to a geometric or physical characteristic of the machine such as the number of blades, gear teeth, etc.

9.12.2 Fatigue

As the plant is load cycled, both thermally and physically, then components are subjected to fluctuating stresses. With the presence of stress raisers such as sharp changes in section or non-homogeneous material, an initial crack site may be located within the structure. Under cyclic loading and with a crack initiated, significantly lower stresses can cause crack propagation with ultimately final overload failure.

9.12.3 Overspeed

All rotating power plant hardware may suffer from overspeed which is simply an increase in the revolutions per minute rate beyond design parameters. This most commonly occurs when a turbine generator suddenly loses load and the resistance to rotation is dramatically reduced. It is important that control systems have been maintained and tested so that they react quickly to this effect to avoid substantial damage. Passive protection such as overspeed bolts should be installed and proved operational.

9.12.4 Erosion

Erosion is a concern on all plant with moving fluids, *e.g.*, turbines, boilers, and valves, pipeline joints. It is a particular problem with fluidised bed boilers due to the particulate size in the boiler, the gas velocity and its path. A carefully controlled maintenance and inspection programme is needed to manage this exposure.

9.12.5 Corrosion

Chemical corrosion comes from acids produced by hydrolysis of salts. This corrosion need not be feared in water or steam installations except where there is insufficient alkalinity to neutralise these acids — oxidation occurs when the pH of the water is less than 9.7; when the pH is between 10 and 12 the metal becomes covered with a magnetic oxide film. Above this, the acid is oxidised and dissolved.

Corrosion by electrolysis may appear in pipework as a result of normal product flow, following ineffective isolation of a nearby electrical installation or by the appearance of a cell phenomenon. It is favoured by conductive water.

Steps can be taken to prevent or slow down corrosion and to utilise the corrosion products as a protective screen. Certainly acid waters must not be used in any system. Ideally, the pH should be adjusted to 10, a value at which the iron becomes oxidised into magnetite to create a protective film of several microns. In the case of a boiler, a blowdown system can be used to remove some unwanted solids from the system.

An increase in the surface tension of the water due to too high a ratio of dissolved salts and organic matter favours priming and carrying of droplets in the superheater where they can cause corrosion or vaporise violently leaving deposits (like the boiler water they contain dissolved salts). This priming may lead to erosion or even destruction of blades if the water droplets reach the turbines. In addition to erosion, corrosion may result from excessive chemical concentrations in steam. For example, stress corrosion cracking in turbine blades can be a consequence of high levels of unreacted oxygen scavenger in steam.

External components in wet atmosphere (*e.g.* HRSGs) can suffer from extreme corrosion and a suitable temperature resistive coating may be required.

(The subject of corrosion is a very broad and complex issue in its own right and it is not the purpose of this Study Report to describe the phenomenon in detail but to identify it as a very significant concern in virtually all power plants.)

9.12.6 **Cable fires**

A power plant has extensive cabling, typically concentrated on cable trays. Cables may run in specially designed basement areas and pass through various walls and fire breaks. It is important to understand that cables passing through firewalls must be packed correctly and to a recognised standard to avoid negating the effect of the separation. Cable insulation can often be flammable and responsible for rapid spread of fire, particularly when running vertically. In addition to spreading fire, the combustion of cables often releases toxic and corrosive fumes that can cause extensive damage to sensitive control equipment. Various factors can influence this exposure:

- the use of cables with non-combustible sheaths
- the design and size of cables arrangements
- nature of the cable clamps: metal, not plastic
- use of an intumescent coating before and after installation
- dividing up of the cable galleries into isolated sections to maintain controllable areas for fire fighting
- unitisation of critical cabling
- sealing of the cable passages to the electric or other rooms to prevent the spread of fire,

In the largest cable galleries the installation of temperature detection equipment with alarms in the control rooms is desirable. These cable galleries might warrant automatic sprinkler protection.

9.12.7 **Other fires**

Oils are utilised throughout a power plant for both lubrication and insulation purposes. These products will support combustion and their containment and fixed fire protections can be a significant factor in the case of an incident.

Fire and explosion problems arise with electrical equipment and these are generally the result of short-circuits due to insulation failure. This is particularly true of transformer (ageing of the dielectric, insulants, and windings). Sound maintenance programmes and condition monitoring are the best mitigating practices to avoid such problems.

9.12.8 Maintenance and overhaul

Already covered are a number of areas in this chapter where maintenance activity and its importance have been detailed. For further guidance the reader's attention is drawn to Chapter 5, 'Loss Prevention'.

9.12.9 Operating/management regime

Some plants such as hydroelectric schemes have never experienced a genuine emergency. Staff may no longer question their operational actions or consider their emergency procedures. Modifications may well have been carried out which fundamentally alter the way in which a plant responds under emergency circumstances. Plant staff should be encouraged to review both their actions and the plant responses to certain deviations from normal operation.

It should be remembered that as for most machinery, mechanical failure is predominantly associated with poor or incorrect maintenance and operator error. With those units that are reliant on new materials and designs such as the latest gas turbines, failure associated with design and materials tends to be more common.

A full permit-to-work system should be in use that controls hot work, entry into confined spaces, electrical isolation, impairment of protection systems, etc.

9.12.10 Contingency planning

An important aspect for plant operators and insurers alike is the state of preparedness in the case of an unwanted event. This should take the form of immediate short-term actions as laid out in an emergency plan as well as a plan for resumption of business and commercial continuity. The plan should include a list of suppliers able to provide services and hardware, which may be required at short notice. Spares pooling arrangements with another site may form part of such a plan.

9.12.11 Technology and updates

All facets of the power generation industry face the continual drive for increased efficiency levels that ultimately should lead to bigger returns for investors. The gas turbine sector has, over recent years, been one of the upper most developers in this sector. Operators and insurers must keep themselves abreast of updates in hardware and best operating practice. Very often, generator user groups exist which allow competitors using the same machines to discuss all manner of issues and mutually share information.

9.12.12 Manning levels

With increased automation and remote operation, manning levels reduce.

There is a need for increased fixed plant protection and more sophisticated communication systems to manage unexpected deviations from normal operation.

Control systems must have the correct trips, alarms and interlocks installed. For example, on boiler plant, loss of burner flame, failure of or low primary air should all trip the pulveriser, closure of the burner valve should trip the pulveriser feed and primary air, pulveriser failure should trip the fuel and primary air. On a steam turbine the loss of lube oil should alarm and trip the unit as should high lube oil temperature and loss of seal air pressure.

9.12.13 **The environment**

An ever increasingly important issue is the damage to and protection of, the environment. Many restrictions are placed upon power plants to ensure that they conform to environmental discharge consents, for example consents for sulphur oxides and nitrogen oxides (SOx and NOx). The legal framework in which standards are set and enforced is highly variable from country to country.

9.12.14 **Plant design**

It requires a great deal of knowledge and skill to properly critique a power plant design. The analysis of process and instrumentation diagrams (P&IDs), machinery details and electrical schematics although time consuming is the only comprehensive way to fully understand the plant. Losses do occur, resulting from failures in the logic of the control systems, the design itself and the emergency shut down systems. For example, a single event might render the AC and back-up DC power-supply systems ineffective even to priority boards. Clearly this is not desirable and designers would have attempted to avoid this exposure. However, if a unique set of circumstances were to occur, which was unforeseen, or perhaps a station modification has been made during the plant's operational lifetime, undesirable results can occur.

9.12.15 **Spares**

The ability to quickly obtain plant items for routine or unplanned replacement is a crucial aspect of modern plant operation, particularly in respect of gas turbines with a significant inventory of items with finite lifetimes. Spares can either be held in an appropriate location on site or held by suppliers. In both cases their availability in an operational condition is essential.

9.12.16 **Accessibility**

In all power plants, the ability of any staff or external persons, such as the fire brigade, to access the site and its plant is important in order to react quickly in the event of a problem. For example, a significant number of hydroelectric stations are located underground and are remotely operated. In the case of significant fire or flood, access to the station may prove impossible. This is also a factor relevant to the evacuation of staff in an emergency. It should be noted that in mountainous regions, the stations themselves may be isolated as a result of normal weather conditions at certain times of the year, which can significantly increase the downtime following an event and the intervention times for emergency response.

9.12.17 **Training and education**

Not only is initial training for staff essential but also re-education is equally important. Technology and best practice all evolve over time and staff must be kept aware of changes.

9.12.18 **Security**

The need for site security is obviously influenced by the plant location but in all cases unwanted persons should not be permitted to enter or approach any equipment.

10   Oil, gas and petrochemicals

10.1   History — oil and petrochemicals

People have been aware of surface deposits of crude oil for the last 5000 years. Initially, how-ever, the uses to which this oil was put were very limited. It was not until the middle of the nineteenth century that the first oil wells were drilled and provided lighter, more useful and a more plentiful supply of oils in their crude state, hence 'crude oil'.

Edwin L. Drake drilled the first commercial oil well during 1857–59 in north-west Pennsylvania, USA. By the end of the century oil fields had been discovered in fourteen states of the USA and also in Europe and East Asia. Significant oil deposits were found in the Middle East before the Second World War. With the advent of the motor car, a better understanding of how crude oil was formed and what were its major constituent parts, the first plants were designed and built to separate the various products, hence 'oil refinery'.

The original oil refineries consisted of very simple processes and were designed around a distillation column. Distillation involves the heating of the crude oil and separation of the constituent parts by their different boiling points.

Through the early part of the twentieth century, scientists' knowledge increased and oil refineries became more technically advanced and more efficient. Eventually technology progressed further with the advent of larger, more sophisticated machinery. The result of this was that large blocks of machinery (or 'units') were built and this enabled the previously discarded residue from the distillation process to be broken down further to provide more useful products. Examples of these units are hydrocrackers and fluid catalytic crackers.

As more products from the oil refineries were made available, and the availability of these products increased due to the building of a larger number of oil refineries, scientists and engineers raced to develop new types of machinery which could utilise the products to make new consumer goods. The outcome of this was the formation of the petrochemical industry from which all types of products such as plastics were made (*e.g.*, polyvinyl chloride (PVC) was first produced in 1912).

Oil is now the major provider of the world's energy needs and is, in many countries, the cornerstone for the whole economy. Therefore, the continued running of the oil refineries and petrochemical plants throughout the world is of significant importance.

10.2   History — gas

The first known natural gas well was drilled in China in 211BC to a reported depth of 150m. However, natural gas was unknown in Europe until its discovery in England in 1659. The first commercial application of a petroleum product in North America was the utilisation of natural gas from a shallow well in Fredonia, New York in 1821. The major barrier against the development of natural gas as a commercial commodity was the difficulty of transportation over any distance. An important breakthrough occurred in 1890 with the invention of a leakproof pipeline coupling. Long distance transmission, however, only became practical during the late 1920s due to yet further advancement in pipeline technology.

In the early days of the discovery of oil the associated gas would be flared off at the refinery or used to keep the pressure up in the oil field by re-injection into that field. More recently the gas industry has come into its own with the development of large gas fields around the world. Natural gas is now utilised as a major fuel both for industry and domestic use and to a lesser extent as a feed stock for the petrochemical industry, *e.g.* in the production of methanol or ammonia.

Large plants known as liquefied natural gas (LNG) plants have been built in certain parts of the world to liquefy the natural gas, thereby dramatically reducing its volume. This LNG is then transferred by ship to the country where the gas is required. It is subsequently heated and vaporised to provide natural gas for fuel or as a feed stock to the petrochemical industry.

10.3   Basic processes

The major components of the oil, gas and petrochemical industry can be summarised as

- exploration and production
- oil refining
- gas separation/liquefaction
- petrochemical production.

The terms 'upstream and downstream' are commonly used within the industry. 'Upstream' is normally defined as exploration and development, whereas 'downstream' is normally defined as the processing (refining) through to production of the final commodity.

Upstream areas include both the below ground drilling and well completion to the well head and the transportation from the well head to the refinery or separation plant. Machinery insurers are normally only required to cover machinery from the well head 'Christmas tree' to the production of the final product. The well head 'Christmas tree' is the control system consisting of various valves and blowout preventors attached to the top of each oil or gas well.

Downstream areas generally commence at the refinery or separation plant until the production of the final product.

The processes involved in the oil, gas and petrochemical industry generally either involve separation, reaction or both. Examples of some processes are:

- Gas plant   Separation only

- Basic refinery (*e.g.* hydroskimming)   Separation only

- Sophisticated refinery
  (*e.g.* hydrocracker, fluid catalytic cracker) Separation followed by reaction

- Petrochemical plant
  (*e.g.* ethylene, polyethylene)   Reaction followed by separation

- Liquefied natural gas;
  liquefied petroleum gas   Separation followed by liquefaction.

Most of the above processes are continuous and because of this the machinery will be running under operating conditions for many months or even years without shutting down. Some smaller, more specific reaction processes may occur as non-continuous, or batch, processes.

10.4   Major feedstocks

The feedstock for a refinery or gas separation plant is crude oil or crude gas respectively. These first stage processes either produce finished products themselves or 'intermediate' products which become the feedstocks for other subsequent processes. Subsequent processes may include further breakdown of heavy molecules to lighter ones as in a hydrocracker unit or the production of petrochemicals such as plastics.

10.4.1   Preparation of feedstocks

Depending upon the process being utilised, the product required and/or environmental needs, the feedstock may need to be cleaned. Cleaning is normally required so that the conversion/separation is at its most efficient; the associated impurities do not effect the reaction or 'poison' any of the catalysts or damage other machinery and/or allow pollutants into the atmosphere.

Cleaning of a feedstock may take many different forms from simple removal or separation (by weight or boiling point) to passing the feedstock through sieves (molecular or mechanical) to chemical reactions.

The purity of the feedstock required will normally depend upon the product to be produced, the reaction to be undertaken, the equipment involved in the process, environmental controls/limitations or economic considerations.

The result of feedstock impurities passing through the processes can result in damage to subsequent machinery by erosion, corrosion, increase in wear and tear and/or poisoning, reduction of conversion rates, product impurity having an affecting on the sale price or an increase in costs of product manufacture.

10.5   Principal processes

The majority of the processes involved in the oil, gas and petrochemical industry concern either the separation of hydrocarbon mixtures into their constituent parts, or the reaction of hydrocarbons to produce further, generally more valuable, products. The plants where these processes are carried out use a wide range of machines, both static and rotating.

10.5.1   Static and rotating machinery

As their names suggest, static machines have no moving parts and the hydrocarbons simply flow through them undergoing either a reaction or separation process. Rotating machines are generally used to convey the hydrocarbons through the plant or alternatively to mix them.

Some examples of static machines are columns, reformers, heat exchangers, furnaces, process vessels, boilers, piping, and storage tanks. Some examples of rotating machines are turbines, pumps, compressors and extruders.

A large refinery or petrochemical plant will comprise various units, each performing a specific task. A large plant may, for instance, contain between six and twenty different 'process units'.

10.5.2   **Distillation**

Distillation units simply separate a mixture by heating up the liquid in a vertical column, which may exceed 45m in height. The column consists of multiple stages or trays characteristically being between 20 and 40 in number.

The constituent parts separate out at different levels throughout the column due to their different boiling points. The most common types of distillation column trays are sieves or bubble caps. Sieve trays are simply perforated plates with small holes of about 5-6mm in diameter. Bubble cap trays have an upturned cup (or cap) over each hole in the tray, which lifts whenever the pressure below exceeds the downward force of the cap. The vapour therefore bubbles up through the liquid held on the tray. The products are taken off at differing levels within the column. Heavier products fall to the bottom of the column while lighter ones move towards the top. The products are then cooled or condensed and either form a final product or become intermediates for further processing.

From a feedstock of crude oil the products produced from simple distillation are, from the top of the column downwards — butanes and lighter hydrocarbons, gasoline/petrol, naphtha, kerosene, light gas oil, heavy gas oil and residue. Distillation forms an important part of the refinery and many petrochemical processes.

10.5.3   **Cracking**

In general terms in the oil industry the larger the hydrocarbon molecule the less valuable it is. Although distillation was the first process in a refinery, the refiners soon found ways to generate smaller hydrocarbon molecules by breaking down the larger, less useful ones. Cracking is therefore the most common term used in the oil industry for breaking down larger molecules into smaller molecules. This term, however, can have a slightly different meaning in the petrochemical industry where more commonly the term relates to the breaking down of a molecule.

There are various types of cracking methods including straight heating to more than 500°C (thermal cracking) and heating in the presence of catalyst (catalytic cracking/fluid catalytic cracking). Cracking may be carried out at high or low pressures depending upon the specific process or feedstock being used.

The cracking of these larger hydrocarbon molecules means that there are not enough hydrogen atoms to go around, therefore rather than just producing hydrocarbons a by-product of cracking heavy oils/residues is pure carbon in the form of coke. This coke is removed from the process stream via the coker unit.

As mentioned above, a result of traditional cracking methods was that there were not enough hydrogen atoms once the larger molecules had broken down. Hydrocracking was therefore introduced to obtain lighter hydrocarbons from heavier ends. This process involves the cracking reaction occurring in the presence of additional hydrogen and a fixed bed (as against fluidised bed) catalyst.

The cracking process is likely to take place in more than one reactor.

Cracking, especially thermal cracking, is used in various processes within the petrochemical industry. One major example is the production of ethylene, in the course of which ethane is pumped through tubes with diameters of four to six inches and heated to more than 800°C. Ethylene is the product of the cracking process.

10.5.4 **Alkylation**

One result for refiners of the various cracking methods mentioned above was that too many lighter hydrocarbons were produced. The alkylation process was therefore invented and this recombined lighter hydrocarbons into heavy hydrocarbons. In simple terms this process involves the conversion of a mixture of lighter hydrocarbons such as olefins and propane/butane to alkylate. Alkylate is produced by first cooling the feed, mixing this with isobutane and a catalyst (normally sulphuric acid). Once the reaction has occurred the acid is removed. The hydrocarbons are then passed through a caustic soda vessel to remove any remaining acid before being fed into distillation columns to separate the alkylate from saturated gas.

10.5.5 **Reforming**

Reforming processes cause chemical changes to occur to the feedstock generally by applying significant heat in the presence of a catalyst.

In a refinery, a major reforming process will be at the catalytic reformer where a naphtha stream is passed through multiple reactors, which have a catalyst of alumina, silica and platinum. The reactors operate at between 200 and 500 pounds per square inch (psi) and at between 480 and 525°C. The chemical composition of the feed changes as it passes through the reformer.

In the petrochemical industry one of the major reforming processes is the production of synthesis gas for the production of methanol or ammonia. The two most well used processes involve either the reaction of methane with steam (steam reforming) or by partial oxidation of methane. Both processes utilise high temperatures and pressures and therefore require substantial equipment similar to a cracking furnace.

10.5.6 **Catalysts**

Catalysts play a very important part in the oil, gas and petrochemical industries. Catalysts can vary greatly in composition, value, durability, ability to be 'poisoned', useful lifetime, brittleness and ability to be regenerated. Many catalysts are made from metals (including precious metals such as platinum). They are generally specially made for specific processes and are protected by patents.

10.5.7 **Process units**

Large refineries or petrochemical plants consist of a multitude of pieces of machinery and equipment. Generally, the machinery and equipment is aligned in such a way that certain areas on the site are allocated to a particular type of process. The combination of the various pieces of machinery and equipment required to complete a certain process is known as a 'process unit'. Examples of process units include distillation units, crude units, coker units, ethylene units and alkylation units. These 'process units' are made up of static and rotating pieces of machinery of varying complexity and size. These machines operate under varying conditions (temperatures, pressures and loads) depending upon the job required of them.

In general terms, and as can be seen from the descriptions above, oil refineries or petrochemical plants take a feedstock and either break it down or build it up to produce useful products to sell. The art of a refinery or petrochemical plant owner is to produce a greater amount of the more valuable product and either minimise, or find other ways to use, the less useful products/by-products.

10.5.8 **Polymers and monomers**

One of the most important groups of products emulating from the petrochemical industry is polymers. Polymers are large molecules formed by the joining in a repetitive pattern one or more types of smaller molecules known as monomers. The monomers can either be attached in a linear chain (linear) or in branches (branched). Different qualities accrue to the polymer if the monomer is attached in either a linear or branched fashion. The number of repeat monomers is called the degree of polymerisation. Most useful polymers have molecule weights between 10,000 and 1,000,000.

Some common examples of polymers and monomers are

Polymers	Monomers
Polyethylene	Ethylene
Polystyrene	Styrene
Polyvinyl chloride	Vinyl chloride

Generally, manufacturing methods for the polymer entail flammable fluids being reacted in large vessels at significant temperatures and pressures. The final product (the polymer) is generally produced as a solid before being further processed to make the final product.

Products from polymers are an important part of everyday life and therefore the methods for making them and the associated risks need to be understood.

The main methods for making plastics are

● Separation followed by liquefaction moulding (compression, injection, blow and rotational)
● extrusion (normally via a reciprocating-screw extruder)
● blowing film and tubing
● calendering
● casting.

Basically, the polymer is heated and/or compressed and/or injected into various types of machine. The polymer liquefies due to the temperature and/or pressure and is forced to take the shape of the mould, nozzle or rollers, etc. Therefore, other than the normal exposures to machinery which often work in corrosive environments (corrosion, natural wear and tear, etc.) the main exposure to this type of process is machine failure either from its own fault or where the power supply to that machine fails. If for instance the power supply to an extruder fails, the liquid polymer cools and solidifies within the machine leaving a nasty mess to be cleaned up. It has been said that the results of this type of loss are not dissimilar to a pot freeze in an aluminium or steel plant. However, generally the machinery values associated with polymer production are lower.

10.5.9 **Utilities**

Each process unit requires various utilities (*e.g.*, water, steam, electricity and air) and therefore most oil, gas and petrochemical plants have large utility sections within the site boundaries. These include gas turbines, steam turbines, transformers and boilers. For greater detail on the subject of utilities, the reader should refer to Chapter 9, 'Power generation' and Chapter 16.8, 'Gas turbines'.

Air liquefaction plants are also built to supply hydrogen, oxygen or nitrogen to the processes.

10.6   Maintenance

Like other industries utilising heavy and complex machinery, the maintenance of the refinery plant is extremely important. As mentioned previously, many of the machines forming part of a refinery or chemical plant will not be shut down for a full maintenance turnaround for anything between one and three years. In light of the time between maintenance turnarounds, it is important to have extremely sophisticated predictive maintenance and inspection procedures and first class control and monitoring systems.

Machines in the refinery, if maintained correctly, can operate continuously and safely for many years. Therefore the type of maintenance that is carried out is of fundamental importance to the operator and the insurance industry. Maintenance may be split into two types — preventative and breakdown. Preventative maintenance in turn may be broken down further into routine and predictive maintenance.

Static and rotating machinery receive different types of maintenance. Most of the maintenance for static machinery occurs during a specific plant shutdown (turnaround). This would generally involve opening up of the equipment and inspection for corrosion (both internally and externally under the insulation) and looking for other faults. Any faults are then remedied so as to enable the machine to remain in good working order until the next turnaround.

Rotating machines usually have an installed spare and so much of their maintenance occurs while the plant is running (*e.g.*, oil change, seal changes on pumps, etc.). Where no installed spare exists it is likely that the plant turnarounds will take place at shorter intervals.

10.7   Control systems

Good monitoring of the operating conditions of machines is of great importance as a variance in reading could be the first sign that a part should be changed or that there is something wrong within the machine.

Other than control systems for controlling the processes, it is important that there is sufficient monitoring of levels, temperatures, pressures, flow rate, vibrations and, where applicable, vapour and/or toxic fluid levels. The positioning of any probes or level detectors is also of great importance. Maintaining these detectors/probes/control systems in good order and at a reasonable degree of accuracy is of paramount importance to the safe running of any plant.

In the event that a problem is detected, the control systems in place must shut down the machinery in the quickest and safest manner. This may involve shutting down one machine and at the same time switching to a spare machine or it may involve the shutting down of the whole unit or plant. It is also important that if any changes are made to the plant that a subsequent hazard and operability (HAZOP) study is carried out to confirm that the settings for the control systems are still valid.

In the event that a control system fails, valve settings and the like should automatically fail to 'safe' which means that valves may fully open or fully close in the event of the failure depending upon the safest position for that particular valve or process. In a computer controlled plant it is important to be able to bring down the plant safely via manual means in the event that the computer controls fail.

10.8 Planning

As in any other industry, a strategic operating plan is of paramount importance to the safe running of the plant. This will require good line management and a proactive teamwork mentality. For a plant of this nature this will include:

● Detailed risk management assessment.

● Extensive maintenance procedures allowing for preventative, and breakdown maintenance to be carried out (this will include full plant turnarounds, continuing general maintenance including the replacement of worn parts or machinery).

● Planning to continue to support customers and suppliers as full shutdowns are required at regular intervals.

● Updating of operating instruction manuals, including procedures for isolating systems for maintenance activities.

● Updating stand-by spares and/or spare parts/equipment generally.

● Replacement of outdated or inefficient equipment.

● Staff training (both on an operational level and for emergencies).

● Detailed emergency procedures, if followed, should shut down the facility as safely as possible in the circumstances and minimise the risks to both staff and third party personnel and property.

● Auditing of safety systems and procedures.

● Emergency plans that fully outline what should be done in an emergency situation and this should include the available alternative working practices, alternative sources of supply for equipment, materials or feedstock.

● Financial business plan that deals not only with normal sales projections and budgets but also outlines investment in new plant, all maintenance including turnarounds and any upgrading/modernisation or de-bottlenecking.

10.9 Critical areas

The oil, gas and petrochemical industry involves the utilisation of specialist machinery, with high capital costs and which must continue to operate for very long periods without being shut down.

The processes involve the use of highly flammable fluids (mainly hydrocarbons), in large amounts, under extreme conditions. These extreme conditions may involve high (or low) temperatures and pressures, large quantities of solids or fluids being processed (high loads) and working in corrosive atmospheres. Therefore the machinery must be carefully designed to take account of the intended working conditions allowing for the specific processes being used and the part of the world in which the machinery is going to operate. Understanding the specific requirements of a machine, its design criteria and the controls systems needed to regulate that machine are of critical importance to its long term safe operation.

The main issues for the use of machinery in the oil, gas and petrochemical industry are likely to relate to the following.

10.9.1 High capital costs

Refinery and/or petrochemical plant values generally vary between values below one hundred million to a few billion US dollars. Individual process units can range in value from a few million to six or seven hundred million US dollars.

10.9.2 Extremes in temperatures, pressures, loads and environments

Machinery is often required to perform under extremes of pressures, temperatures, and loads and in some cases under corrosive conditions.

Temperatures may vary from many hundred degrees Celsius to many degrees below zero Celsius. Pressures may vary from many times atmospheric pressure to no pressure (vacuum units). Heavy loads can be applied to machines due to large inventories of fluids being held up in units and/or being transported from one unit to another. In some cases machinery has to operate in either very acidic or alkaline conditions.

10.9.3 Highly specialised machinery

To take account of the extremes in operating conditions mentioned above, machinery has to be specially designed and built so that these requirements can be met. In addition to this the machinery is required to work continually for between one and three years before being shut down for a full maintenance turnaround. It should be noted that machines are generally at their safest when they are working in a steady state. Start-ups, shutdowns and cyclic operations can put tremendous strains on machinery, especially emergency shutdowns.

Plant is in many cases very large and can weigh a great deal (some columns are over 50m high, a few metres in diameter and can weigh over 1000 tonnes. Some reactors have a wall thickness of some inches).

10.9.4 New technology

Technology is permanently moving forward with new processes, new materials and new designs coming to the market place. These advancements normally

● enable machines to be designed better using new materials or new methods to contain the fluids under more extreme conditions

● increase efficiency but often at higher capital expense

● mean that it takes longer to replace the machine due to the limited number of manufacturers equipped to supply a replacement

● may cause lower tolerance to upsets and systems are more reliant upon control systems with increases in efficiency

● provide better control over the processes and safety systems.

However, it should be noted that although the energy companies are always looking to improve their processes and therefore improve their designs, materials and plant integrity, continuity of service and therefore revenue earning is an all important consideration.

10.9.5 **Failures**

Although the frequency of major machinery failures in this industry is relatively low, when a failure does occur, its effects can be catastrophic. The major exposures relate to chemical explosions and/or severe fire due to the handling of extremely flammable fluids and mechanical type explosions.

For processes involving light hydrocarbons there is the risk of a vapour cloud explosion (VCE). Where there is a large-scale hold up of light hydrocarbons under pressure (*e.g.* storage spheres full of butane) there is the risk of a boiling liquid expanding vapour explosion (BLEVE). Past experience has shown that these types of explosions can cause damage on a devastating scale.

10.9.6 **Fire protection systems and fire fighting**

As fire and explosion risks are major exposures to this industry it is important to understand the different methods available to fight fires.

Fire protection systems are either fixed or mobile. Fixed fire protection may involve release of fire-fighting fluids (generally water or foam) over a particular machine by either dedicated fire protection or by general fire monitors. Depending upon the situation, the fire may be best controlled by a mist type spray or by a deluge system. It is important to understand that with the types of equipment being used, the flammable fluids being processed and the significant temperatures and pressures involved that it is unlikely that fixed fire-fighting systems attached to particular machines will be able to control a large fire alone. The reason for this is that the original explosion or fire often destroys the fixed systems. Therefore it is important to have powerful fire monitors stationed around the site in such a way that all of the machinery is covered by at least one monitor. The majority of all of these systems will need to be automatically controlled. These monitors should be regularly tested as part of the overall plant maintenance.

In addition to the fixed systems there will need to be a fully manned fire brigade at the site. The size of this fire brigade will depend upon the type of plant, location, what support can be obtained from local authority fire brigades or other local companies. For instance, along the Houston Ship Canal in the USA, where there are many refineries and chemical plants next to each other, there is a mutual aid agreement whereby if one party has an emergency all other local companies will, if required, go to their aid. It is always important however to have quick response fire-fighting capability at the specific site.

10.9.7 **Spread of damage**

As machines in the oil, gas and petrochemical industries, in many cases, operate under extreme conditions in the presence of very flammable fluids, the risk of explosion or serious fire is always present. While these highly volatile fluids are contained within the designed machine then all is well. However, when something goes wrong or failures occur, the results can be catastrophic. These plants are normally quite congested areas with machines of individual high values in close proximity to one another. Therefore damage can be widespread across the plant when a major fire or explosion occurs. This possibility needs to be appreciated when considering the maximum probable loss.

10.9.8 **Human factors**

In the oil, gas and petrochemical industries, the majority of losses can be traced back to human intervention. Machinery should, where possible (other than for maintenance), be left well alone. These plants operate best under steady conditions and technology advancements have taken day-to-day control of these facilities out of the hands of the operators. Computer-driven control and monitoring systems play a vital part in all plants and generally safety, although these may create problems of their own. However, if systems are upset, control systems made inoperable, and control rooms destroyed or damaged, plant operators must be able to shut down the facility as safely as possible.

10.9.9 **Prolonged business interruption**

These plants represent higher exposures to business interruption than most other industries due to the lengthy periods that are required to reorder, rebuild and reinstall damaged machines due to their specialist nature (long lead times). Lead times of 18–24 months are not uncommon.

Most refineries and chemical plants are unable to run at low throughputs, due to either safety or process considerations. Therefore a plant will shut down once the first constraint is reached. The point when the plant must be shut down is known as the 'turndown ratio'. A plant may typically be shut down at between 40% and 50% throughput.

One vessel or machine may be crucial to the operation of the whole plant.

The excessive size and weight of many machines or equipment mean that very large crane or other specialist equipment is required to install new machinery. This can cause significant problems when replacing a machine in an existing facility. Machinery life (especially for fixed machines) can be very long, spare parts can therefore be difficult to obtain.

A complex refinery or chemical plant may be able to significantly mitigate a loss by rerouting streams and/or making different products.

There may be significant contingent/interdependency exposures as one plant or machine will feed another plant or machine in a continuous process. If a machine/plant/company cannot obtain its feedstock then that machine/plant/company will have to shut down. In certain circumstances it may be possible to obtain feedstock from alternative sources. However the practicality of this needs to be carefully assessed.

It is likely that there would be intervention by the local authority or national government following a major incident due to health and safety implications.

To summarise, the most frequent cause of failures is human intervention and other major causes are design defects, inherent defects and natural peril events. The nature of these exposures may be further categorised, as below, divided between the inherent machinery risks ('internals') and outside influences ('externals').

Internals

● The specific features of the particular machinery, *e.g.* manufacturer, type, size, value, process, etc. Specialists are required to build this type of machinery. Very little can be bought 'off the shelf'.

● All machinery has been successfully commissioned and tested.

● The condition of the machinery.

● The quality of installed control/monitoring systems.

- The effect of new technology, which may for instance involve the use of new or unproven materials, designs or size upgrading.

Externals

- The risk management and maintenance philosophy of the company.

- The quality of staff training.

- The emergency provisions that are in place.

- The fixed fire fighting and mobile fire fighting equipment that is available.

- The general housekeeping philosophy of the owner.

- Is the control room for the unit/plant/site in an exposed area from the point of view of fire and/or explosion? If so, is it blast-proof?

- Exposure to natural catastrophes such as flood, hurricane, volcanic eruption or earthquake (with regard to this exposure, it should be noted that in many cases it is usually not the natural peril itself that causes the major damage but the fire or explosion that subsequently occurs after flammable fluids have been released from, for instance, a pipe flange that has broken).

11 | Pulp and paper plants

11.1　History

Humanity has been driven by the need to record and depict real and artistic impressions of life and the recording medium initially involved the use of stone, rock, bark, leaves and ivory.

As early as 2500BC, Egyptians made and used paper produced from the pith of the papyrus reed that grew along the banks of the River Nile. It was made from *Cyperus papyrus*, an aquatic plant of the sedge family, which was prepared by laying strips of the reed side by side and then crossing them with other strips. It was then soaked in the water of the Nile, and this created an adhesive and glued together the strips. Finally the sheet was hammered and left out to dry in the sun with any surface roughness removed by polishing with ivory or smooth shell.

Later clay brick, wax-coated boards were used and the Babylonians and Romans also used dried animal skins (parchments). However, it was not until about AD105 that the Chinese invented the method of making paper that we know today.

Methods were improved and the technology spread further afield until the thirteenth century, when paper making was known in southern Europe. Watermarks were introduced at this time and continue to be used on documents and bank notes as a guarantee of authenticity.

Paper making in Europe was well established by the seventeenth century and the first paper mill in the United States was built in 1690. In 1799 a Frenchman, Robert Nicholas-Louis, patented the first papermaking machine. It made paper in great lengths using a continuous conveyor or belt system and was driven by turning a handle. The prepared mixture of water and pulp was poured into an oval chest, then picked up on rotating copper bars and discharged on to the upper surface of an endless wire mesh running on two end rollers. The pulp passed between felt-covered squeezing rollers, removing most of the water so that the web lifted off the wire and could be coiled on a roller. A screw adjusted the tension of the wire, while a crossbar shook the wire. This crossbar could also be raised or lowered to alter the slope of the wire and thus the rate of water loss. This fourdrinier technique remains basically unchanged to this day for modern papermaking.

In addition to fulfilling the need for recording, paper is also used for clothing, as containers for food and drink, packaging, building materials, currency and for decorative uses.

11.2　Developments

Notable milestones in pulp and papermaking have included:

1799　The French invented a continuous paper machine with a moving sheet or wire screen. This is known as the fourdrinier and this technology is still used.

1809　Cylinder paper machine invented.

1826　Steam heated drying rolls first used.

1851　Soda process developed; not used extensively today.

1867　Sulphite process invented by an American, Tilghman.

1884   Rags had been the feed stock for paper production but the scarcity of rags at this time prompted the introduction of the mechanical process of making pulp from wood.

Dahl of Danzig invented the sulphate process.

1955   Mechanical pulping achieved through grinder stones before this time supplemented by refiner mechanical pulping.

11.3   Principal processes

Most modern paper consists of interlaced fibres derived from wood, although some papers may also contain fibres from rags, other vegetable sources and in some cases synthetic materials. The basic principle is to chop up the wood, separate the fibres, purify the resultant material, mix with water, deposit in a semi-finished condition and then remove excess water.

The overall process of making paper can be separated into two basic operations — making pulp and then using the pulp to make paper.

11.3.1   Pulp production

Although material other than wood, such as rags, bagasse (a by-product of producing sugar from cane) and other synthetic materials are sometimes used, the majority of pulp comes from the harvesting and processing of wood.

Logs arrive at the pulp mill either by river, road or rail from the forest areas, and are cut into manageable lengths before being debarked in large rotating drums with high power water jets. At this stage the next part of the process depends on whether mechanical or chemical processed pulp is being produced.

11.3.1.1   Mechanical process

In mechanical stone-ground pulp processing the debarked round wood logs are ground by large grindstones. Alternatively, in mechanical refiner pulp processing wood chips, sawdust, edgings, slabs, and veneer refuse are shaved by closely positioned rotating discs.

The grinding or refining is normally a multi-stage operation with typically between 25 and 30% of water being added. Screening or filtering also occurs following each stage. Finally, the pulp is cleaned in centrifuges and thickened to a consistency of about 15%.

11.3.1.2   Chemical process

Debarked round wood logs are chipped in a chipper, which consists of closely positioned rotating cutter discs; the chips are mechanically screened and washed.

The chemical pulp process is designed to separate the two principal constituents of wood — cellulose and lignin. The lignin holds the cellulose fibres together and the chemical cooking process separates and removes the lignin.

There are a number of chemical processes utilised and these are briefly described in the following paragraphs.

11.3.1.3 Sulphate or Kraft process (alkaline)

This process, producing a long fibre strong pulp makes most pulp and from which the process derives its name — from the German 'kraft', meaning strength.

The chips are fed into digesters of which there are two types generally used. Batch digesters are about 6m diameter and 12m high and continuous or 'Kamyr' digesters are about 6m diameter and 80m high. The digesters are giant cookers fed with wood chips, pulping liquor and steam. The 'cook' is carried out at a pressure of about 7 bars and 175°C temperature for 2–3 hours. The pulp yield is about 45% of the weight of the original wood.

Digester relief gases are used to produce by-products such as tall oil, which is made into soaps, greases and emulsions, and turpentine.

The pulping liquor is made up of sodium hydroxide and sodium sulphide and is known as white liquor. After the cooking process in the digester, the spent liquor consists of the process chemicals and solid and dissolved organic material which is concentrated in evaporators to produce black liquor and then burnt in black liquor recovery boilers. The organic components are burnt, thus providing significant energy recovery for the plant, and the melted inorganic chemicals (smelt) are recovered for reuse of the valuable chemicals.

It should be emphasised that within the black liquor recovery boiler there is severe potential exposure to explosion as the smelt reacts energetically when in contact with any water. The pulp from the digester is washed in counter-flow, multistage vacuum washers and then bleached or left unbleached depending on final use. Unless there are paper making facilities at the mill, the pulp is dewatered, dried, pressed and baled for shipment.

11.3.1.4 Sulphite process (acidic)

This process utilises the same method for debarking and chipping as for the sulphate process but in this case the feed material is spruce, hemlock and balsam. This gives a shorter fibre, weaker in strength but with a fine bond type of paper. The cooking liquor for the batch type digester is a solution of magnesium, sodium or ammonium bisulphite with an excess of sulphur dioxide. The operation is carried out at about 8 bars pressure and 150°C temperature for 6–12 hours. As with the sulphate process the chemicals are recovered in a boiler and the raw pulp is treated in a similar way.

11.3.1.5 Neutral sulphite semi-chemical process

This process is principally used to produce pulp for use in making corrugating material for cartons. Hardwood chips are partially cooked with sodium sulphite and sodium carbonate and then turned into fibres in disc refiners. Alternatively a cold caustic treatment followed by grinding to produce fibres may be used.

11.3.2 Papermaking

Pulp produced by the mechanical or chemical process will have different characteristics that will also be governed by the type of wood feed stock. Fibre length, which equates to final paper strength, will generally be greater for chemical pulp. However, it is normal to mix the various pulps to arrive at a paper that has the desired properties and quality.

Increasingly integrated pulp and paper mills are being designed and commissioned and in these the semi-liquid pulp can be drawn from bulk storage and directed to the paper making facility. Alternatively pulp may be partially dried and pressed for economy of shipping and delivered to a stand-alone paper making facility or to supplement another plant's pulp quality. In this case the dry pulp is reconstituted in a hydrapulper at the papermaking facility.

Pulp fibres are 1–3mm long and 0.01–0.03mm in diameter with paper being formed when the dispersed fibres in slurry are dewatered and dried. Pulp is usually cleaned, refined, bleached and pigments added at the pulp mill. However, some of these actions may be incorporated in to the paper plant process.

Bleaching removes traces of lignin and leaves the pure carbohydrate fibres. Bleaching is not a single operation but consists of a combination of a number of processes — chlorination; extraction with caustic soda and oxidation with sodium or calcium hypochlorite, chlorine dioxide, or hydrogen peroxide. High-pressure oxygen is also used. Increasingly, for environmental reasons, chlorine is not favoured and is being replaced by elemental chlorine free (ECF) processes using chlorine dioxide and totally chlorine free (TCF) processes using hydrogen peroxide. With continuing environmental pressures, significant developments are taking place in identifying alternative bleaching chemicals such as peracetic acid and Caro's acid (permono-sulphuric acid); and the use of enzymes such as those from genetically modified trichoderma fungus and E. coli.

Paper stock preparation can be divided into two main areas — first, preparation of the 'furnish' which is the water slurry of the fibres with the additives and second, the mechanical treatment of the furnish' by beating or refining. The additives can consist of fillers to reduce the proportion of expensive wood pulp, improve the paper opacity and reduce sheet thickness; and historically have involved the use of clay, chalk, calcium carbonate and titanium dioxide. Increasing use of precipitated calcium carbonate (PCC) has now been adopted by the industry.

A further additive at this stage can be an 'internal' size that is added to the pulp as an emulsion. Originally rosin was used but due to the swing to neutral or alkaline pulp processes, the industry now uses synthetic sizes such as alkyl ketene dimer (AKD) and alkenyl succinic anhydride (ASA). Size is applied to improve the print quality of paper. 'Surface' sizing can also be used where the size is applied as a coating on the finished paper product. Refiners are either cone or disc type with closely positioned knives or blades. The 'furnish' to the paper machine is slurry containing about 0.5% fibres.

11.3.2.1 Paper machines

These can be divided into two types — fourdrinier and the cylinder type.

A fourdrinier machine can measure up to 15m wide by 100m long, the process including filtering, pressing and drying the fibres into paper. Process speeds range between 300 to 1000m per minute and tissue machines can run excess of 1500m per minute.

The progressive stages of dewatering and drying the 'furnish' is carried out on the rolls, felts and screens. These are normally driven by a single electric motor or steam turbine through a reduction gearbox and various shafting. The 'furnish' or stock is fed to the wet end of the paper machine through a head box and on to a travelling wire screen, which is now generally made of plastic. A number of suction boxes at this stage remove about 15% of the water with a 'dandy' roll used to smooth the top surface of the wet fibre mat. Travelling felts pick up this fibre mat and it is progressively fed through press rolls and steam heated drying rolls. The final stage is carried out on polished colander rolls before being rolled for storage.

Tissue machines use a polished 'Yankee' dryer roll, which can be up to 6m in diameter and 7m in length, and weighing in the region of 70 tonnes and operating at steam pressures of about 10 bar. In certain machines this roll can have supplementary gas fired heating to aid in the drying process. The finished product from the machines has moisture content in the region of 5%.

Over the 'dry' end of the machine there is a hood, which collects and exhausts the moisture-laden hot air through a heat exchanger for energy recovery.

The cylinder machine is used to make speciality and multi-ply laminated papers and boards such as are used in cardboard boxes having a low-grade base with a cover of fine paper. The machine can be about 5m wide and have up to eight woven wire-covered cylinders, each picking up fibres from a separate tank, and operates at 75m per minute. Miniature fourdrinier machines operating at much higher speeds now are used to produce the same products.

As mentioned, a number of plants already integrate pulp production with papermaking. It is also becoming common for the semi-finished product, paper, to be converted to finished products at the same site and involving corrugating, box manufacture, lamination, coating and printing and utilising specialised machinery.

11.4   Major feedstocks

As indicated in earlier parts of this chapter, the raw pulp feedstock can consist of many fibre-based materials both natural and synthetic. Natural materials include many forms of wood and bagasse. Synthetic and previously used materials include rags and waste paper and these require special attention to remove dyes and inks.

Other materials critical to the production of pulp include chemical solutions of sodium — hydroxide, sulphide, bisulphite and carbonate; magnesium and ammonium-bisulphite depending on the process. Most plants will have their own production facilities to produce these chemicals from raw material such as sodium chloride (salt) and calcium carbonate (limestone).

Chemicals used for the refining of the pulp include chlorine, caustic soda, sodium or calcium hypochlorite, chlorine dioxide, hydrogen peroxide and high-pressure oxygen.

As with the pulp chemicals most plants will produce the process chemicals from raw material; additional to those already mentioned are sulphuric acid and hydrochloric acid.

Where pulp and paper plants are fully integrated with their own chemical production and recovery facilities, it can be seen that the type of risk now includes characteristics similar to chemical operations, although the scale may be reduced.

11.5   Maintenance

It is believed that the significant maintenance issues arise through the characteristics of the feedstock and chemicals, process conditions, machinery involved and intermediate and final product.

The characteristics of the feedstock, chemicals, intermediate and final products include their significantly combustible, corrosive, explosive and abrasive nature.

In the maintenance philosophy these features must be taken into account in terms of safe working practice in explosive environments, where hydrogen from chemical production may be present. Well-trained maintenance personnel or contractors who carry out gauging of black liquor boiler tubes, use of correct repair or replacement materials for corrosive environments and awareness of potential wear patterns where erosion can be expected also need to be taken into account.

Process conditions give rise to intermediate pressures and temperatures, together with similar characteristics detailed above. In these conditions, effective maintenance needs to take account of the effects of caustic and stress corrosion cracking especially in the debarking drums and digester vessels. With significant levels of humidity in the plant from process steam and water, special attention needs to be given to the integrity of electrical equipment such as motor winding heaters for stand-by equipment.

Major 'machinery' can be grouped as vessels and boilers, rotating machines and electrical machines. The maintenance of the vessels and boilers requires that water level devices, over pressure and temperature safety devices remain in good condition and are tested regularly. Vessels include dryer rolls and 'Yankee' dryers, the latter of large diameter, of considerable length, operating at pressure with significant thermal loadings and rotating speeds. These are factors that can contribute or be conducive to certain failure mechanisms.

11.5.1   Black liquor recovery boilers

As previously indicated, the black liquor recovery boiler has given rise to very significant losses. For several years the industry has had a special Black Liquor Recovery Boiler Committee made up of industry, industry research association and insurers representatives, which has been charged with investigating boiler smelt explosions and providing recommendations to prevent reoccurrence. Very detailed guidelines are now available providing for more stringent standards than previously and these have gone a long way to reducing the number of losses arising out of smelt bed explosions in black liquor recovery boilers.

The BLRB Committee recommendations include a significant section on maintenance.

11.5.2   Other machines

The rotating machinery includes large pumps — both pressure and vacuum, chippers, drums, steam turbines and the paper machine which can be regarded as an assembly of component parts, etc. Most have very small clearance tolerances for bearings, seals and rotating/stationary elements. A high level of engineering capability is required for maintenance personnel in these areas. Electrical machines include large high-powered motors (AC and DC), transformers and switchgear. Once again high-quality personnel are required, and sparing and repairs must be carried out to the same or higher standards than the original supply conditions. Potentially aggressive chemical environments and high humidity require maintenance of a standard where attention to detail is the rule rather than the exception.

11.6   Monitoring and protection

Taking the same approach as set out in 11.5 above, and focusing specifically on pulp and paper, the issues in regard to feedstock, chemicals, intermediate product and final product include the potential for combustion and explosion. Depending on the various areas of the plant it may be necessary to install, maintain and periodically test heat and flame detectors and hazardous atmosphere sensors. In the processing of chemicals for the digester it is necessary to use a lime kiln and all of the monitoring precautions mentioned in Chapter 12, 'Cement plants', need to be carefully evaluated. These precautions include infrared thermographic monitoring of kiln shell temperature.

The process conditions that primarily affect monitoring and protection are the high caustic environment and the need for driving off large quantities of water vapour. Detailed effective material selection should reduce the potential failure of vessels from caustic-related failure mechanisms. However based on experience, careful monitoring of vessels such as the debarker drums and digester should be carried out for early evidence of attack; 'Yankee' dryers require periodic non-destructive examination and under BLRB Committee guidelines the periodic thickness gauging of black liquor boiler tubes is required.

In terms of the process itself, the black liquor boiler when fed with weak liquor — below 60% solids — has a high potential for explosion without the addition of further water. The BLRB Committee recommendations include the provision of two in-series refraction index density meters, which are continuously monitored with regular laboratory validation tests.

High humidity will detrimentally affect electrical equipment. Motor and generator windings should be checked for insulation resistance before energising and transformers should have periodic oil monitoring tests to ensure moisture contamination has not occurred.

As can be appreciated in a pulp and paper plant there is a considerable amount of rotating equipment. Some of this may be subjected to severe shock loading such as for the chippers or fluctuating cyclic loading as for de-barker drum, pumps, motors and paper machine cylinders. Vibration monitoring can be very useful in identifying trends and allows action to be taken prior to failure. Paper machine cylinders, which may flex in service owing to their length and are therefore susceptible to fatigue type failure, are normally subjected to non-destructive testing at periodic intervals.

Most plants are complex operations and increasingly a single distributed control system is utilised to ensure safe and efficient operation throughout the plant. This system is computer based, and normally includes features that monitor and allow protection of the process together with the keeping of detailed records.

11.7 Planning

The majority of pulp and paper plants are single stream operations with limited spare capacity or alternative methods of working.

A coherent planning strategy in this type of process is critical to a trouble free operation or for the prevention of major downtime in the event of a failure.

Significant areas include sparing philosophy where critical plant items need to be identified and 'what if' scenarios worked through to ensure that risk and cost effective spares or access to spares through mutual aid agreements are in place.

Equally important is the need to plan any de-bottlenecking operations such that, at the critical time of tying in any new systems and machines to existing plant, all control, protection and safety integrity is maintained. Changes, both major and minor, are common in the life of a pulp and paper plant.

Where plants rely on bagasse as the feedstock for pulp production, planning will centre on the need to operate the plant around a seasonally available and/or limited stock piled feedstock. Maintenance outages also need to take this factor into account.

11.8 Operations

Feedstocks receiving areas and chipping operations are particularly severe operating areas, with a high volume of logs being processed rapidly. From a fire risk point of view, housekeeping and separation distances are critical and for machinery a high degree of operator attention and initiative is required in an arduous and potentially dangerous environment.

Metal foreign objects entering the process at this stage can lead to catastrophic failure of chippers and as a consequence presents a danger to operators. Automatic devices for detecting metal and also the general machinery monitoring equipment need to maintained and kept operating in what can become a rough-and-ready area of the process.

The utility areas within pulp and paper plants include the steam power boilers, grid and own electricity generation facilities and water production, treatment and effluent plants. For a modern plant these are significant operations in their own right. Operators and managers with specialist training and experience are required to ensure that a safe and effective operation is maintained.

The above comments apply to the chemical preparation and recovery areas of the plant, which require the same high level of expertise to run as stand alone chemical plants producing chlorine, chlorine dioxide, hypochlorite, hydrogen, etc. Transfer of chemicals is particularly important and can give rise to potentially dangerous situations where tanks may rupture when incorrect transfer has occurred with 'unsuitable cocktails' spontaneously reacting. Once again the black liquor recovery boiler requires to be carefully operated to prevent catastrophic failures.

In the pulp and paper areas of the process, modern plants have sophisticated distribution and control systems in place. However, as already described, these plants operate in an environment that has potentially aggressive chemicals, heat and humidity. Levels of maintenance of the sophisticated monitoring and control equipment need to be high, with operators encouraged to be vigilant to trends and indicators of potential process upsets to be identified before an incident. This is particularly important with regard to the paper machine as the speed of this machine results in very limited time to take appropriate action.

11.9 Critical areas

Many of the physical areas have already been covered in the preceding text and although in the section on 'Operations' (11.8), there is mention of the quality of personnel, it is believed that the most significant influence on the safe running of a pulp and paper plant is the expertise, experience and motivation of its personnel. Therefore profiling of new staff, induction and ongoing training, involvement in problem solving and integration of staff across operating areas is believed to be critical.

Additionally, in terms of machinery, the following areas are regarded as critical.

- Kiln
  - Cracking of support rollers
  - Roller and driver failures
  - Cracking of tyres
  - Refractory failures leading to shell hot spots and deformation

- Transformers
  - Lightning
  - Age-related insulation deterioration
  - Oil quality deterioration in insulation and acidic properties

- Generators
  - Winding insulation failure
  - Wedge integrity
  - Winding support systems

- Turbines
  - Foreign object damage after maintenance
  - Fatigue and detachment of rotating blades
  - Rotor flexing leading to impact on stator

- Debarking drums
  - Shell failure due to cracking

- Chippers
  - Fatigue through shock loading on motor, gearbox and chipper
  - Insulation deterioration on motor, high variable loading, heat

- Digester
  - Cracking of shell internally
  - Erosion at washout areas
  - Corrosion at interfaces of liquid/vapour

- Black liquor recovery boiler
  - Explosion from weak liquor
  - Explosion from water leaking from perforated tubes into smelt bed
  - Explosion from changeover from liquor to/from fuel oil/gas
  - Explosion from firing instability of liquor

- Paper machine
  - Drive motor or turbine failure
  - Failure of cylinders through fatigue — specifically 'Yankee' dryers, with limited manu-
    facturers and long lead times
  - Bearing failures through loss of lubrication

- Pipe systems and pumps
  - Erosion from pulp and flow rates
  - Turbulence leading to fatigue and metal loss

12 Cement plants

12.1 History

Although there may have been earlier attempts at concrete manufacture, the earliest concrete discovered dates from about 5600BC and was found on the banks of the River Danube in Yugoslavia. It formed the floors of huts in a Stone Age village inhabited by hunter-fishermen and was made from a mixture of red lime, sand, gravel and water.

Coming down through the ages a form of concrete was used in the great pyramid at Giza in Egypt, where it was used primarily as an infill material for stone walls. Its use spread initially as a relatively weak mix in what was known as 'pseudo concrete', *i.e.* roughly broken stone bound together with a mortar of lime and sand. From around 300BC to 500AD it was developed by the Romans, who produced a stronger material known as Pozzolanic cement, using volcanic ash. Unknown to the Romans, this ash/sand contained silica and alumina that chemically combined with lime and was therefore a milestone in concrete manufacture. The Romans also attempted to make reinforced concrete but due to the use of bronze for the strips and rods, there was considerable differential expansion leading to spalling and cracking of the concrete.

In Britain, the Romans used lime concrete and this was used in the construction of the 120km long and almost 3m high Hadrian's Wall, stretching from the Solway Firth to the River Tyne.

With the decline of the Roman Empire, the use of concrete almost disappeared due probably to the loss of knowledge of how and where it could be utilised. It is thought that the Normans reintroduced concrete usage into Britain for castle and cathedral construction and in the eighteenth century a Leeds engineer, John Smeaton, developed the first really good quality cement since Roman times.

In the early nineteenth century, Portland cement was first produced and patented. The name relates solely to the colour of the product in its resemblance to Portland stone rather than its area of origin.

Although cement was being produced in large quantities its cost was extremely high due to use of the static kiln method of production, but in the 1880s the continuous process rotary cement kiln was designed and went into service reducing costs to a level that builders could reasonably afford. This rotary kiln process was not widely utilised in Britain and it was left to the United States to develop the design and reintroduce it to Britain at a later date.

Concrete had become popular as a method of construction and many houses, river banks, docks, bridges and the original Thames Tunnel used it extensively, and at this time the use of reinforced concrete using wire ropes or 'T' beams as the reinforcement also came into vogue. A French engineer, François Hennebique, was responsible at this stage, for development of reinforced concrete, and concrete generally came into use in Europe as an accepted method of construction with ferro-concrete being used to build boats and ships.

To produce more intricate and less bulky expensive structures the research and development of prestressed concrete took place from 1920 onwards and a French engineer, Eugène Freyssinet, was instrumental in this important advancement of structural techniques. In fact the famous Mulberry Harbour, which played a vital part following the D-Day landings was constructed in reinforced concrete and towed in sections across the English Channel to Normandy.

Due to a shortage of steel in and around 1945, concrete usage became commonplace in all types of structures and in variously sophisticated forms is now used in the construction of bridges, tunnels, buildings, oil production platforms, barriers, dams, etc. In fact without it, it is fair to say that the face and functionality of the modern world would present a different picture.

12.2   Developments

Some milestones in the history of cement are

1758	Observation, by John Smeaton, of lime-pozzolana as a hydraulic binder (pozzolana has the effect, when mixed with mortar, of enabling the latter to harden either in air or under water)
1800	Invention of Roman cement by Parker
1824	Patent of 'Portland cement' by Joseph Aspdin
1840	Invention of modern 'Portland cement' by I. C. Johnson
1850	Intermittent shaft/bottle kilns in use
1858	Invention of jaw crushers, screw and worm crushers
1876	Introduction of continuous screen ball mills
1877	Rotary kiln patented by Crompton
1890	Improved mill designs, centrifugal ring ball mills, spring ball mills, vertical ring roller mills
1891	Invention of tube mills
1896	Practical development of rotary kilns in USA by Hurry and Seamen
1928	Lepol grate kiln designed by Lelep
1950-51	Suspension preheater commercialisation by Humboldt
1963-66	Conception of precalcination system with the first German trials in 1966

Most cement is now made in what is known as the dry process and there are further developments in the processing plant, product, quality and cost savings. The use of precalciners, high efficiency multi-channel burners, reciprocating grate coolers, high performance separators, improvements in ball mill internals and vertical spindle mills for both raw material and coal grinding, high pressure roll presses for comminution are all adding to product efficiency and cost savings. However, with machinery of increased complexity there is a need for enhanced planning, vigilance and highly efficient maintenance arrangements in order to avoid forced outages.

12.3   Principal processes

12.3.1   Portland cement

The principal type of cement known as 'Portland' cement is made in a so-called dry process. Limestone, the calcareous component, and shales/clays, the argillaceous component, are quarried at their respective supply points. They are then crushed in primary crushers to a reduced size suitable for storage and blending prior to grinding, which in the case of modern hammer crushers or vertical spindle mills can be up to 125mm. Crushing will probably be done in two stages and in some cases by a primary crusher at the quarry. The material is then transported to the cement plant for secondary crushing prior to blending and stockpile storage.

From the stockpile material is transferred to grinding mills which reduce the stone to fine powder known as raw meal and this process will probably include heating to dry the product, cyclones to remove meal from the gas stream and an electrostatic precipitator. Any additives to produce a certain cement composition would also be added at this stage. The fine powder is then fed into blending silos and raw meal buffer storage.

From storage the raw meal enters the preheater cyclones heated by kiln exhaust gases as they flow upward through them. The exhaust gases pass to atmosphere via dust extraction systems, *i.e.* electrostatic precipitators. Heated raw meal now passes down a rotating inclined cylindrical kiln that rotates at around 1–4rpm. The meal flows in a counter-direction to the heated gases that are produced by a combustion section located at the opposite kiln end to raw meal introduction and is fired on pulverised coal, fuel oil or gas. A coal-fired plant would include coal-grinding mills, which would utilise kiln clinker cooling air. The cyclones and kiln are of steel construction but have suitable refractory linings to protect the shell from temperatures they could not possibly handle.

In the kiln the raw meal is dewatered, subject to thermal decomposition and formation of clinker which in the white hot condition as it exits the kiln (maximum temperature around 1450°C) is cooled by air blown across it. This air is used for combustion and in a coal-fired plant for the coal pulverisation mills.

Cooled clinker is taken via a conveyor system to covered storage as a buffer area and will be used to match cement production to contract requirements as at this stage it is a relatively inert material.

For the final production of Portland cement, the clinker is ground in ball or other mills with a proportion of gypsum to the fine white/grey powdery material we know as cement. It is then transferred by conveyor to storage silos and bulk loading/weighing, truck or railway facilities, or bagging and weighing systems for market distribution.

It is not uncommon for cement plants in remote locations to incorporate their own electrical power generation plant as a supplement to or as an alternative to grid supply. This can be by the use of diesel engines or more recently the use of combined heating and power plant.

12.3.2 Wet process

The wet process of cement production is little used and refers mainly to the raw meal being fed to the kiln in slurry form where it is clinkerised, as in the dry process. This process has been used where the raw materials are suitable and easier grinding processes are allowed but it consumes a significantly greater amount of energy in the kiln.

Some wet process plants have been converted to semi-wet process, where the slurry mix is partially dewatered to form a cake that is then broken up and fed into a long re-chained kiln or a preheater such as a 'Lepol' grate and into a short kiln.

12.3.3 Semi-dry process

There is also a semi-dry or 'Lepol' process, in which the raw meal is prepared in the same way as the dry process and is then nodulised or palletised into spheres with approximately 12% moisture content. This material then passes over a moving Lepol grate preheater and into the kiln to be clinkerised as normal.

12.4 Major feedstocks

The major raw materials used in cement production will vary in content, consistency, size and handling capability dependent upon source, and therefore the methods of processing and end product will vary and need more or less additional input as necessary. This will also apply to the kiln-heating medium.

Apart from additives used to give specialist cements, the materials forming basic cement are

- Limestone
- Shale or clay
- Gypsum (hydrated calcium sulphate).

12.5   Maintenance

It is not the purpose of this Study Report to provide a detailed maintenance directive, as the nature of plant, its location and its economics are all factors to be taken into consideration in such an evaluation. There are, however, several basic rules to be applied that will determine an underwriter's viewpoint as to the nature of and insurability of a cement plant whether it is new or whether it has been in production for many years. Loss prevention is discussed in some detail in Chapter 5, and this highlights much of the detail regarding risk analysis that will feature prominently in any successful plant operation.

Any programme, whether using planned preventive or predictive techniques, requires careful study and formulation to prevent over- or under-application, both of which can result in unnecessary expenditure and loss of production. There is a fourth method of maintenance known as breakdown; this is not considered an option with regard to machinery breakdown or other insurance, as although it could possibly be justified in certain cases by some plant operators on economic grounds, it leaves insurers with a normally high and unacceptable risk factor and possible catastrophic results.

The programme therefore must be carefully chosen and tailored to the particular plant in question, although many aspects will be common to any machinery or cement plant. Computerisation has provided an important tool in organisation of any maintenance programme and manufacturers or specialist companies can provide basic or bespoke programs. Where an older log or 'cardex' system is in use, the system can be easily updated except, for example, for an old plant with copious records, in which case the transfer process could be costly in time and monetary terms. However, once completed the footprint provided would have an invaluable nature for long-term safe and reliable operation. In the case of new plant it is to be recommended that the programme be instituted immediately operation commences, with reference to construction and commissioning data that could provide invaluable assistance in any failures or problems that arise following plant acceptance.

Record keeping has to be of a high standard and monitored by the risk/technical division of the plant management. This extends to ensuring that the programmed tasks are being implemented and accurately recorded. Records are useless if no monitoring and trend analysis takes place. Analysis leads to programme alterations that can, it is admitted, cost money but there can also be savings through the extension of maintenance periods and prevention of costly breakdowns.

An inspection department plays a vital role in keeping the machinery operational and in which it is responsible for vibration and other condition monitoring, NDT and other systems, and the inspection of pressure or other plant and machinery, either during service or in maintenance periods. Valuable condition and trend data with regard to wear and operational patterns are obtained in this way and provide useful input into programmed planning for maintenance or replacement of electrical or mechanical components or even whole machines. Information gathered will also provide diagnostic evaluation of recurring incidence of problems or failings that can be used to avoid forced outages and highlight operational or manufacturing defects. The inspection department would also be responsible for testing and certification of any safety devices installed in the plant and to ensure that any government or other statutory tests/ inspections are carried out correctly and to date.

Instrumentation in any plant is critical for its safe operation and regular monitoring. Testing and maintenance of the various gauges, recording and logging devices, computers, as well as checking the set, alarm and shutdown points is essential. There seems little point in installing expensive plant monitoring systems if they are then assumed to be infallible and their upkeep ignored.

Correct proportions of electrical, mechanical, instrumentation engineers and support staff are important to retain a balance of safe operation and economical maintenance and the accessibility of these staff deserves consideration. There is some trend towards utilisation of manufacturers or specialist maintenance companies that remain on 24-hour call, and can provide experienced and well-qualified staff with modern equipment at competitive rates.

This option has several advantages and, depending upon plant location, it can be a distinct advantage, provided plant management still monitors the work carried out and seriously consider any recommendations made by the company concerned.

Minor and major overhauls must be programmed in so that machinery internals or refractory can be renewed, motors overhauled, gearboxes inspected, mill liners changed and tests and inspections carried out. Insurers' appointed surveyors would seek to inspect records of such overhauls or even be present at a major overhaul to ascertain the extent of maintenance and to witness the actual plant condition. Delays in the overhaul of major items should be notified to insurers otherwise any consequent breakdowns and production losses could possibly be viewed as being the result of faulty maintenance and therefore at least contributory to the breakdown.

As previously stated, all work carried out during overhauls should be recorded and any contractors/subcontractors should provide detailed reports of their scope of work and any alignment, test or other readings taken. These records should be held and incorporated in the maintenance-recording programme.

A major factor in an insurance evaluation of any risk, especially where business interruption is being considered, is the provision of spare parts. This refers in the main not to regular consumable parts such as bearings, mill liners, balls refractory, etc., but to mid to long term parts such as kiln rollers and tyres, trunnion bearings, motors and gearboxes. Sophisticated effective repair procedures do exist, but they can be short term. Actual parts will in most cases eventually have to be obtained, and there are long delivery dates, up to 18 months or more, on some items.

In some countries economic and government restrictions on foreign currencies and imports can extend the procurement of spares. In these cases long-term planning is essential and strategic planning programmes should also take in alternative production methods and/or base material suppliers in.

12.6   Monitoring and protection

There are several areas, some already mentioned, which are elemental in reducing the risk of breakdown and loss of production. Some are specific to plant location, and these are as follows:

● Vibration   This is important in relation to all rotating plants and especially for gear-boxes, motors and bearings. All types of vibration are omnipresent in cement plants and cannot be avoided. Additionally, the starting up of heavy machinery and increasing revolutions generate vibrations over a large frequency range. It would be logical to assume therefore that every power plant will be, more or less, stimulated from resonance and subjected to additional stress. As well as normal design and installation, levels of vibration can be added to and reach unacceptable levels because of

- wear and tear of bearings, gearwheels, etc.
- misalignment
- material fatigue and breakage
- turbulence and other process related effects.

● Thermal   The kiln requires sophisticated shell temperature monitoring but thermal readings are required on many other components.

● Lubrication   Regular oil sampling, analysis and oil renewal, as required, are critical on modern machinery, not only because of service life but also as a valuable machinery condition monitoring tool.

● Refractory   A constantly renewable item that can, if neglected, cause major break-downs.

● Electricity   An especially important item where business interruption insurance is in force. Supplies can be intermittent in some parts of the world and partial or total self-sufficiency of supply to the plant requires competent maintenance. In the case of grid supplies the transformer and circuit capacities and their protection need careful design and maintenance. Infrared thermal imaging equipment is now in wide use and is an invaluable tool for diagnosis of a fault prior to it causing a breakdown, and in plotting deteriorating windings so that replacement or rewinding can be effected before failure occurs. This equipment has the advantage of being used for on-line monitoring and is a supplement to off-line testing.

● Gears   Without stopping production, some gears can be inspected using a stroboscope for unusual wear, deformation or pitting, etc.

● Dust   All cement plants create greater than average quantities of dust, the amount of which depends upon location and can be subject to severe government control of the output to atmosphere. This entails more intricate production, equipment and monitoring. However dust control in relation to the plant, electrical and lubrication sections must be kept under control otherwise machinery failures can result.

● Noise   Again, dependent upon plant location, noise levels can be subject to government restrictions but acoustic measurements is also used as a condition-monitoring tool.

● Records/ analysis   This area of plant operation cannot be stressed too highly and with computerised systems in place then it becomes a simple routine task of keeping data under electronic filing and easily retrievable for regular technical analysis.

12.7   Planning

Planning and strategy are infinitely preferable to the alternative, and this can be highlighted as applicable to the majority of successful plant operations. Teamwork with good management control is essential in all plants, but where breakdown philosophies are applied then it is important to eliminate this and top priority should be given to the implementation of dynamic predictive maintenance systems. Without this, the insurability of a plant and the value of available cover is restricted with the inevitable result that when claims occur disputes will arise and cause unnecessary dialogue and adjustments.

Planning and good quality maintenance cost money to implement, and in a tight economic environment may not appear as entirely logical to financially orientated management. However, overall savings can and will result with regard to higher plant availability figures and lower operating costs if co-ordinated planning techniques are applied to

- risk management
- expenditure
- maintenance
- plant revisions
- alternative production methods
- material supply
- modernisation.

12.8   Operations

When a cement plant is being proposed for machinery insurance and a survey is produced or a survey being conducted there are several major points with regard to plant operation that will be looked at in close detail. Evaluation of the results along with other factors previously mentioned, will ultimately affect the extent of cover and rate of premium. These can be as follows:

- Bottleneck identification   Where are the critical areas that will stop or reduce production for extended periods?

- Product revisions   Are there revisions to the production process in progress or planned which could lead to losses, new bottlenecks, and use of improved technology, etc?

- Fuel   This is always an important item, as the change of fuel supplier or grade or conversation from oil to coal for example will lead to installation of pulverising mills and change in kiln firing regimes which can have serious knock on effects.

- Access/ departmental co-operation   Plant accessibility with regard to outside maintenance, spare parts, etc., and the co-operation actual and planned all affect smooth operation.

- Loadings   A plant running at from 50% to 60% of design capacity generally has few problems but plants running at full rated capacity or over are most at risk.

- Emergency contingencies   These should be catered for in the risk management programme. For example, kiln emergency electrical supply for kiln turning on main supply failure.

- Manufacturers' involvement
  This is an arguable point as the cost involved is a major consideration. However the makers' input and expertise can be invaluable and their utilisation of resources and up to date techniques are often put to great advantage.

- Staff training
  A vital factor in running a successful plant. New technology and actual plant operational experience should also be in the training curriculum.

- Safety
  Again this should be the responsibility of the risk management team. It plays a vital role in operations and can and will prevent accidents and forced outages. For example, a machine running with high vibration levels and/or high temperature is unsafe and both machine and personnel are at risk.

12.9 Critical areas

Described below are those areas where major failures have occurred and problems are known to exist that are potential failure points. These areas are thus potential producers of claims against machinery insurers. The list provided has no significance in the order of items in relation to severity of risk or frequency of failures.

- Crushers
  - Contamination of feedstock by foreign objects leading to breakdown of internals
  - Gearbox and motor failures

- Ball mills and rod mills
  - Liner failures
  - Trunnion failures
  - Head plate fracturing
  - Gearbox and motor failures
  - Girth gear or pinion teeth fractures and cracking

- Kiln
  - Cracking of support rollers
  - Roller and driver failures
  - Cracking of tyres
  - Incorrect alignment of shell and supports
  - Refractory failures leading to shell hot spot and deformation

- Precipitator
  - Dust causing collapse
  - Corrosion due to condensation
  - Erosion and corrosion leading to collapse
  - On a coal-fired kiln there is also an explosion risk

- Vertical mills
  - Motors and gearbox failures
  - Internal failures
  - Coal mill explosions
  - Cone mills cracking of internal parts

- Cyclones
  - Refractory failure and resultant mechanical and thermal damage

- Conveyors
  - Belt failures
  - Drive and roller mechanism failures

- Transformers
  - Lightning, overload or age-related failures

- Electrical
  circuits

- Vermin-related failures
- Overload
- Inadequate protection

- Power supply
  (internal)

- Diesel engine breakdowns
- Generator breakdowns

It is important to mention here that the majority of machinery failures are related to inadequate or defective maintenance, operator error or plant overload since faulty design or materials currently provide only a minor amount of breakdowns. This ratio could alter in the future as plant design and materials used are subject to more stringent load bearing design and cost parameters which materially affect their capacity to absorb adverse conditions and their life expectation.

13 | Mineral extraction and primary processing

13.1 History

Mining, the extraction and subsequent use of the earth's natural resources has been common-place since prehistoric times. Flint has been used extensively for making fire as well as weapons. The manner in which history is defined using terms such as the Bronze Age (from 4500BC) and the Iron Age (1100BC) is a clear indication as to the importance of metals and minerals and their use.

As societies became more sophisticated and the ability to process metal ores, albeit crudely at first, developed, so a mining industry evolved around those minerals which were of value both commercially, such as gold and silver and because of their physical properties, such as iron and coal. Although this primary motivation has not changed with time, the manner in which the process take place has advanced dramatically.

Modern mining using machinery started during the Industrial Revolution. The first rotary drill was used in England in 1813 and the first pneumatic drill in Germany in 1853.

Mining has always been labour intensive but prior to the Industrial Revolution relied almost exclusively on manual labour. Mines were generally shallow surface arrangements with mini-mal underground workings. As the industry started to exploit underground reserves without fully understanding the exposures, so there were numerous explosions, cave-ins and floods.

13.2 Developments

Modern techniques have reduced the need for labour and improved the safety in which under-ground extraction can take place. Mining practices, instrumentation and machinery develop-ments have all contributed to the evolution of the mining industry.

The use of explosives in mining for blasting also brought change. Larger volumes of ore could be moved more quickly and allowed development of resources that would otherwise have not been accessible or economically viable.

In the extraction and primary processing industries, significant changes continue to arise. New territories are being exploited to recover minerals and metals. These new environments are challenging, with remote deserts, Arctic tundra and sub-sea among the new environments encountered. Commercial mining in remote areas also has associated political considerations and exposures.

The extraction companies are forming mutuals and conglomerates with ever-larger capital bases. They are also expanding their operations into downstream processing and by-product plants and in so doing are reducing the sensitivity of their businesses to dynamic commodity markets. Holistic, raw product to final product businesses are present where, for example, a company will own and operate the coal mine that provides the coal for the power station, and the distributor of the electricity — all as one company.

Political changes include privatisation and deregulation of what in the past have been strategic national industries. World economic stability influences demand for raw material and process-ing and over the past few years, commodity prices of metals has dropped significantly. Mines frequently stop operating or are mothballed if commodity prices (or longer-term contracts)

make the operation uneconomic. The manner in which a mine is put into 'care and maintenance' operation and machinery mothballed should be carefully monitored to ensure that
machinery and the mine remain serviceable.

Technology changes are also evident and required for commercial reasons in terms of deeper
mines and continuous smelting processing of some metals.

All of these factors have an impact on machinery insurance. A comparatively recent development in underground mining has been the introduction of remotely controlled equipment such
as continuous miners and scoops. While such units reduce the operator's exposure to roof falls
in the face area, it usually means that the unit is repeatedly exposed to an unsupported roof
during the production cycle and is prone to damage from collapse.

13.3   Mineral classification

Minerals are composed of elements combined in specific amounts and patterns with rocks
being large masses of minerals that have been combined through thermal and/or compression
forces or have been deposited together in a sedimentary environment. As a result of these different origins, some rock types are more likely than others to be associated with a form of economically valuable resource that can be exploited. It is their exploitation through the processes
that is described in this chapter.

Minerals can be divided into two categories, namely metallic and non-metallic. Metallic minerals are those containing metallic elements such as gold, silver, iron, copper etc. These elements
are reasonably non-reactive and tend not to be found in combination with other elements.
Non-metallic minerals do not, by definition, contain metallic elements and include nitrates,
clays, limestone and quartz and the generic category, stone.

Coal is not actually considered a mineral owing to its organic origins but is invariably included
in all mining documentation because of the similar methods of extraction and its economic
importance.

13.4   Deposits

Mineral and coal distribution obviously varies around the world with some countries being
more 'rich' in natural deposits than others. Brazil, Australia, China and Russia, for example,
have substantial reserves of iron ore.

Mineral deposits can be found either within existing rock structures or cutting across geological structures in veins, dykes or similar.

With the exception of sedimentary deposits such as limestone, salts and coals, most ore bodies
are created in geologically active areas when existing rock is brought into contact with molten
rock (magma) with the result that metallic elements tend to be consolidated into economically
viable concentrations

Copper porphyry deposits are good examples of ore bodies created by the interaction of molten
magma and existing rock. These deposits, typically between 0.5% and 2.5% copper, form the
vast majority of the world's copper reserves.

Gold is also found in volcanic or tectonic (geologically active) areas. Gold does not form compounds and tends to crystallise with irregular distribution. Economic grades are typically

between 3 and 9 parts per million (ppm) of gold. 'Placer' gold deposits can also be mined for gold. These are formed in the bed of rivers as gold-rich rock, eroded by river action and the gold itself left on the riverbed. These types of deposit are 'panned' for gold.

13.5   Principal methods and processes

The mining industry is facing new challenges, including the introduction of new complex technologies and techniques, deeper mines and continuous smelting. Diversification into added value and greater margin downstream manufacturing of intermediate and final products, cooperative trading arrangements with mutual organisations and conglomerates, are current day features. Political changes such as in privatisation and deregulation and developments in new territories are also present.

These activities are in addition to the existing financial pressures on businesses. This has resulted in a heightened awareness of risk and insurance and the need to protect assets and revenue streams from undesirable fortuitous events.

In this chapter, extraction and primary processing are dealt with in separate sections, addressing the techniques, machines and services that may be found in typical operations although inevitably there may be some similarities and duplication. At this point it may be of interest to raise a number of points that will highlight some of the issues that influence the insurance of machinery in extraction and primary processing.

During construction and operation the issues that predominate revolve around effective planning and management especially for early identification of hazards and appropriate actions for early minimisation or eradication of these. For example, projects may be near completion before consideration has been given to the provision of fire prevention and protection, control of combustible and flammable materials and the availability and testing of emergency plans. Significant losses have also resulted from inadequate storage of critical capital equipment.

Differences between soft and hard rock extraction can be illustrated by considering copper mining, which has very limited fire hazards both from the rock and burden itself and the method of mining, since the mine galleries are likely to be self supporting. In the case of a soft rock such as coal, outbursts can be experienced where there is a sudden release of methane and/or carbon dioxide and coal under pressure from the seam. Asphyxiation and/or explosion can follow.

Machinery such as electrical equipment and conveyor systems can contribute to a higher hazard rating as sources of ignition and interruption to transfer of ore. Adequate geological surveys should be conducted to identify the presence of aquifers in order to avoid the risk of having to recover machinery and equipment from a flooded mine.

As with most soft rock mines, subsidence is a potential risk not only from the existing mine but also from previous workings and neighbouring mines. For coal specifically, spontaneous combustion of stockpiles needs to be considered.

Primary processing can involve heavily stressed machines and chemical processes with aggressive chemical environments. Increasingly the process may be a single stream, 100% production facility, being extremely sensitive to any interruption of any individual machine or service.

Extraction and primary processing is dealt with in more detail in the following sections.

13.6 Extraction

Minerals and coal are mined either from a surface pit or via underground workings and the nature of the ore body determines the most appropriate method. Clearly, ore deposits close to the surface can be most efficiently mined by the open-pit method.

Underground mining is much more complex than surface mining with issues relating to blasting, ventilation, access, ore transport, overburden pressure and workforce safety all making underground ore removal more challenging and more costly.

13.6.1 Mobile plant

All modern mining risks including surface and underground, make extensive use of mobile equipment (sometimes called 'contractor's equipment' or 'mobile plant') to do the actual mining of the mineral or ores with equipment ranging both in size and value. Mobile equipment, by its nature, is subject to more hazards and exposures than buildings because it can suffer losses arising out of collision, upset, overturn or those presented by the environment of use. There may also be fuels, lubricants, hydraulic fluid and other flammables onboard that can make for a high fire hazard. The equipment is subject to heavy use in harsh conditions with a key consideration being the quality and training of equipment operators.

13.6.2 Surface workings

Common surface mining methods include contour mining, mountain top removal, area mining, auger/high-wall mining and open-pit mining.

Contour mining occurs in mountainous or hilly terrain and begins where the ore/mineral seam and surface elevation are the same (commonly called the cropline) and proceeds around the side of the hill or mountain on the cropline elevation.

Area mining occurs where the seams (usually coal) lie in a relatively level plane beneath a level of gently rolling surface terrain.

Mountain top removal is carried out in those areas where seam(s) outcrop on the hills and all overburden is removed. This results in a hill or mountain whose top has been completely removed and left relatively flat or level.

Auguring/high-wall mining occurs where overburden heights make existing area or contour mining no longer feasible. Auguring/high-wall mining utilises horizontal borings into exposed coal seams to remove the remaining coal.

Open-pit mining is common with mineral mining operations where the overburden waste material is removed from the surface to expose the minerals. The minerals are then extracted by taking successive vertical and horizontal production cuts.

Equipment operated above ground is normally less hazardous than underground equipment since it is not exposed to the hazards unique to the underground environment. The above-ground equipment none the less has its own hazards that need to be evaluated. The major exposures are

- collision
- upset/overturn
- fire
- theft

- high-wall collapse
- flood.

Examples of surface mining equipment include

- drag lines — generally so large that they are built on site
- bulldozers
- front end loaders
- striping shovels
- hydraulic shovels
- bucket wheel excavators
- high-wall or thin seam coal mining machines
- augers
- haulers
- drills.

13.6.3 Underground workings

Initially the common elements of underground operations are described and followed by specific sections referring to coal and hard rock mining.

13.6.4 Common

The process of underground mining creates unnatural openings under the surface of the ground. Basically there are two types of opening. Those that create access into the mine and those that are created during the extraction of the ore or mineral. These mine openings go by many technical and slang names. The most common of these are

- adits
- crosscuts
- declines
- drifts
- entries
- ore passes
- raises
- rooms
- shafts
- slopes
- stopes
- tunnels
- winzes.

While they all have specific meanings within the context of mining, in common with each other they are all types of openings inside a mine. The creation of these openings is the process of mining. Some of them are permanent and essential for continued access into the mine to conduct operations and are continually maintained, while others are temporary openings that will eventually be abandoned, filled in or collapse.

All of these terms can be collectively referred to under other terms such as mine development, which generally refers to the permanent openings created to access the ore body, or the underground workings, which generally encompasses all types of mine openings. Collapse of any of these openings may temporarily or permanently interrupt the mining activities.

13.6.5 **Collapse**

Collapse is an obvious hazard underground. Some mining techniques rely on collapse as part of the stress-relieving process and thus only unwanted collapse presents a mining hazard. Roof support may or may not be necessary in a mine depending on the nature of the rocks and the amount of geological activity.

Roof supports might be timber (often treated with fire retardant) or steel. Commonly, roof bolting is used and the process consists of the insertion of a long steel bolt driven into a drilled hole in the roof and anchored at its innermost end. A steel plate can then be pulled on to the exposed end and tightened against the roof. This will help hold an unstable roof in place when the rock-bolting programme is correctly planned and implemented.

In extreme cases of roof instability, a technique of polyurethane resin injection (PUR) can be used. In this process, resin is injected in the roof and cured, the objective being to simply bond the loose roof material together.

13.6.6 **Ventilation**

Ventilation is essential in any confined environment in which humans are present. Fans are used to draw fresh air throughout a mine for a number of reasons:

● Air is provided for workers.

● The ventilation air sweeps the mine of unwanted gases — carbon dioxide, methane, carbon monoxide, hydrogen, hydrogen sulphide

Fans are generally surface mounted and are provided with a degree of redundancy. Generally, alarms sound if mine ventilation is lost or the power supply to mining equipment trips out.

13.6.7 **Electricity supply**

Virtually every aspect of a modern mining operation is heavily dependent on a reliable electrical supply. This is true for both above ground and below ground applications, although surface equipment will be more conventional.

Underground applications generally will all require the following:

● A surface sub-station.
● Portable switches — which includes protective breakers to distribution circuits.
● Underground power load centres — which includes transformation to the voltage for use.
● Low voltage distribution centres.
● Capacitor packs to correct power factor effects.
● Conversion equipment to convert AC to DC as necessary.
● Numerous cables for all connections.

The environment in which the above equipment is installed and used makes it more vulnerable to loss and damage.

Mobile equipment used underground faces the same risks as those for surface plant but with a higher likelihood of loss or damage due to the limited options to mitigate loss. Mobile plant unique to underground applications are

- continuous miners
- remote control continuous miners
- remote control roof bolting machine
- mobile loading machines

13.6.8 Types of coal mines

The three basic types of underground mines are classified by the method in which the opening from the surface to the mineral seam is made. A drift mine occurs when a nearly horizontal mineral seam outcrops to the surface in the side of a hill or mountain, and entry to the mineral seams is made via a horizontal shaft. Slope mines utilise downward inclined shafts to access mineral seams. Shaft mines (also called deep mines) utilise vertical shafts to access mineral seams. These openings are the hub around which the mine expands and develops.

13.6.8.1 Drift mines

These are less common and are used in hilly or mountainous areas where the coal seam is exposed. The entries into the mine are horizontally into the hill following the coal seam. Both belt and rail haulage is used in drift mines.

13.6.8.2 Slope mines

These are commonly used for coal that is buried at shallow depths. Most slope mines have one entry that is divided into two compartments — one having a belt for transportation and the other having a track system for supporting miners, supplies and equipment to and out of the mine.

13.6.8.3 Shaft mines

Cut straight down from the collar to the seam, this type of mine is normally used where the coal lies at a depth of more than 600ft. Elevators or cages as they are sometimes called transport miners and supplies in the shaft. Coal is brought to the surface in skips or vertical conveyors through a separate shaft served by a heavy-duty electric hoist.

13.6.9 Coal removal methods

Underground coal mines use three different production methods to remove coal. The conventional mining system utilises a cutting machine to undercut the coal seam, blasting to loosen the coal, and loading machines or scoops to remove broken coal.

The continuous mining method utilises a single machine (continuous miner) to rip coal from the seam and automatically load it on to shuttle cars or mobile conveyors.

In the long-wall mining system, large blocks of coal are completely extracted in a single continuous operation. Hydraulic jacks are used to support the roof at the immediate face as the coal is removed. As the face advances, the strata are allowed to cave-in behind the support units.

Other underground mineral mines primarily utilise a conventional mining method to extract the minerals. The mining sequence generally consists of drilling and blasting the mineral and loading it with loading machines.

13.6.10 **Mineral mining**

Due to the nature of most mineral or metal deposits, the ore is typically embedded within hard rock strata. This reduces the exposure of roof collapse compared with that in coal mines and also creates greater 'space' in which to work. Some underground hard rock mines are huge with immense caverns, accommodating large haulage and crushing equipment.

There is still only one main method in hard rock mining, which is the conventional drilling, blasting and haulage. The equipment used for this is similar if not the same as that for above ground mining — drills, bulldozers, front-end loaders, trucks, gathering machines.

Three sub-categories exist for underground hard rock mining which are, in basic terms, as follows:

● Where stopes are naturally supported, room and pillar mining or sub-level stoping can be carried out.

● Where stopes are artificially supported, shrinkage stoping cut and fill, square set mining and long-wall mining can be considered.

● Where it is intended that the stopes collapse, sub-level caving and block caving methods can be used.

There is ample information published about each of these techniques in various mining handbooks but it should be realised that each ore body is unique and variations in removal technique will always be present.

The selection of an appropriate method effectively to extract an economically viable ore body is complex. Geology (dip, rock strength, etc.), ore grade, reserves size and the availability of suitable machinery all influence the system chosen.

Once the ore has been blasted and gathered, haulage can be carried out either by truck, conveyor or locomotive and is either taken directly to the surface or is crushed underground in order to transport it with greater efficiency. A crushing machine such as a 'jaw crusher' typically carries this out, which is explained in greater detail later on in the primary processing section.

The need for supporting the roof is not as great as it is with coal mining. However, when it is used it is typically of wood frame structure (normally within the tunnels and supporting the working face).

Again, slope, shaft or drift mines can be used for hard rock depending upon the proximity of the ore to the surface and the same access and haulage devices are used as for coal — elevators (cages), skips, conveyor systems, etc.

13.7 Primary processing

For primary processing this Report looks at the methods for carrying out the initial processing of both metals and non-metals. The processes involved can be likened to 'material cookery' with various methods of cooking and appropriate machines to assist in the process.

Careful examination of some rocks will reveal that they are made from small crystals or grains, but within a matrix of other material. Each kind of crystal grain consists of one compound or, more rarely, one element. It is unusual to find the mineral that is being recovered to be in a pure state. Normally, the ore produced from the mining or extraction process will require to be worked on to prepare the ore so that a concentrate is available and then for this concentrate to be treated to remove the economic valuable material.

As discussed earlier, generally those elements that are reactive with oxygen are found as compounds while those that are not reactive with oxygen will be found naturally as an element. Examples of low reactivity series metal elements are gold and silver, while higher reactivity series ones include copper, iron, aluminium and potassium. This difference is significant in terms of any subsequent primary processing.

In the case of low reactive metals such as silver and gold, the ore contains the metal element that is being sought for economic benefit, and the processing is primarily to recover the available element. Where there are higher reactive metals to process, such as copper, the ore will contain a compound of copper such as sulphides of copper — copper pyrites or chalcopyrites. In this case the recovery involves the separation of the compound into its constituent elements.

When processing different materials, similar or even identical technology may be used with machines that are of a similar type being utilised for a range of materials.

The following sections first look at the technology for concentration of ores — known as mineral dressing or benefication, and secondly at the extractive methods to recover the target metal or non-metal from the concentrate, although concentration may also include a degree of extraction.

In preparation for the following sections it may be of help to summarise the mineral characteristics which we can use to concentrate and extract the valuable metal or non-metal. These are summarised in the table on page 159.

13.7.1 **Mineral characteristics and processes**

The table opposite charts the mineral characteristics, means of separation and processes.

13.7.2 **Ore concentration and sorting**

Ore concentration includes comminution or size reduction involving breaking, crushing and grinding; screening and classification; and separation or concentration through gravity, magnetic and electrical, and flotation.

However, sorting of the ore as the first part of the process remains important, although manual methods have been overtaken by the use of powerful electromagnets to remove tramp metal. Mechanical ore sorters based on detecting differences in optical or other characteristics of ore and waste, use of a remote form of detector to measure variations in electrical conductivity and/or magnetic characteristics as individual rocks pass through the sorter are also used.

In the case of certain minerals, a high-capacity electronic laser sorter is used. This is effective in the case of limestone, where the blue laser enhances the reflectance difference between the limestone and the gangue or waste minerals contaminating it. This results in very effective separation of the limestone, which separates waste rock from the ore before it is fed to the concentrator.

A further method of sorting works on the principle of irradiating the feed material and measuring the scattered gamma radiation. This allows the high-grade material to be directed to the next part of the process by air blast and the waste to disposal.

Mineral characteristics and processes

Mineral characteristic	Means of separating	Process
Specific gravity	Differential movement due to mass, usually in fluid streams	Dense media separation. Sluice, shaking table, spiral.
Colour	Visual, manual, automated	Hand sorting, or may use fluorescent lighting, or impulses triggered by reflected light.
Surface reactivity	Differential surface tension in a fluid	Aerated pulp with froth-flotation.
Chemical reactivity	Solvation by appropriate chemicals	Hydrometallurgy. Ore or concentrate exposed to chemicals with heat and pressure, then filtered. Dissolved element(s) recovered from filtrate, chemically, electrolytically or by ion exchange.
Chemical reactivity	Oxidation or reduction	Pyrometallurgy. Ore or concentrate exposed to heat and chemical environment with tapped raw metal further treated in furnaces and/or electrolytically.
Ferro-magnetism	Magnetic	Magnetic devices remove the target mineral.
Conductivity	Electrostatic charge	Particles pass through high-voltage zone. Rate of dissipation of induced charge influences subsequent deflection. Differential conductivity.
Radioactivity	Alpha or beta rays	Sensor detectors which also activates a separating device.
Shape	Frictional	Sliding force is opposed by drag of article. Drag depends on cross-section and area.
Texture	Crushing, screening and classifying	Characteristic shapes and surfaces are developed during size reduction.

Comminution

Comminution, or size reduction, of the ore usually incorporates two crushing stages (primary and secondary — in some cases a tertiary crushing stage is used) followed by grinding of the ore. A preliminary size reduction process sometimes occurs when large lumps of ore result from the mining process.

The main type of primary crusher is the jaw crusher, which consists essentially of one fixed and one moving jaw. In modern underground mines it is becoming increasingly common to have a primary crusher underground, as this offers a number of advantages in transporting the ore out of the mine. An example of such an underground crusher is one that is able to crush some 550 tonnes per hour of ore to 200mm. The crusher chamber for this installation is 23m long x 10m wide x 14m high. In open pit mines there is also a trend towards use of a primary crushing unit within the pit — usually a mobile crusher which can be shifted about as work proceeds.

Gyratory crushers also are used as primary crushers. The gyratory crusher consists of a hollow, cone-shaped fixed surface or anvil, containing a cone-shaped spindle or hammer that gyrates around the vertical axis of the fixed surface. The annular space between the hammer and anvil changes in width as the spindle revolves. Materials feed in as the gap opens, is crushed as it closes and falls through as it opens again. An example of a primary gyratory crusher would be one that had a feed size of 1.4m, product size of 200–300mm, capacity of 6000 tonnes per hour and power absorbed of 1000 horsepower.

Cone crushers are similar in principle to gyratory crushers. The crushing head may be a short frustrum and gyrates eccentrically. Cone crushers are designed to deal with feed material up to about 380mm, reducing this to 40–60mm, at a rate of 950–1300 tonnes per hour. Models at the lower end of the range take a feed size of about 25mm and reduce it to 3–6mm; through-put rate is about 10–13 tonnes per hour.

Grinding

Grinding is carried out using ball, rod or autogenous mills, or combinations of these. Fine grinding of the ore tends to involve the largest power consumption in a concentration plant and consequently much attention has been paid to developing different milling methods and machinery to reduce power, capital and associated running costs.

In the past large tonnages of ore were processed by the installation of a large number of mod-erately sized mills. An example of this is where grinding was accomplished in eleven 2.75 x 2.45m ball mills each handling 48 tonnes per hour of feed. Now, various approaches are taken, including the use of very much larger ball mills, on their own or in combination with rod mills, the use of autogenous and semi-autogenous milling techniques; and the use of multistage and combination grinding circuits. An example of a large ball mill is one that has a 6.5m diameter drum and is 9.65m long. Drive is by a 9.65MW ring motor constructed integrally with the drum.

Autogenous grinding is accomplished in large diameter, short length mills fed with run-off mine ore without preliminary crushing. The diameter to length ratio of the mill is between 2 and 3 to 1. In pure autogenous milling the ore acts as its own grinding medium; in semi-autogenous milling, a small proportion of steel balls is added. Achieving true autogenous milling is not easy, as several important requirements have to be met. The mill must be large enough to lift the ore to a suitable height so that sufficient energy is developed for crushing. The ore fragments entering the mill must be of sufficient size to accomplish crushing, and most importantly, the ore must be hard enough so that there is always an adequate supply of cor-rectly sized particles in the mill to achieve the correct grind.

Rod and ball mills are essentially a cylindrical drum charged with the crushing medium, either steel balls or rods, the cylinder revolving about its horizontal axis: they are usually run wet in view of the dust problems resulting from dry grinding. Many mills of this type have wear-resis-tant linings such as steel or rubber.

Screening and classification

Screening and classification of the crushed ore is an essential part of the ore preparation process, and this is usually done on wire mesh screens; for very large sizes of ore, a series of steel bars forming a grid are used. Alternatively, screens made of reinforced rubber or polyurethane, which give considerably longer life with abrasive ores, are used.

Shaking or vibrating screens are usual and sometimes revolving screens are used. Cyclones are also used as classifiers, frequently in closed circuit with ball mills in the grinding circuit. The liquid-solid hydrocyclone consists of a cone with a cylinder at the top. When mineral pulp is fed tangentially into the cyclone at the top, a vortex is generated about the longitudinal axis. The accompanying centrifugal acceleration increases the settling rates of the particles, the coarser of which reach the wall of the cone. Here they enter a zone of reduced pressure and flow downward to the apex, through which they are discharged. At the centre of the cyclone is a zone of low pressure and low centrifugal force that surrounds an air-filled vortex. Part of the pulp, carrying the finer particles, moves inward toward this vortex.

Separation and concentration

Separation and concentration is achieved by various methods such as froth flotation, gravity methods, and magnetic electrostatic and associated techniques. The particular method chosen depends on its effectiveness for the particular ore being processed. For example, tin does not lend itself to froth flotation separation but can be concentrated by gravity techniques.

Froth flotation

In froth flotation, the technique utilises the phenomena of the weak bonds that exist at an interface between the air bubble and the particle. For this to work the particle has to be small enough so that the gravity force tending to cause it to fall is overcome by the buoyancy of the air bubble and the weak bond. The usual commercial separation entails the lifting of particles by the agency of air bubbles rising through a pulp. This buoyancy results from the adhesion of the particle to a comparatively large bubble. The generation of the bubble stream is achieved by mechanically driven impellers or agitators or through direct injection of compressed air. Depending on the type of process the incoming feed is either introduced as a pulp or directly from above on to the froth bed. The vessels may be open baths or columns. The size of these cells is increasing but a typical single cell could have a capacity of 85 cubic metres. The reagents are selected for the particular ore being concentrated to enable the correct property for the bubble and surface bonding.

Gravity

In the gravity process, this depends on the difference in specific gravity between the valuable mineral and the gangue or waste. The medium used for the carrying of the ore is not limited to water, although historically suspension within water has been the most common. Heavy media, such as suspensions of ferro-silicon or finely divided magnetite in water, are used.

Magnetic and electrostatic separation

Magnetic separation is applicable to minerals in which a natural or induced degree of polarity can be sustained during passage through a magnetic field. High intensity or electrostatic separation is applicable where one particle species is relatively non-conducting and the feed to the system is sufficiently mobile and close-sized to allow the delicate electrical forces of repulsion and attraction. This acts on particles gathering charge as they move through a field of high electrical intensity, and on into one where insulation is suitably controlled and charge dissipation becomes a discriminating force.

13.7.3   Coal processing

Although not mentioned specifically in the preceding paragraphs, the processing of coal does utilise some of the above mentioned techniques prior to being made ready for distribution and sale. However, the following details address some of the specific coal issues.

The preparation of coal is primarily concerned with providing consistent product quality such as ash, moisture, and sulphur content as well as the removal of non-combustible material such as clay, shale and sulphur and impurities added during the mining process such as shot wire, wood and cutting bits.

The process also sizes and dries the coal to customer specification. The machinery involved in the various stages includes for separation and washing for large size bath and drums, and for small centrifugal machines; electromagnets for ferrous metal removal; float baths for wood removal; blenders, which allow operators to change ratios of component coals. Other operations include crushing to remove pyrites in the desulphurisation process and to pre-treat before flotation where reagents and residence time are critical. These processes carry a risk and thermal coal dryers, for example, have been subject to fires and explosions on numerous occasions.

13.8   Recovery/refining

As already mentioned, concentration may also include a degree of recovery or refining of the target material. However, this section focuses on two generic refining processes: pyrometallurgy — oxidation or reduction, and hydrometallurgy — solvation by appropriate chemicals.

Pyrometallurgy

In pyrometallurgy, two examples will illustrate the overall process concept.

In the first case, iron ore is concentrated into pellets that can be regarded as iron oxide. These are transported to a steel plant where the objective is to remove the oxygen to form pure iron before additives and processing make the iron into steel. In modern plants this is achieved by exposing the pellets to a reducing environment such as hydrogen-rich gas so that the oxygen from the pellets joins with the hydrogen to form water or vapour. Process equipment involved includes tall shaft furnaces that are likely to operate at 1000°C where the intimate mixing occurs and reformers where the gas production and energy recovery takes place. The sponge or pure iron is then processed further with scrap iron, lime and other additives in an electric arc furnace with electrodes to melt the feed, allow high temperature interaction of the chemical components and then cast into billets. The furnaces which are also refractory lined are exposed to severe thermal loadings and may suffer 'pot freezing' in the event of power being lost before action can be taken to empty the contents.

In the second example, copper ore generally will be in a form of copper sulphide. In this case the process is to feed the ore of the right size into a furnace which has an environment which allows oxidation of the sulphide. This is removed as off-take gas possibly to a by-product acid plant, and to leave basic copper. This copper is then cast into electrodes for subsequent electrolysis, which produces high-purity copper of 99.9% purity. The plant used for this type of processing will involve high temperature operation with refractory lined and water-cooled wall furnaces. Owing to gas velocities and the nature of the material, erosion is likely to be a significant factor as will the possibility of explosion from water leakage into the furnace area. Break-out of molten material could then occur.

Hydrometallurgy

In hydrometallurgy the objective is to use a solvent in which the concentrated ore is exposed to that and it efficiently removes the target metal. Examples of this are to dissolve silver and gold in mercury or more likely now, cyanide, to form an amalgam. Various types of aqueous solutions are used to leach or percolate the metals from the ore, normally in large bath vessels.

Electrolysis

A further stage for the refinement of metals employs electrolysis. In an aqueous solution, an anode electrode of semi-refined metal has a current passed through it, so that pure metal is deposited at the cathode. Metals that are refined in this way are copper, nickel, zinc, silver and gold. Alternatively, for metals such as aluminium, barium, calcium, magnesium, beryllium and sodium, these are refined in electrolytic furnaces.

13.9   Maintenance

The maintenance for extraction and primary processing may well have specific needs, although in the following section maintenance is addressed in a general approach with the introduction of particular areas as examples.

Working machines are expected to operate in environments which can be physically aggressive and subject to significant explosion, erosion, vibration, turbulence, cavitation, fatigue, creep, and stress — straight and thermally induced. This environment may also at the same time or independently be aggressive from a chemical point of view with corrosion, stress corrosion, embrittlement, or preferential element removal resulting.

In these types of environments it is important first, to recognise the working conditions under which the equipment is intended to work and to be satisfied that this is the actual operating condition. Selection of equipment and subsequent maintenance strategies should be made against this position of knowledge.

Increasingly, industry is using condition monitoring to identify trends in machine health so that preventive action can be taken to prevent an unplanned outage. By way of example, there is the use of trend records for vibration analysis of heavily loaded bearings for conveyor drive motors and processing mills; oil analysis of high energy transformers for services underground and electric arc furnaces and infrared thermal imaging of refractory lined process vessels and critical switch gear. All of these can provide an opportunity for early identification of a potential problem. In hazardous explosive environments the integrity of electrical equipment is critical, as is the case where explosive material is stored, ensuring that earthing can reliably prevent a build-up of static electricity.

Preventive or reliability based maintenance linked to condition monitoring and with a management system to allow feedback of experience into the planning process, will critically depend on the human factors of selection, training and motivation of personnel. All of these issues are within a commercial environment of larger capital investment projects and a dynamic world commodity market.

13.10   Critical exposures

There are a number of key extraction activities, which, due to the process or the environment in which they occur, present exposures which, once understood, can be managed to reduce risk. In this section no distinctions are made between surface, underground, extraction or process exposures. Some comments are generic and some specific but it will be apparent to the reader, which of these apply uniquely to a key activity.

13.10.1   Blasting

Blasting takes place extensively in mining operations. The risks to mine personnel are reasonably obvious and therefore operating procedures need to be tightly controlled and staff suitably trained.

Unintentional and accidental damage to surrounding property can also be an issue. Pre-blast surveys may be necessary on nearby dwellings to ensure that any damage caused by blasting is identifiable.

Explosive handling and storage is clearly important. Ammonium nitrate and fuel oil (ANFO) is commonly used for surface blasting and is often made and stored in large quantities on site. Only suitably trained and, in many countries, licensed staff should handle explosives. Detonation risks from external sources such as radio frequencies must be carefully controlled.

13.10.2 **Fire**

The risk of fire is present in mining operations, often exacerbated by the fact that mines are very often extremely remote and fires must be fought without external assistance. Certain areas and mine types are however more susceptible to fire. Due to its calorific value, coal will obviously present a higher fire hazard than other mined products. That said, most environments both above and below ground have enough combustible load to sustain fire. Sources of ignition must be controlled and unnecessary build up of combustible material managed. Fire is generally more feared than explosion with naked lights, internal combustion engines, matches, electrical arcing, explosives and spontaneous combustion all presenting sources of ignition. The hazard of electrical ignition is the most significant source of ignition in a modern mine with arcing, damage to cables and high-voltage underground installations.

Fire prevention is best achieved with the building of fire-resistant structures, good control of combustible materials, the use of proper and appropriate electrical installations and where practical the installation of fire protection.

Fire protection includes hand-held extinguishers, fixed deluge and sprinkler systems in certain areas, foam machines, mobile water cars and a fire water ring main/hydrant system throughout the site.

Under the heading of fire, a reference to coal storage is appropriate. Whether clean or raw, coal is often stored in large quantities, regularly outside and exposed to the weather. Coal storage is not as inert as it might seem, and less than satisfactory stockpile management can be an important factor in the likelihood of loss to fire. Coals are often susceptible to spontaneous combustion, which can only occur in the presence of oxygen. Stockpiles may, for this reason, be compacted to exclude oxygen and therefore prevent spontaneous combustion. In the event that a stockpile does ignite, it is extremely difficult to extinguish and often the best course of action is to isolate the burning portion of coal from the stockpile by moving it with a shovel.

Mobile mining plant can also give rise to some fire concerns. Large surface plant such as drag lines or bucket wheel excavators should be fitted with their own fire suppression equipment. Hydraulic shovels have been lost on many occasions to fire. The hydraulic oil or the fuel driving the machine is itself often the main cause of fire.

Haulage trucks have also been lost to fire. The most significant losses generally happen either while the trucks are being maintained or when not working and parked up. The large truck tyres burn well and a number of trucks may become involved in the same event when parked together. A good management practice is to stipulate minimum distances between parked trucks.

13.10.3 **Storage**

Storage can lead to relatively high concentrations of combustible material. On the surface, mines will always have a stores in which flammable liquids, consumable items and maybe high value critical spares might be stored. A large fire loss could well have a significant impact on the whole operation. Stock control, storage philosophy, *e.g.*, with separate flammable liquid store, and fire protections are important factors in avoiding loss.

Underground storage is also an issue. Fuels, oils and consumables will be stored underground in any sizeable operation. Strict controls for inventory control, product handling and fire protection are critical.

13.10.4 Explosion

There are two factors that influence the likelihood of an explosion. These are

- the presence of methane
- the presence of suspended dust.

Methane is an explosive gas between 5 and 15% concentration (by volume with air) and is often given off by coal seams and adjacent strata. It can be easily detected and managed with adequate ventilation. Particular attention must be paid to dormant areas of the mine where a 'pocket' of methane might build up and cause an explosion hazard.

Dust can be a major problem in the mine environment. Dust is an explosion problem when suspended in air but less so if lying undisturbed. Blasting or impact can obviously cause settled dust to lift and to become suspended in air and potentially sustain an explosion. Unlike a methane explosion, which is usually reasonably localised, a dust explosion can be propagated over a much larger area and is both more damaging to property and more life threatening. Housekeeping and dust suppression are the principal methods used to help control the dust explosion problem.

13.10.5 Flooding

Flooding can be an issue in many mines where a safe and acceptable working environment is only achieved with the use of pumps to remove unwanted water. In broad terms, a mine can be flooded by underground water ingress or via the surface openings (shafts and/or tunnels).

Nearly all mines have some water 'make' which seeps into the mine. Mines with unusually large make (in an aquifer area for example) should be fully assessed and understood since a number of mines have been entirely lost owing to uncontrollable flooding.

Dams are often associated with remote mining operations in order to provide a reliable supply of process water. These dams introduce an additional flooding risk. Construction to appropriate engineering standards, monitoring and maintenance methods are essential to ensure long-term reliable operation. In many countries, statutory regulations will be applicable to large dam monitoring and operations.

13.10.6 Pollution

Pollution is a significant exposure from hard rock mineral processing. Tailings dams often retain residues with an element of metallic and chemical content. It is paramount that this does not escape from the containment pond. Monitoring of the dam stability along with the liner used significantly reduces this exposure, especially if the dam is situated near a river, potable water supply or dwellings.

Similarly, heap leach pads and pregnant ponds which often rely on the use of heavy pollutants for ore extraction, must be carefully managed and maintained.

13.10.7 **Rock burst**

Rock burst is the name given to the violent failure of rock as a result of excessive stress. Following excavation, stresses in rocks need to be redistributed and as this happens there may be fracturing at or near the rock surface in the tunnel. These rock bursts can cause damage to equipment and injury to personnel and in areas where this occurs, wall and roof support should be installed.

13.10.8 **Subsidence**

Subsidence is the term given to sinking, lowering or descending of the ground surface and can occur on the surface above underground mine workings.

Factors such as the dimensions of the ore reserve, the depth and type of overburden, the inclination of the strata with respect to the surface and the structural support offered by the collapsed roof material (gob) all affect the likelihood of subsidence.

13.10.9 **Collapse**

Collapse accounts for half of all fatalities in coal mines. The likelihood of collapse influences the mining system used and roof control, particularly in soft rock coal mining, can often represent the largest single expenditure in the mine operation.

The type of roof strata, such as slate, shale, sandstone or limestone all influence the chances of collapse and as more ore is removed so the forces influencing collapse change.

Those areas of the mine which are designed as permanent features should be supported with more substantial structures since they will be regularly used as access routes to the working faces of the mine over a long period.

A unique feature with underground coal mines is a production method known generically as 'retreat mining'. The practice can also be referred to as 'second mining, pulling pillars and pillar recovery'. Coal pillars are intended to support the main roof during advance mining. Since these pillars can contain a vast amount of coal, it may be practical or even desirable to mine them.

Partial pillar recovery can be found in certain mine areas and continuous miner sections. The intent of partial pillar recovery is to recover as much ore as possible from the roof supporting 'pillars' without collapse. The practice should allow the immediate and main roof to remain intact and usually involves either taking a cut through the centre or small cuts from the sides of the pillar.

Because of roof fall fatalities, the Mine Safety and Health Administration in the United States, along with the various state regulatory agencies has been increasingly proactive in reducing the number of mines that practice full pillar recovery. However, the practice is still encountered. With full pillar recovery, the extraction of the coal pillars will cause the immediate and main roof to fall, hopefully in a planned and predictable manner. Unplanned roof falls can produce miner fatalities and extensive damage to equipment and is usually caused by the failure to closely adhere to the approved roof control plan. Some of the more common causes of these unplanned roof falls during retreat mining are

● the failure to install the proper number of breaker posts
● moving of the continuous miner beyond the supported roof

- full pillar recovery in an area with unusual geological conditions (fault lines, massive sandstone roof, etc.)
- the accidental knocking down of temporary roof supports
- the failure to install roof bolts during pillar extraction
- the failure of personnel to detect and react quickly to roof hazards.

Mobile face equipment such as continuous miners, cutting machines and roof bolters should be pulled back from the face of the mine during non-working hours.

When a mine is close to previously mined areas it is important to understand the physical relationship between old and existing workings. With multi-seam mining, the lower deep mine should not extract pillars below active working sections above.

13.10.10 Mechanical breakdown

As has already been mentioned, the environment in which machinery works in extraction and primary processing can be regarded as demanding.

Breakdown mechanisms experienced in mining and extraction equipment can include failure through material fatigue, which may be induced through vibration and cyclic loading. Serious failures of this type have occurred in winding gear involving large loss of life. Other results of this failure mechanism include cracking of large grinding mill shells and rotating furnace kilns. The time taken to return the machine to service can be lengthy. Large surface walking dragline machines may suffer this type of failure in their booms. A dragline boom may represent up to 25% of the total machine value. Other physical failure mechanisms are also experienced. These include overload ductile failure of drive shafts and overload brittle failure of crane hooks due to material selection and low ambient temperatures. Refractory failure through erosion may also be encountered in furnaces.

Deterioration may be experienced in furnaces through aggressive attack of refractory constituents by metal oxides. Overheating of the metal containment will follow and there will be a possible breakout of molten metal. Stress corrosion cracking may be found in processing, for example where stressed copper and ammonia come into intimate contact.

The use of condition monitoring is becoming increasingly common in the extraction and processing industry. Machine reliability, efficiency and longevity can be improved with a comprehensive predictive maintenance programme

The provision of power and removal of water underground is critical to ensure adequate ventilation and to prevent flooding. Electrical system failures through ingress of moisture into switchgear and motor windings can occur, and the failure of insulation may result in unplanned shutdown of the operation or putting the mine at risk from flooding. Transformer tap changer failure on electric arc furnaces may occur from repetitive changes and deterioration of contacts. Unless timely action is taken to remove the liquid contents, the metal may freeze within the vessel causing significant cost of replacement and downtime.

14 ▌Iron and steel

14.1 Introduction

This chapter concerns itself with the production of iron and its alloys, particularly those containing a small percentage of carbon. Steel in general is an alloy of iron and carbon, often with an admixture of other elements. Some alloys that are commonly called irons actually contain more carbon than some commercial steel. Open-hearth iron and wrought iron contain only a few hundredths of 1% carbon. Steels of various types contain from 0.04% to 2.25% of carbon. Cast iron, malleable cast iron, and pig iron contain amounts of carbon varying from 2% to 4%. A special form of malleable iron, containing virtually no carbon, is known as white-heart malleable iron. A special group of iron alloys known as ferro alloys is used in the manufacture of iron and steel alloys. They contain from 20% to 80% of an alloying element, such as manganese, silicon, or chromium.

Why is alloy iron used with other elements? The principle reason is that iron by itself is relatively soft but it can be made harder with the addition of carbon. Other alloying elements will allow it to be 'worked' more easily into different shapes and to withstand different environments that are corrosive, through acid and alkaline attack and also low temperatures such as in cryogenic uses.

Through the ages, iron and steel has been an area of continuing development, with trial and error playing a significant part.

14.2 History

The exact date when the technique of smelting iron ore to produce usable metal was invented is not known. The earliest iron implements, discovered by archaeologists in Egypt, date from about 3000BC and iron ornaments were used even earlier. The comparatively advanced technique of hardening iron weapons by heat treatment was known to the Greeks in about 1000BC.

The alloys produced by early ironworkers, and, indeed, all the iron alloys made until about the fourteenth century would be classified today as wrought iron. They were made by heating a mass of iron ore and charcoal in a forge or furnace with a forced draft. Under this treatment, the ore was reduced to the sponge of metallic iron filled with slag-composed metal impurities and charcoal ash. This sponge of iron was removed from the furnace and beaten with heavy sledges to drive out the slag and to weld and consolidate the iron. The iron produced under these conditions usually contained about 3.0% of slag particles and 0.1% of other impurities.

Ironworkers learned to make steel by heating wrought iron and charcoal clay boxes for a period of several days and by this process the iron absorbed enough carbon to become true steel.

After the fourteenth century, the furnaces used in smelting were increased in size, and an increased draft was used to force the combustion gases through the mixture of raw materials. In these larger furnaces, the iron ore in the upper part of the furnace was first reduced to metallic iron and then took on more carbon as a result of the gases forced through it by the blast. The product of these furnaces was pig iron, an alloy that melts at a lower temperature than steel or wrought iron. Pig iron (so called because it was usually cast in stubby, round ingots known as 'pigs') was then further refined to make steel.

14.3   Developments

Some milestones in the history of iron and steel production are

- The inventor of the modern blast furnace was Abraham Derby (1711–63), an ironmaster from Coalbrookdale.

- Henry Bessemer (1813–96) perfected a converter in 1856 that allowed him to remove the carbon from pig iron and to produce steel of a good quality.

- Charles William Siemens (1823–83) took the next step forward by using the waste heat from gases inside the furnace to heat the air sent in by the bellows. In 1861, together with his brother Frederick, he designed an open-hearth steel furnace, which both utilised waste heat and incorporated a gas producer, which allowed the use of low-grade coal as fuel.

- Sydney Gilchrist Thomas (1850–85) improved the Bessemer process in 1876, making it possible to refine phosphoric pig-iron and to eliminate the various other impurities due to a basic lining of the converters.

- Frenchman Paul Heroult (1863–1914) made possible the melting of scrap iron in an electric arc furnace. The first industrial application took place on 9 October 1900.

14.4   Principal processes

14.4.1   Pig iron production

The basic materials used for the manufacture of pig iron are iron ore, coke, and limestone. The coke is burned as a fuel to heat the furnace. As it burns, the coke gives off carbon monoxide, which combines with the iron oxides in the ore, reducing them to metallic iron. This is the basic chemical reaction in the blast furnace. The limestone in the furnace charge is used as an additional source of carbon monoxide and as a 'flux' to combine with the infusible silica present in the ore to form fusible calcium silicate. Without the limestone, iron silicate would be formed with a resulting loss of metallic iron.

Calcium silicate, plus other impurities, forms a slag that floats on top of the molten metal at the bottom of the furnace. Ordinary pig iron as produced by blast furnaces contains iron, about 92%; carbon, 3–4%; silicon, 0.5–3.0%; manganese, 0.25–2.5%; phosphorus, 0.04–2.0%; and a trace of sulphur.

14.4.2   Blast furnace

A typical blast furnace consists of a cylindrical steel shell lined with refractory material that is a non-metallic substance, such as a firebrick. The shell is tapered at the top and at the bottom and is widest at a point about one-quarter of the distance from the bottom. The lower portion of the furnace, called the bosh, where the melting takes place, is equipped with several tubular openings or tuyeres through which the air blast is forced. It is above the hearth and below the stack. Near the bottom of the bosh is a hole through which the molten pig iron flows when the furnace is tapped, and above this hole, but below the tuyeres, is another hole for draining the slag. The top of the furnace, which is about 27m in height, contains vents for the escaping gases and a pair of round hoppers closed with bell-shaped valves through which the charge is introduced into the furnace.

The materials are brought up to the hoppers in small dump cars or skips that are hauled up an inclined external skip hoist.

Blast furnaces operate continuously. The raw material to be fed into the furnace is divided into a number of small charges that are introduced into the furnace at 10–15 minute intervals. Slag is drawn off from the top of the melt about once every two hours, and the iron itself is drawn off or tapped about five times a day.

The air used to supply the blast in a blast furnace is preheated to temperatures between approximately 540° and 870°C. The heating is performed in stoves that comprise cylinders containing networks of firebrick. The bricks in the stoves are heated for several hours by burning blast-furnace gas, the waste gases from the top of the furnace and when the flame is turned off the air from the blast is blown through the stove.

The process of tapping consists of knocking out a clay plug from the iron hole near the bottom of the bosh and allowing the molten metal to flow into a clay-lined runner. It then runs into a large brick-lined metal container, which may be either a ladle or a rail car capable of holding as much as 100 tons of metal. Any slag that may flow from the furnace with the metal is skimmed off before it reaches the container. The container of molten pig iron is then transported to the steel-making shop.

Modern blast furnaces are operated in conjunction with basic oxygen furnaces and sometimes the older open-hearth furnaces as part of a single steel-producing plant. In such plants the molten pig iron is used to charge the steel furnaces. The molten metal from several blast furnaces may be mixed in a large ladle before it is converted to steel, to minimise any irregularities in the composition of the individual melts.

14.4.3 Other methods of iron refining

Although almost all iron and steel is made from pig iron produced by the blast-furnace process, other methods of iron refining are possible and have been used to a limited extent. One such method is the so-called direct reduction method of making iron and steel from ore without making pig iron. In this process iron ore and coke are mixed in a revolving kiln or passed through a vertical furnace and heated to a temperature of about 950°C. A reducing gas such as hydrogen comes in to contact with the oxides of iron. Carbon monoxide is given off from the heated coke just as in the blast furnace and reduces the oxides of the ore to metallic iron. However, the secondary reactions that occur in a blast furnace do not occur, and the kiln produces so-called sponge iron of much higher purity than pig iron.

Virtually pure iron is also produced by means of electrolysis, by passing an electric current through a solution of ferrous chloride.

14.4.4 Open-hearth process

Essentially the production of steel from pig iron by any process consists of burning out the excess carbon and other impurities present in the iron. One difficulty in the manufacture of steel is its high melting point, about 1370°C, which prevents the use of ordinary fuels and furnaces. To overcome this difficulty, the open-hearth furnace was developed. This type of furnace can be operated at a high temperature by regenerative preheating; the exhaust gases from the furnace are drawn through one of a series of chambers containing a mass of brickwork and give up most of their heat to the bricks. Then the flow through the furnace is reversed and the fuel and air pass through the heated chambers and are warmed by the bricks. Through this method open-hearth furnaces can reach temperatures as high as 1650°C.

The furnace itself consists typically of a flat, rectangular brick hearth about 6m x 10m, which is roofed over at a height of about 2.5m. In front of the hearth, a series of doors open out on to a working floor in front of the hearth. The entire hearth and working floor are one storey above ground level, and the heat-regenerating chambers of the furnace take up the space under the hearth.

The furnace is charged with a mixture of pig iron (either molten or cold), scrap steel, and iron ore that provides additional oxygen. Limestone is added for flux and fluorspar to make the slag more fluid. After the furnace has been charged, the furnace is lit and the flames play back and forth over the hearth as their direction is changed by the operator to provide heat regeneration.

Chemically, the action of the open-hearth furnace consists of lowering the carbon content of the charge by oxidisation and removing such impurities as silicon, phosphorus, manganese, and sulphur, which combine with the limestone to form slag. These reactions take place while the metal in the furnace is at melting heat, and the furnace is held between 1540° and 1650°C for many hours until the molten metal has the desired carbon content. The melt is usually tested by withdrawing a small amount of metal from the furnace, cooling it, and then subjecting it to physical examination or chemical analysis.

When the carbon content of the melt reaches the desired level, the furnace is tapped through a hole at the rear. The molten steel then flows through a short trough to a large ladle set below the furnace at ground level. From the ladle the steel is poured into cast-iron moulds that form ingots usually about 1.5m long and 48cm square. These ingots, being the raw material for all forms of fabricated steel, weigh approximately 2.25 tonnes in this size.

Recently, methods have been put into practice for the continuous processing of steel without first having to go through the process of casting ingots. By this method, after leaving the electric furnace where the steel composition has been achieved, the liquid metal enters a partly enclosed, heated continuous casting machine. The liquid is continuously cast into billets of steel.

14.4.5   **Basic oxygen process**

The oldest process for making steel in large quantities, the Bessemer process, made use of a tall pear-shaped furnace, called a Bessemer converter, that could be tilted sideways for charging and pouring. High volumes of air were blown through the molten metal and its oxygen united chemically with the impurities and carried them off.

In the basic oxygen process, steel is also refined in a pear-shaped furnace that tilts sideways on trunnions, for charging and pouring. Air is utilised in conjunction with an oxygen lance. The water-cooled tip of the lance is usually about 2m above the charge although this distance can be varied according to requirements. Thousands of cubic metres of oxygen are blown into the furnace at supersonic speed. The oxygen combines with carbon and other unwanted elements and starts a high-temperature churning reaction that rapidly burns out impurities from the pig iron and converts it to steel. The refining process takes approximately 50 minutes or less and approximately 275 tonnes of steel can be made in one hour.

14.4.6   **Electric-furnace steel**

In some furnaces, energy is produced by electricity for the melting and refining of steel, because refining conditions in such a furnace can be regulated more strictly than in open-hearth or basic oxygen furnaces. Electric furnaces are particularly valuable for producing stainless steels and other highly alloyed steels that must be made to exacting specifications.

Refining takes place in a tightly closed chamber, where temperatures and other conditions are kept under rigid control by automatic devices. During the early stages of this refining process, high-purity oxygen is injected through a lance, raising the temperature of the furnace and decreasing the time needed to produce the finished steel.

Most often the charge consists almost entirely of scrap. Before it is ready to be used, the scrap must first be analysed and sorted, because its alloy content will affect the composition of the refined metal. Other materials, such as small quantities of iron ore and dry lime, are added in order to help remove carbon and other impurities that are present. The additional alloying elements enter the charge at this point or enter the refined steel as it is subsequently poured into the ladle.

After the furnace is charged, electrodes are lowered close to the surface of the metal. The current enters through one of the electrode arcs to the metallic charge, flows through the metal, and then arcs back to the next electrode. Heat is generated by overcoming the resistance to the flow of current through the charge. This heat, together with that coming from the intensely hot arc itself, quickly melts the metal.

In another type of electric furnace, heat is generated in a coil. Alternatively the electrical path may be between the electrode, metal charge and furnace body.

14.4.7 Heat treatment of steel

The basic process of hardening steel by heat treatment consists of heating the metal to a temperature at which austenite is formed, usually about 760°C to 870°C, and then cooling it rapidly in water or oil. Such hardening treatments, which form martensite, set up large internal strains in metal which is relieved by tempering, or annealing which consists of reheating the steel to a lower temperature. Tempering results in decrease in hardness and strength and an increase in ductility and toughness.

Metallurgists have found that a change from austenite to martensite occurs during the latter part of the cooling period and that this change is accompanied by a change in volume that may crack the metal if the cooling is too swift. New processes are continually being tried and tested to assist in the prevention of this cracking. For example, in time quenching, the steel is withdrawn from the furnace and transferred to a quenching bath of metal or salt where it is maintained at the constant temperature. Here the desired structural change occurs and the steel is held in this bath until the change is complete. The steel is then subjected to the final cooling.

Other methods of heat-treating are used to harden steel. In case hardening, a finished piece of steel is given an extremely hard surface by heating it with carbon or nitrogen compounds. These compounds react with the steel, either raising the carbon content or forming nitrides in its surface layer

14.4.8 Finishing processes

Steel is distributed in a wide variety of sizes and shapes, such as rods, pipes and railroad rails. These shapes are produced at steel mills by rolling and other methods of forming heated ingots to the required shape. The working of steel also improves its quality by refining its crystalline structure and making the metal tougher.

The basic process of working steel is known as hot rolling. In hot rolling the cast ingot is first heated to bright-red heat in a furnace called a soaking pit and it is then passed between a series of pairs of metal rollers that squeeze it to the desired size and shape. The distance between the rollers diminishes for each successive pair as the steel is elongated and reduced in thickness.

The first pair of rollers through which the ingot passes is commonly called the blooming mill, and the square billets of steel that the ingot produces are known as blooms. From the blooming mill, the steel is passed on to roughing mills and finally to finishing mill that reduces it to the correct cross section. The rollers of mills used to produce railroad rails and such structural shapes as I-beams, H-beams, and angles are grooved to give the required shape.

Modern manufacturing requires a large amount of thin sheet steel. Production mills process thin sheet steel rapidly, before it cools and becomes unworkable. A slab of hot steel over 11cm thick is fed through a series of rollers, which reduce it progressively in thickness to 0.127cm and increase its length from 4m to 370m. Continuous mills are equipped with a number of accessories including edging rollers, descalers and machines for coiling the sheet automatically when it reaches the end of the mill.

The edging rollers are sets of vertical rolls set opposite each other at either side of the sheet to ensure that the width of the sheet is maintained. Descaling apparatus removes the scale that forms on the surface of the sheet by knocking it off mechanically, loosening it by means of an air blast, or bending the sheet sharply at some point in its travel. The completed coils of sheet are dropped on a conveyor and carried away to be annealed and cut into individual sheets.

A more efficient way to produce thin sheet steel is to feed thinner slabs through a blooming mill in order to produce slabs thin enough to enter a continuous mill.

By devising a continuous casting system that produces an endless steel slab less than 5cm thick, German engineers have eliminated any need for blooming and roughing mills. In 1989, a steel mill in Indiana became the first outside Europe to adopt this system.

14.4.9 Pipework

Certain grades of pipe are shaped by bending a flat strip, or skelp, of hot steel into cylindrical form and welding the edges to complete the pipe. For the smaller sizes of pipe, the edges of the skelp are usually overlapped and passed between a pair of rollers curved to correspond with the outside diameter of the pipe. The pressure on the rollers is sufficient to weld together the edges.

Seamless pipe or tubing is made from solid rods by passing them between a pair of inclined rollers that have a pointed metal bar, or mandrel, set between them in such a way that it pierces the rods. This forms the inside diameter of the pipe at the same time that the rollers are forming the outside diameter.

14.4.10 Tin plate

By far the most important coated product of the steel mill is tin plate for the manufacture of containers. The 'tin' can is actually more than 99% steel. In some mills steel sheets are hot-rolled and then cold-rolled and are coated by passing them through a bath of molten tin.

The most common method of coating is by the electrolytic process. Sheet steel is slowly unrolled from its coil and passed through a chemical solution. Meanwhile, a current of electricity is passing through a piece of pure tin into the same solution, causing the tin to dissolve slowly and to be deposited on the steel.

In electrolytic processing, less than one half of a kilogram of tin will coat more than 18.6 square metres of steel. For the product known as thin tin, sheet steel and strip steel are given a second cold rolling before being coated with tin, a treatment that makes the steel plate extra tough as well as ultra thin. Cans made of thin tin are as strong as ordinary tin cans, yet they contain less steel, with a resultant saving weight and cost. Lightweight packaging containers are also being made of tin-plated steel foil that has been laminated to paper cardboard.

14.4.11 **Wrought iron**

The process of making the tough, malleable alloy known as wrought iron differs markedly from other forms of steel making. The development of new processes using Bessemer converters and open-hearth furnaces allowed the production of larger quantities of wrought iron.

Wrought iron is no longer produced commercially, however, because it can be effectively replaced in nearly all applications by low-carbon steel, which is less expensive to produce and is typically of more uniform quality than wrought iron.

The modern technique of making wrought iron uses molten iron from a Bessemer converter and molten slag, which is usually prepared by melting iron ore, mill scale, and sand in an open-hearth furnace. The molten slag is maintained in a ladle at a temperature several hundred degrees below the temperature of the molten iron. When the molten iron, which carries a large amount of gas in solution, is poured into the ladle containing the molten slag, the metal solidifies almost instantly, releasing the dissolved gas. The force exerted by the gas shatters the metal into minute particles that are heavier than the slag and that accumulate in the bottom of the ladle, gathering into a spongy mass. After the slag has been poured off the top of the ladle, the ball of iron is removed and squeezed and rolled.

14.5 Major feedstocks — the classification of steels and their uses

Steels are grouped into five main classifications according to the method of manufacture and their constituent parts.

The physical properties of various types of steel and of any given steel alloy at varying temperatures depend primarily on the amount of carbon present and on how it is distributed in the iron. Before being heat treated, most steel is a mixture of three substances — ferrite, pearlite and cementite.

Ferrite is iron containing small amounts of carbon and other element in solution and is soft and ductile. Pearlite is an intimate mixture of ferrite and cementite having a specific composition and characteristic structure, and physical characteristics intermediate between its two constituents. Cementite, a compound of iron containing about 7% carbon, is extremely brittle and hard.

The toughness and hardness of steel that is not heat-treated depend on the proportions of these three ingredients. As the carbon content of a steel increases, the amount of ferrite present decreases and the amount of pearlite increases until, when the steel has 0.8% of carbon, it is entirely composed of pearlite. Steel with still more carbon is a mixture of pearlite and cementite.

14.5.1 **Carbon steels**

More than 90% of all steels are carbon steels. They contain varying amounts of carbon and not more than 1.65% manganese, 0.60% silicon, and 0.60% copper. Machines, motor car bodies, most structural steel for building and ship hulls are among the products made of carbon steels.

14.5.2   **Alloy steels**

These steels have a specified composition, containing certain percentages of vanadium, molyb-
denum, or other elements, as well as larger amounts of manganese, silicon, and copper than do
the regular carbon steels. Automobile gear and axles, roller skates, and carving knives are
some of the many things that are made of alloy steels.

14.5.3   **High-strength low-alloy steels**

High-strength low alloy (HSLA) steels are the newest of the five chief families of steels. They
cost less than the regular alloy steels because they contain only small amounts of the expensive
alloying elements. They have been specially processed, however, to have much more strength
than carbon steels of the same weight. For example, railway freight wagons made of HSLA
steels can carry larger loads because their walls are thinner than would be possible with carbon
steel of equal strength. Moreover, a HSLA freight wagon is lighter in weight than the ordinary
wagon and it is less of a load for the locomotive to pull.

Numerous buildings are now being constructed with frameworks of HSLA steels. Girders and
beams can be made thinner without sacrificing their strength, and additional space is left for
offices and apartments.

14.5.4   **Stainless steels**

Stainless steels contain chromium, nickel, and other elements that keep them bright and rust
resistant despite the presence moisture or the action of corrosive acids and gases. Some stainless steels are very hard and some have unusual strength and will retain that strength for long
periods at extremely high and low temperatures. Because their surfaces can be processed to a
highly polished degree, architects often use them for decorative purposes.

Stainless steels can be used for the pipes and tanks in petroleum refineries and chemical plants
where resistance to corrosion is required. Surgical instruments and equipment are made from
these steels, and they are also used to patch or replace broken bones because the steels can
withstand the action of body fluids. In kitchens and in plants where food is prepared, handling
equipment is often made of stainless steel because it does not taint the food and can be easily
cleaned.

14.5.5   **Tools steels**

These steels are fabricated into many types of tools or into the cutting and shaping parts of
power-driven machinery for various manufacturing operations. They contain tungsten, molyb-
denum, and other alloying elements that give them extra strength, hardness, and resistance to
wear.

14.6   Maintenance and monitoring

This industry can be likened to the 'cooking' of metal and as such the preparation and processing involves the correct selection of ingredients, treatments of the ingredients to the correct
size and quality, the cooking (smelting and conversion). All these processes having been
described in earlier paragraphs.

The production equipment and machinery handles large volumes of abrasive raw material and
off-take gases. The process also involves the preparation and use of processing chemicals that
can be corrosive at high or low temperatures, in vacuum and at very high pressures. Machinery

is designed to be robust in this industry, but effective maintenance and monitoring is essential to ensure there are no unplanned shutdowns.

In almost all furnaces, the off-take gas ducts and in some cases the furnaces themselves, are water-cooled. In a number of cases where the jackets have failed and have allowed water to come into contact with the liquid metal or slag, explosions have resulted.

In the preparation of raw products in mills, heavily loaded rotating machines will be monitored for vibration to allow early prediction of wear and possible breakdown. Similar equipment is used in the downstream areas of rolling where gearboxes and drive systems are used.

As previously noted the raw products and off-take gases can be very abrasive and where furnaces and the exhaust systems are subjected to high glow rates with entrained particulates, wear rates are extremely high even when special inserts, linings or coatings are used. Ultrasonic thickness gauging is used extensively in the industry to prevent unplanned outages by providing wear profiling and this is supplemented by infrared thermal imaging which detects 'heat leakage' from reduced integrity of the containment.

Many plants have become automated to a high degree. Reduced numbers of operators and speed of product throughput has made the process more sensitive to minor failures in computer sensors, monitoring equipment and software. In rolling mills, incidents have occurred relating to forming stand cooling failures which has led to major damage from product damage leading to a fire before the process could be halted.

The iron and steel industry also uses high quantities of energy in the form of electrical power. Because the processes are subject to high temperatures and vibration the environment is aggressive for the electrical equipment. Although physical inspection can be undertaken, this would entail off-load working and interruption to processing. The utilisation of thermal imaging means that on-load surveys can be carried out with reliable results.

Good quality planning strategies and maintenance programmes, although expensive to implement and continue with, should be encouraged together with loss-prevention programmes for analysis profiling and trending utilising various techniques such as vibration monitoring, ultrasonic thickness gauging and infrared thermal imaging.

Refractory linings have a very limited service life and must be replaced regularly. Some of the fireproof bricks, such as dolomite, used in refractory linings are very delicate. If stored incorrectly they may absorb moisture from the atmosphere and very quickly disintegrate. Particular attention must therefore be given to protecting them during storage. Fire clay bricks are less of a problem. Also, after installation it is important that refractory linings are dried carefully in accordance with the designated procedures.

14.7   Critical areas

The risks presented at iron and steel factories relate to high temperature processing of iron and steel, the generation, storage and use of combustible and potentially explosive gases within these processes and the use of combustible hydraulic oils in the presence of hot steel. Other combustible gases required in the processing of steel, such as oxygen and hydrogen are produced and stored. There is also a high level of impact risk emanating from the transport of heavy loads of steel over and adjacent to capital plant and equipment.

In addition, a range of normal industrial risks prevail in the form of high speed rotating equipment, compressed-air production and storage, electrical equipment, and the presence of lubricating oil in areas subject to high temperatures. The presence of electronic equipment in buildings that are subject to high temperatures from both ambient and process heat sources is also a particular risk.

14.7.1   **Fire**

Fires can occur in

- electrical switch rooms, cable tunnels and motor rooms
- hydraulic pump rooms
- desulphurisation filter bag house
- coal tar storage tanks farms.

14.7.2   **Explosion**

Among the causes and locations of explosion are

- blast furnace explosions with potential collapse of refractory lining and consequential structural damage
- gas explosions in coke ovens, steam generators, annealing ovens and furnaces
- explosions in basic oxygen steel-making vessels from the escape of lance and gas hood cooling water, damaging vessel refractory and hood integrity
- gas explosions in oxygen generating plant.

14.7.3   **Operational failure**

Causes of operational failure include

- turbine-generator and turbo-compressors disintegration and consequential fire
- electric generator and motor short circuits and potential resultant fires
- refractory lining failures
- breakout of molten metal owing to vessel failure or malfunction
- failure of electricity supply, for example, following damage to a key transformer, resulting in pot freezing and solidification of molten metal, as work in progress.

14.7.4   **Impact**

Impact damage can result from

- crane accidents
- collision with ground level transportation facilities
- impact and consequential fire damage from hot billets, slabs, rolled products, etc., falling from roller tables etc.

Some of these critical exposures are illustrated in the following example of incidents occurring at steel plants.

- In a direct reduction plant iron oxide pellets are fed into a tall tower some 100m in height. As the pellets drop through the tower, hydrogen gas is fed into the furnace to react with the oxygen and reduce the iron oxide to iron. The hydrogen gas is produced in a reformer where natural gas is heated. Serious fires have occurred where reformers and furnaces have failed, gas has leaked and it has been ignited. Large compressors are used in this process also and there have been incidents of component failure due to hydrogen embrittlement.

- In furnaces that are refractory lined, premature failure has come about from inappropriate selection of refractory or mortar. In this case the iron or steel or the gases present have attached to the lining, leading to failure. There has also been experience of the installation of a new lining, which has been followed by incorrect drying out of the mortar or cast refractor, which has subsequently led to cracking. Premature failure has followed.

- Pot or furnace freezing can lead to large business interruption exposures. Increasingly iron and steel works are becoming integrated and feature iron ore to finished product facilities on one site. Electrical demands are high especially where electric arc furnaces are utilised. Incidents have occurred where, owing to electrical supply failure from the grid or site transformers failing, liquid metal freezing has resulted.

See also Chapter 16, 'Other manufacturing industries', 16.2 'Smelting'.

15 Integrated circuit manufacturing plants

15.1 Introduction

Owing to the rapid advance of technology in the field of integrated circuit manufacturing and the standard of construction and materials used it is probable that some of the information contained in this chapter will be outdated by the time of publication. This situation is obviously outside the control of the Study Group but realistically reflects the pace of development in this industry.

Additionally, the commercial sensitivity of the various manufacturers and the unique nature of the process machines themselves render it more difficult for the insurer to ascertain full underwriting information in some circumstances.

Unfortunately, therefore, the content of this chapter may be more general than the Study Group would wish. Furthermore, this is compounded because internationally recognised loss prevention standards and codes of practice are still developing.

However, it is hoped that even with these recognised limitations the reader will gain a significant understanding of this industry sector.

15.2 History and developments

Although mechanical computers in the form of processing machines and electrical — valve operated computers have been extensively used, their performance in terms of speed of processing, power requirements and reliability and costs were serious limitations. This changed with the advent of electronic computers using transistors in the late 1950s and integrated circuits (ICs) in the late 1960s.

The development of integrated circuits has been driven by the demands for higher speeds of operation, smaller size of computers and components and relative cost. This drive has resulted in revolutionary product development, and production machines and methods of equal revolutionary design.

Unlike other industries covered in this publication, the history of integrated circuits and their manufacture is only traceable to the early 1960s. The dynamic nature of this industry suggests we need to take a different approach to reviewing 'history' and to this end we will look at the 'future' history!

Computer performance in terms of speed, size and power consumption/heat dissipation requires that integrated circuits and their production systems need to be innovative in the use of more effective materials, miniaturisation and integrating techniques. Cost reduction or stability of prices needs efficient production systems and economies of scale, with large throughputs.

Current examples and predictions of the future include the following.

15.2.1 More effective materials

Microchip ('chip') technology using copper, instead of aluminium alloys, for the metallic circuit lines linking transistors on a chip. Copper is a better conductor of electricity than aluminium, so it can carry currents more efficiently.

Silicon-based microprocessors have clock cycle times of between 40 and 5 nanoseconds and the fastest, which use gallium arsenide, are between 2 and 3 nanoseconds. By the 2007 the clock cycle time is likely to be below 1 nanosecond.

15.2.2 Miniaturisation

Production of chips in the current form and size would not be possible without clean room technology. Government laboratories and microchip makers are developing a new generation of chip production equipment and techniques aimed at shrinking chip dimensions below 0.1 microns. Current chips have features just 0.25 microns wide — 400 times smaller than a human hair. The research will focus on the use of extreme ultraviolet light, X-ray or electron beam technology to create circuit patterns on chips to provide finer definition and smaller images. Early in the new millennium it is expected that sizes as small as 0.025 microns will be in use.

15.2.3 Integrating techniques

Researchers are also exploring the potential of organic materials that might be used to create 'bio-chips'. Some scientists expect that optical devices will ultimately displace the semiconductor chip.

Fibre optics has significant advantages as message carriers and provides a good interface for cryogenic devices.

Through cryogenically induced superconductivity, Josephson Junction technology, clock rate speeds will be up to twice the magnitude of current technology. Cryogenic superconductivity benefits from low consumption of power and lower heat dissipation than conventional conducting media, although cryogenics has limits with regard to high density memory devices.

Early in the new millennium the 'PetaFlop' will be in place and will probably require all three technologies. A PetaFlop is a measure of computer performance and is comparable to being more than ten thousand times faster than the world's most powerful current computer.

15.2.4 Production and scale

Arthur Rock, a veteran Silicon Valley venture capitalist and one of the original investors in Intel, penned an acerbic corollary to Moore's law a few years ago. He wrote, 'The cost of capital equipment to build semiconductors will double every four years'.

He may have been optimistic. Already, a large-scale state-of-the-art chip plant costs $1.5bn. This will double within the next two or three years, and double again over a similar period, Mr Maydan (President of Applied Materials, the world's leading supplier of semiconductor production equipment) predicts that, 'Within 10 years, it seems, the $10bn chip factory may be with us'.

15.3 Principal processes

A microelectronic device based on silicon as the semiconducting material is manufactured by creating components and interconnections in a silicon substrate by depositing on it several thin films of dielectric and conductive material. A thin wafer of silicon, several inches in diameter, is modified to create several hundreds of identical miniature circuits. These circuits are only separated from each other by dicing the wafer as the final stage in producing the chip.

The various stages of IC manufacture are wafer manufacture, circuit design and mask making, and wafer processing. These activities are critically affected by the cleanliness of the process environment and the subject of clean room technology is central to integrated circuit manufacture. It could be said that clean room technology has had to be a prerequisite for effective integrated circuit manufacture. However, clean room technology is also important in other industry sectors such as aerospace, pharmaceuticals, medical, etc. The Study Group has recognised the importance of clean room technology by including a separate section on this topic. Within this section reference is made to clean room technology but for a deeper commentary on the subject the reader is referred to Chapter 17 and its section on clean room technology.

15.3.1 Wafer manufacture

Wafer manufacture is highly specialised and starts with crystal pulling from high purity silicon, where atoms attach to a small seed crystal and form a single crystal ingot. The ingot is machined to a cylindrical shape with flats introduced to identify crystal orientation and to aid the following automated activities. The cylinder of a single crystal is sliced into wafers of uniform thickness and then polished to a very high finish.

15.3.2 Design and masking

In the design and masking stage, an enlarged design of the integrated circuit is generated using computer-aided design that details components and interconnections. A pattern for each layer is duplicated on a glass photo-mask or reticle, which are manufactured with the use of similar techniques as those employed for silicon wafers, described later in this chapter.

15.3.3 Wafer processing

The various stages of wafer processing can result in typically 50 discrete steps. During deposition, circuit components and their interconnections are produced on the wafer or in thin layers of material. Complex ICs may need to have up to 20 separate layers. Wafer processing consists of deposition, photolithography, etching, and diffusion or implanting and back end.

15.3.4 Deposition

Various deposition film processes are used and in the case of epitaxial silicon a thin layer of silicon with different electrical characteristics to the underlying wafer is deposited on the wafer surface by using high-energy ions in a vacuum chamber.

Chemical vapour deposition deposits silicon nitride, silicon dioxide or polysilicon from gaseous or liquid organometallic raw material by cracking them at high temperature in a furnace and or with the use of electrical discharge plasma.

15.3.5 Other film processes

Other film processes include sputtering, where metals and their alloys and inorganic compounds are deposited from material targets in high-vacuum equipment. This is achieved by bombarding them with high-energy inert ions such as argon.

Evaporation is similar to sputtering but the source material is heated in a crucible and oxidation induces a layer of insulating silicon dioxide to be formed on the wafer surface by the introduction of oxygen or water vapour which reacts with the wafer at high temperature.

15.3.6   **Photolithography**

During the group of process steps described as photolithography, the pattern from the reticle is transferred to a mask on the wafer. A photo-resist coating is spread on to the wafer by using a jet while the wafer is spinning. The coating is a mixture of organic chemicals with photosensitive properties dissolved in a solvent. The wafer is then soft-baked at low temperature to remove residual solvent and improve the adhesion. Pattern transfer takes place when the wafer is exposed to ultraviolet light through the reticle, exposing to ultraviolet the unmasked areas of photo-resist and converting them to insoluble polymers.

During pattern development the pattern is developed in a chemical solution, typically an alkaline mixture with sodium hydroxide or ammonium hydroxide as the primary constituent. This solution removes the soluble portion of the photo-resist. The post-bake, which is carried out at a higher temperature than the soft-bake, is to increase adhesion and durability during further processing.

15.3.7   **Etching**

To replicate the pattern from the mask to the underlying material, exposed parts are etched. The etching is required to modify material selectively, leaving unaffected photo-resist and underlying layers. It is normally a tightly controlled chemical process. In wet etching the wafers are placed in baths of chemicals, normally acidic, such as in the case of etching of silicon dioxide by hydrofluoric acid. Alternatively dry etching uses a reactor chamber in which the wafers are placed and through which relatively inert gases are introduced but with a short electrical discharge. This results in reactive but short-lived etchants. The etchant and substrate products are volatile and removed with the gas stream.

15.3.8   **Diffusion/implanting**

To create IC components, such as diodes or transistors, small areas of the deposited layers or substrate silicon are doped with impurity atoms. This is achieved in the diffusion/implanting part of the process. The doping modifies the conductivity depending on the concentration of dopant. The most common dopants are arsenic, phosphorus and boron. There are two techniques — diffusion and ion implantation. In diffusion the wafer is heated and the dopant either as a vapour, gas or oxide source permeates into the wafer. Ion implantation occurs at high vacuum with the ionised dopant species, such as arsine or phosphine, bombarded on to the target wafer.

15.3.9   **Back end**

The back end operation consists of testing, assembly and packaging of the ICs. This includes characterisation of the wafer, dicing into separate chips by diamond saw, mounting of bond pads and leads and sealing.

Now that the overall process has been looked at, it may be of assistance to look at the typical construction and layout of a wafer processing plant.

15.4   Typical wafer plant

The following details illustrate what could be expected in a silicon wafer plant producing monthly some 10,000 units of 8in wafers of 0.4 microns with various types of processors such as DRAM (dynamic random access memory) and SRAM (static random access memory). As with many such fabrication facilities it is likely that the operation is a joint venture.

The construction is likely to be of a reinforced concrete frame, externally tile clad, roofs and floors of reinforced mass concrete slabs. Above and below the clean room environment on the third level reinforced concrete latticework would be in place to allow airflow. The clean room floor will have some form of sealing, such as an epoxy coating, to the porous concrete slabs. This fabrication building is also likely to be interconnected to other fabrication, support and office buildings.

Typically, the supply and exhaust air handling ducting is made of either stainless steel or polypropylene. This ducting and electrical power, lighting and control cabling will of necessity be routed between floors. The fire detection systems will include ionisation smoke detectors, thermal and flicker sensors.

The plant consists of a ground floor with a further four building floors and roof, occupying some 100,000sq ft of floor area. The ground floor would house various support operations such as the uninterruptible power supply (UPS), electrical switch rooms for gas and chemical handling equipment and vacuum pumps.

The first floor is likely to be a void under the clean room floor but will house scrubbers and supply and exhaust ducts for the clean room. Additionally, small specialised rooms for failure analysis and with high precision optical equipment and trial clean room would be located on this floor.

The clean room located on the second floor would house the photolithography equipment, which consists of high-value optical steppers, dopant introduction equipment consisting of electrical cabinets, furnaces, chemical cabinets and plasma machines.

The third floor will be essentially a void area above the clean room, but will house significant electrical switchgear for the clean room and air and chemical handling ducting will pass through this space.

Administrative offices and sealed make-up air-handling plants would be located on the fourth floor. A significant amount of computer equipment is likely to be present and this will include servers, mass storage devices and workstations.

Sprinkler fire protection is likely to be limited to the ground, first and fourth floors. The clean room is unlikely to have sprinklers. The computer system in the administrative area on the fourth floor will have carbon dioxide flooding protection.

Finally, flues, blowers, ducting, water scrubbers for the exhaust system and associated cooling towers will be sited on the roof.

15.5   Major feedstocks

Apart from the substrate materials, such as silicon and germanium, each of the processes involves a range of other substances as raw materials, carrier substitutes, dopants, solvents or etchants. For example, in chemical vapour deposition (CVD) where polysilicon is the deposited film, the raw material would be silane, the carrier gases could be argon or nitrogen and substitutes would be silicon tetrafluoride, silicon hydrides or silicon tetrachloride. Dopants will be arsine, diborane or other boron or phosphorous compounds.

In sputtering, the deposited film is likely to include aluminium, copper, silver, and nickel with the raw material as the deposited film being loaded into the chamber as the 'target'.

The acidic materials involved include hydrogen fluoride, hydrofluoric acid, hydrogen chloride, hydrochloric acid, nitric acid, sulphuric acid, oxides of nitrogen, chlorine and bromine.

Alkali materials include ammonia; and volatile organo-compounds such as butyl acetate, ethanol, acetone and xylene. Metals and their compounds used include arsenic, gallium, phosphorous and indium.

As can be readily understood many of these processes involve a resultant reaction with by-products. For example in the case of polysilicon CVD, the by-products include hydrogen and solid compounds of arsenic, boron and phosphorous.

Many of these substances are toxic and in many countries have statutory occupational exposure limits. Some national statutes and commercial association codes apply and a selection is listed here for reference purposes.

HSE	Health & Safety Executive (UK)
SoSGN	Secretary of State Process Guidance (UK)
SEMI	Semiconductor Equipment and Materials Institute (USA)
BCGA	British Compressed Gas Association (UK)

The use of these substances results in significant risk exposures in the handling, storage, fire, explosion, process and decontamination as a result of spill or fire.

15.5.1 Types of gases and their characteristics

For ease of reference a description of categories of gases is detailed below:

Asphyxiant   gases that in general do not act as poisons, but which may cause death by displacing the available oxygen in the atmosphere and reducing it to a level that will not support life.

Flammable   a gas that can form a mixture with air or other oxidants which will freely propagate a flame.

Pyrophoric   gases which may spontaneously ignite and burn in air or other oxidants. Under some conditions they may not ignite spontaneously but form a mixture with air that may subsequently explode.

Oxidising   gases which will react with flammable gases and other combustible materials in a manner chemically similar to oxygen, *i.e.* they will support combustion.

Toxic   a gas that can cause a health hazard. Various guidance notes give occupational exposure standards.

Corrosive   gases which on direct contact may cause harm to human tissue. These gases can react with some materials causing material damage and possible failure.

15.6 Maintenance

High-precision equipment operating in potentially aggressive environments and which is expected to perform continuously to tight technical tolerances requires well-planned and well-executed maintenance. The drive for this comes from the fact that most of the equipment will have a planned high utilisation with any downtime regarded as having a negative impact on the financial viability and performance of the plant.

In addition to the general issue of maintenance, the issues specific to this industry include the need to overcome limited access both from a physical point of view and also from a need to contend with toxic substances. Permit-to-work systems are required to carefully control safe methods of working, to ensure gas-free areas and environments that safely support human life.

As has already been indicated, the safe systems of work also need to carefully control hot working to prevent fire and explosions.

Not only are the substances likely to be toxic or flammable, they are also likely to include corrosive substances. For containment vessels involving these substances, a programme of non-destructive testing to ensure continuing integrity is required.

With the type of equipment in use, such as optical equipment, it is also likely that specialists from original equipment manufacturers will be employed to carry out any necessary maintenance on a contract basis. This involvement of external contractors can also pose problems that arise because visitors do not fully understand the individual conditions of a particular plant. Therefore induction or assimilation training for contractors is important to ensure accidents arising out of unfamiliarity are avoided.

15.7 Monitoring and protection

Although monitoring and protection of machinery and associated spaces is important, it is suggested that protection should take place at the earliest time in a facility's existence at the time of design and construction.

Selection of materials, methods of fabrication and installation and working practices during construction should be considered in as much detail as when the machinery is operational. For example, although air movement/ventilation systems may use polypropylene piping, this selection of material provides a high fire load construction that will give off persistent toxic chemicals in the event of a fire and is easily ignited when normal repair techniques such as welding or cutting are involved. This selection in this geometry, *i.e.* tubular ventilation, enables rapid spread of fire and fuelling of a fire. In a set-up that includes tubular ventilation, a fire can be fuelled and can spread very rapidly. Equally important, from a fire exposure viewpoint, is the choice of basic construction materials and services incorporated into the facility, *e.g.* walls, doors, windows, service transfer points, air-conditioning and piping. The presence of liquids and flammable gases are also serious issues.

The environment within an integrated circuit facility is likely, as has already been indicated, to involve volatile materials. The use of these substances results in significant risk exposures in handling, storage, fire, explosion, process and decontamination as a result of a spill or fire. To identify unplanned release, detectors and sensors should be provided and these should be selected for the range of substances and levels of exposure that are acceptable. Indicators will allow for contingent plans to be actioned to minimise any leakage, to remove spillages safely and to protect personnel.

In addition to release and clean-up monitoring and protection, fires are a major cause of losses in integrated plants. These have primarily come about through electrical faults and short circuits and poor working practices when hot work is being undertaken.

In fire monitoring and protection it is important to have sensors to detect atmospheres that are potentially combustible or explosive as well as fire detectors. Smoke and heat detectors are normally provided and are interlinked with fire alarms, fire-fighting, extraction and damper systems. Specifically, very early smoke detection (VESDA) systems may be installed in the return air circuit.

In the past, manufacturing plants have been provided with fire-fighting systems including halon, carbon dioxide and water sprinklers. These may include fixed and portable systems, and significantly, are located within ductwork used for the removal of process fumes. However, it should be noted that there is a significant risk of a violent reaction between halongenated extinguishing agents and diborane and silane process gasses.

A number of fire protection and fire-fighting standards are set out below as a guide to available information and standards that have been used within the industry either specifically or from experience in other industries, but which are in common use.

NFPA-10	Portable fire extinguishers
NFPA-13	Standard for the installation of sprinkler systems
NFPA-70	National electric code
NFPA-72	National fire alarm code
NFPA-75	Protection of electronic computer/data processing equipment
NFPA-318	Clean room detection and protection
BS 5445	Specifications for components of automatic fire detection systems
BS 6266	Code for electronic data processing installations

In addition to environmental and fire risks, significant occupational exposure risks are also present and it is normal to monitor personnel who are considered to be at risk.

15.8   Planning and operations

The machines and processes depend on high accuracy, high speed, miniaturisation, some sterile environments and some aggressive environments, with operations normally 24 hours a day working.

Operations require to be both planned and detailed, with 'what if' contingency plans being in place and that are tested and audited periodically.

Specifically, there should be a fire emergency plan (FEP) which includes 'what to do in the first 24 hours — for damaged electronic equipment and magnetic data.' It should include information on restoration techniques, details of on-call specialists and a plan for final and intermediate stocks of high value to be removed from high risk areas as soon as practicable.

The importance of uninterruptible power supply to this manufacturing process has been stressed. There is a need for independent back-up generators to facilitate a controlled shutdown of the plant, in the event of a failure of public electricity supply, say through a natural catastrophe, so that work in progress may be salvaged.

15.9   Critical areas

The preceding text has covered many of the critical areas of integrated circuit manufacturing. However, the following summarises the critical areas and provides some practical examples.

Two fire incidents involving the manufacturing of integrated circuits in 1996–97 are understood to have resulted in losses estimated in the order of US$150m and US$265m respectively.

In the first of these losses a fire started on the fourth floor outside a clean room, probably originating at one of the CVD cleaning machines. Extensive fire damage affected the support area and the smoke/corrosion damage to the equipment on the fourth floor. Heat and smoke damage affected the facilities on the fifth floor as well as water damage to the facilities on the first and third floors. The plant was in the process of erection, with some buildings and plant having already been handed over and therefore insured by property insurers. The total cost of the claim was in the region of US$150m, which was shared equally between the erection all risks and the property insurers.

The second incident similarly concerned extensive fire damage during the time that an expansion programme was underway. The operational property insurance was affected as well as the erection all risks policy. While repairs were being undertaken to a polypropylene exhaust system a fire was discovered in the pipes. The fire proved impossible to control and the spread was not contained. Total damage sustained was estimated at approximately US$265m, again shared roughly 60%/40% between the property and the EAR insurers respectively.

In both claims damage to plant, machinery and equipment was substantial.

The following critical areas — financial, processes using toxic and contaminating chemicals, fire/explosion, and human factors — should be considered.

15.9.1   Financial aspects

- New projects fast-track construction to take advantage of new technology with rapid handover from the erection policy to the operational policy.

- Rapid redundancy of machinery in dynamic industry.

- High concentration of values.

- Loss values are disproportionate to size of incident, *i.e.* small incident very large loss.

- Loss mitigation delayed by access to site of loss restricted — site controlled by the fire brigade and other statutory bodies.

- Need for contingency and disaster recovery plans.

- Benefit of seamless handover or exposure between EAR/CAR and operational covers.

15.9.2   Processes using toxic and contaminating chemicals

- Time to gain access to mitigate loss due to dangerous environment.

- Toxic compounds and fallout time to decontaminate buildings and machinery.

- Building structure materials, *i.e.* concrete absorbing contaminants in clean rooms following a fire.

- Delay in access to site of loss — site controlled by the fire brigade and other statutory bodies.

- Occupational exposure limits to toxic substances.

15.9.3 **Fire/explosion**

● Some process materials are pyrophoric, such as silane gas, which is commonly encountered.

● High fire loads with process materials such as solvents.

● Clean rooms, large non-compartmented areas.

● Clean rooms large air flows — ventilation and exhaust.

● Reluctance by operators to sprinkler high value/high exposure areas.

● Use of plastic piping increases fire load, speed and spread of fire.

● Production of toxic and process contaminants with difficulty in extinguishing fires.

● Prevention of reignition, *e.g.* one example of fire under control by about eight hours after first noticed. However, some windows which were opened to remove smoke allowed fire to reignite.

● Equipment safety standards. Experience has shown high incidence of fire started from electrical faults in machinery.

15.9.4 **Human factors**

● Contractors unfamiliar with working environment.

● Inappropriate working methods.

● Contractor control and management.

● Personnel selection/motivation.

● In-depth training of response team.

16 Other manufacturing industries

16.1 Introduction

In the preceding chapters the significant or 'major' manufacturing industries were examined. In this chapter some other important industries are reviewed, with their exposure characteristics described in summary format.

16.2 Smelting and refining

Smelting and refining industries can be immediately associated with mining operations where the detailed exposures and characteristics are described in Chapter 13, 'Mineral extraction and primary processing plants'. They do include, however, mobile plant, crushing mills, conveyor belts, material sizing machinery and separation machinery. All of these can be classified as heavy-duty design, and in some cases unusually large with attendant high capacities. This in itself provides problems of replacement related to availability, delivery time and access to remote sites.

In common with iron and steel plants (see Chapter 14), these plants can present the usual problems relating to furnace operations such as fires, breakouts, refractory failures and explosions caused by flue gas or product contamination.

In the product lines, internal/external power supply failures can lead to pot-line freeze-ups with attendant product removal and refractory replacement, all of which can be expensive in terms of both physical damage and business interruption. Where extrusion processes are used there are risks of hydraulic/component failure, fire and uncontrolled product runaways.

An efficient risk management system is essential and an integral or emergency supply system, including a back-up transformer with pot-line shunt equipment is desirable. If power supplies are lost, pot freezing may be delayed by the use of thermic lances, which should be gas powered for preference.

16.3 Food/drink/pharmaceutical

In the food and drink and pharmaceutical industry sectors, the dominant loss potential is contamination and therefore clean/sterile conditions are obligatory. Stock storage facilities are also a common area of losses due to infestations, fires or failure of the ventilation or refrigeration systems. This exposure may be exacerbated by the practice of large single storage facilities.

Many of these industries utilise sophisticated refrigeration machinery and systems where compressor or component failures can lead to heavy production losses or missed critical crop ripening peaks.

A fire in these plants can have disastrous consequences owing to not only physical damage but also to contamination of the product and machinery. Burning chemicals and cables can cause serious corrosion of stainless steel equipment, which may have been selected for hygiene purposes and not for its anti-corrosion properties. Chloride attack can lead to extensive replacement and/or cleaning operations due to microbiological degradation.

The electronic control systems and close tolerance packaging, bottling or other lines can also be affected. When an incident occurs, the rapid use of specialist cleaning and refurbishment contractors is of paramount importance if the loss is to be minimised.

Baking ovens as well as boilers and furnaces used in the supply of process water or steam are sources of fires and explosions. This aspect of risk exposure may be heightened where waste products are used to fire boilers such as in the case of bagasse in sugar processing.

Conveyor systems can jam or become misaligned and storage bins for the raw or finished products can be subject to dust explosions, most notably in the case of ingredients such as flour, pasta, custard powder and similar products.

Some gases or chemicals used in the product lines will be toxic or volatile, and special precautions are necessary in the selection of materials, design and operation of equipment.

The machinery used in many of these industries is very sophisticated and operates at very high production rates. Therefore a failure in a relatively minor component could lead to a serious domino effect. Business interruption losses can escalate quickly and there needs to be an efficient maintenance system in operation along with a suitable spare parts supply. The maintenance system should be supported by contingency plans for replacement of any machinery, either from the original equipment manufactures (OEM) or alternative suppliers.

It will be appreciated that the temperature of storage for frozen foods is critical along with the temperatures attained in the flash freezing process, and in the event of a refrigeration plant failure, there should be a contingency plan to preserve the products, which might include alternative storage arrangements at another cold store.

16.4   Printing works

Apart from the obvious fire hazards due to the presence of chemicals, which are likely to be solvent based, and paper storage and paper usage in this type of industry, the major exposures probably relate to the size and high speed at which the equipment functions.

The machinery consists of rollers, drives, gears, and chains in a series of combinations. Some rollers are heated. A drive breakdown or introduction of a foreign object (a constant risk) could, in the worst case, lead to a complete machine failure. Many of the rollers are highly polished, coated or are very accurately machined and shaped. Therefore, what might be termed minor deformations can lead to the scrapping of expensive components. It is therefore essential that spares are readily available or that there is ready access to manufacturers or competent repair facilities. However, it should be noted that although the overall machine may be highly complex, it is made up of a large number of individual, often basic, components.

Handling of paper supplies is a critical operation, as dropping or mishandling of the often very heavy rolls can lead to machinery damage or misalignment.

Some printing works operate very old machinery and the degree of obsolescence related to obtaining spares or suitably matched machinery should be considered in the context of business interruption insurance cover.

16.5   Glass

This industry utilises fired refractory lined furnaces to produce molten glass to manufacture the various end products, such as sheet glass and bottles. As with other industries of this nature, there are the attendant risks of refractory failures, breakouts and freeze-ups caused by damage to the power supply, complete power failure or chemical attack on refractory or mortar. Flue gas explosions with the attendant associated physical damage and interruption to business are also ever-present risks. Cool-down times prior to assessment of damage and the effecting of repairs along with start-up times can be extensive due to thermal gradients imposed by the refractory materials and construction. Well-maintained control systems, fire protection and an emergency power supply are essential considerations.

This industry utilises high speed production methods with computerised control, and therefore the control and back-up systems together with readily available spares and/or machinery suppliers is necessary to maintain production in the event of a machinery failure.

16.6   Cars/aircraft

It would not be possible within the scope of this section to describe in any great detail these industries, which have some common characteristics.

In general terms they are both heavily reliant upon the supply of finished goods from subcontractors, although in some cases they operate their own production facilities for major components. In the case of car manufacturing, this could include foundry and continuous casting lines, engine production facilities and body panel pressing lines, where the risks are as described on other facilities.

Many car and aero-manufacturing factories are basically assembly plants and the main risks to these are related to ensuring a constant supply of parts to feed production. Multiple quantities of suppliers are involved in this supply chain, each industry having its own individual peculiarities, but having risk factors common to industries already described, such as

● Fire and explosion — paint/oils/plastic/fabrics/chemicals/coatings/solvents/dust/storage/furnaces/gases, etc.

● Automatic production lines — spare parts/supply of new machines/computer control problems/robotic software

● Electric power supply — factory failure/external supply failure/ emergency supplies.

Maintenance, with monitoring and planned or programmed schemes is essential.

Fire or explosion is a constant risk where painting facilities are located. Any computer hardware or software failures can lead to serious losses, therefore adequate back-up systems are a necessity, as well as contingency planning if reprogramming or replacement equipment becomes necessary.

A great deal of specialised tooling and equipment, such as robots, is utilised in the car industry, and therefore de-bottlenecking exercises are essential to identify and reduce and/or eradicate the heaviest risks. CNC spark erosion and other computer-controlled machines are widely used in production facilities, and they can malfunction.

However, except in the case of major fire, flood or other such perils rarely do these plants provide significant losses for machinery insurers. An exception would be a machinery failure critical to production requirements that could not be repaired or replaced in the short term, and resultant business interruption losses accrue.

16.7   Sugar refining

Sugar refineries are normally located near sugar plantations where the sugar crops (cane or beet) are grown and harvested. The production is highly seasonal and the timing of the harvest collection, which has to be closely co-ordinated with the processing, is crucial to output and quality. The season is typically three to five months and during this period the machinery works flat out. This has implications in respect of the business interruption risk. It should be noted that the effects on the business may extend beyond the current harvest season, as an inability to collect the harvest can lead to poorer yields in the next season, if the crop is left to rot in the fields. The harvested crop cannot be stored for long before it starts to deteriorate.

After the raw materials for sugar production are extracted through a process of crushing, heating and refining, the residue materials, known as bagasse, are salvaged. Bagasse is used as fuel to fire the steam boilers, which are important to the overall process.

While this makes economical sense, the combustion of bagasse can create an aggressive environment and if not controlled correctly, and can lead to premature wearing of the boiler. Another feature in the safe operation of boilers at a sugar refinery is the risk of sugary substances entering the boiler feedwater circuit. This may cause damage to the boiler tubes or the boiler plates and in extreme cases this can lead to an explosion.

16.8   Textile mills

The dominant exposure relates to the risk of fire where the fibres are handled or stored. Smoke and pollutants from a fire can spread via service distribution systems or otherwise into production areas. Foreign bodies should be screened from the raw material before the spinning process commences (e.g. magnetic separators).

Dust is a constant fire risk hazard, and so a high standard of housekeeping and dust collection throughout the mill is a vital factor. Fire-fighting facilities should be of the highest standard. Where synthetic fibres are involved, the exposure may be more akin to a chemical works, with the additional hazard of explosion present.

Following a fire and its extinguishment, urgent attention is required in cleaning, preservation and availability of replacement machinery.

17 Cross-industry topics

17.1 Introduction

This chapter deals with some important topics that span more than one industrial sector or apply in general terms to all sectors. These are

- clean rooms
- general maintenance of machinery
- control systems
- industrial gas turbines.

Each topic is important in its own right and should be of wide interest but some may be used to supplement other chapters of this Study Report. For example, 'clean rooms' are found in many different sectors of industry, such as food, pharmaceutical, aerospace and semiconductor plants. Therefore, in the latter case, this topic may be read in conjunction with Chapter 15, 'Integrated circuit manufacturing plants'.

Similarly, the topic of gas turbines will be relevant to those interested in power generation (see Chapter 9) or the oil, gas and petrochemical industry (see Chapter 10), where the use of these rapidly developing machines is widespread. They also represent a high potential risk exposure to insurers.

17.2 Clean rooms

In recent years, the application of clean room technology has spread from manufacturing to such other fields as aerospace, bioscience, pharmaceuticals, medicine, food processing and computing in general. This expansion of technology has brought increased experience and knowledge not only in the diversified requirements for air cleanliness, but also in the methods that should be employed to meet these requirements.

Since the necessity for control of airborne particulates has affected many manufacturers and indirectly governmental activities, the need for standardisation has been recognised, since their mutual aim is to make places of work cleaner and safer. Consequently, established guidelines for design, definitions, and air cleanliness classes for clean rooms and clean workstations have been established, such as in the United States, where they are incorporated within the Federal Standard 209B.

17.2.1 Uses of clean rooms

Clean rooms are commonly used in the following types of operations:

- Electronics industry

  - fabrication of semiconductor devices
  - production of miniaturised parts
  - assembly of electronic instruments.

- Aerospace industry

  - assembly of miniaturised components

- assembly of electronic instrumentation/components of space vehicles
- research in medical biophysics
- testing of space vehicles.

- Research and educational institutions

  - in medical and pharmaceutical research
  - in the fields of biology, chemistry, electronics, physics, etc.

- Pharmaceuticals

  - production of contamination-free pharmaceuticals and biological materials.

- Radioactive materials industry

  - segregation of materials to eliminate radioactive contamination in research and industry
  - production of fuel rods and related materials
  - assembly of components for radioactive devices.

- Others

  - food industry
  - plastics industry
  - photographic industry.

17.2.2   **Basic details**

A clean room is a controlled environment facility in which all incoming air passes through a filter capable of removing 99.97% of all particles which are 0.2 microns in diameter and larger. In a clean room the temperature, pressure, and humidity are controlled. External sources of particulate contaminants are excluded, and internal sources are controlled to required cleanliness levels.

Environment cleanliness is measured as a function of the particle size in microns (micrometer). One micron is equal to 0.000040in (one-millionth of a metre).

An electrical uninterruptible power supply (UPS) or emergency stand-by power system is needed in clean rooms to prevent product damage during minimal power outages. The configuration of the UPS system consists of a rectifier, battery, and inverter operating continuously in the power line. These are available in sizes ranging from 250VA to over 500KVA.

During normal operation, the primary electrical power supplies the system via the rectifier and inverter and also charges the battery that is 'floated' on the direct current (DC) bus and kept fully charged. In the event of a primary power failure the inverter converts battery power from DC to alternating current (AC) for use by the critical loads. It is the inverter which alone governs the characteristics of the AC output, and any voltage or frequency fluctuations or transients present on the utility power system are completely isolated from the critical load.

In the event of a momentary or prolonged loss of power, the battery (which is floated on the DC bus) will supply sufficient power to the inverter to maintain its output for a specified time. This may be for a few minutes to several hours, until the battery has discharged to a predetermined minimum voltage.

17.2.3 Classification of clean rooms (United States origin)

The general classes are Class 1, Class 10, Class 1000, Class 10,000 and Class 100,000. Class 1 rooms are not very common. To put the cleanliness in perspective, normal air is Class 1,000,000 or greater.

- *Class 1* Particle count not to exceed 1 particle per cu ft (0.035 particle per litre) for particle sizes of 0.2 microns and larger.

- *Class 10* Particle count not to exceed 10 particles per cu ft (0.35 particles per litre) for particle sizes of 0.3 microns and larger.

- *Class 100* Particle count not to exceed 100 particles per cu ft (3.5 particles per litre) for particle sizes of 0.5 microns and larger.

- *Class 1000* Particle count not to exceed 1000 particles per cu ft (35 particles per litre) for particle sizes of 0.5 microns and larger.

- *Class 10,000* Particle count not to exceed 10,000 particles per cu ft (350 particles per litre) for particle sizes of 0.5 microns and larger.

- *Class 100,000* Particle count not to exceed 100,000 particles per cu ft (3500 particles per litre) for particle sizes of 0.5 microns and larger.

17.2.4 Technology

17.2.4.1 Clean room airflow design

There are two design concepts for clean rooms in current use — conventional flow and laminar flow.

The conventional flow clean room type uses standard, but filtered, air-handling and distribution systems. The air normally enters from the ceiling and takes a random path exiting near the floor. These rooms are generally used for classes 10,000 or 100,000. However, conventional flow clean rooms can contain workstations with hoods for their own laminar flow conditioned air supply to provide a high degree of control of contaminants for critical operations.

In laminar flow clean rooms the airflow is in one direction and parallel elements of air flow remain parallel in one plane (*i.e.*, flow is not turbulent). In this type of facility, one wall or ceiling is made up of a bank of high-efficiency particulate air (HEPA) filters and on the opposite wall or floor is the exhaust grill. Theoretically, after being forced through the HEPA filters, the air will move directly to the exhaust grill across the room in a straight line. The air stream makes only a single pass through the clean room before being returned to the filters for recirculation. This reduces the likelihood of deposition and re-suspension of light particulate matter.

Laminar flow clean rooms can have horizontal airflow from wall to wall or vertical airflow from ceiling to floor. Laminar flow, however, exists in such a room only when it is unoccupied. Furniture, equipment, personnel, and any movement in the room will interfere with the laminar flow. Because the air streamlines must divert around these objects, eddy currents are created that interfere with the laminar flow. The chief advantage of a laminar flow room is that a large mass of moving air entrains and sweeps particles of contamination downstream as they are generated and made airborne. This is essential when high levels of cleanliness must be achieved. Only a laminar flow clean room can achieve Class 100 or less.

17.2.4.2 **Laminar flow workstation**

The laminar flow workstation is used to provide a small working space of particularly clean environment when this is more economical than providing a complete clean room of that standard. Workstations are often used in conventional flow clean rooms. A laminar flow workstation is a modular unit that usually accommodates one or two operators. It provides a working area of a higher cleanliness environment than the clean room that contains it.

17.2.4.3 **Fume exhaust**

In addition to the general air-handling system for clean rooms, there may also be a fume exhaust system to control hazardous gases and vapours. The fume exhaust system picks up air and fumes from workstations and equipment cabinets, and discharges them outside, typically using a water wash scrubber to remove the contaminants from the air stream. This system normally has an emergency/stand-by power system for the fan(s).

17.2.4.4 **'SuperFab'**

The current trend in the design of microelectronic fabrication facilities is towards the 'Super-Fab', which is a large facility with modularised clean rooms (Classes 1 to 1000) contained within a large service structure, which among other things, acts as a common return air plenum. There is high potential for loss due to particulate contamination.

17.3 Environment

17.3.1 **Hazards**

Clean rooms present loss prevention problems due to their high intrinsic value and importance to other processes, taking full account of the inherent operating complexities and delicate nature of the product. The demands for extreme cleanliness required in the work performed within a clean room makes it susceptible to the combustion products from a small fire and other types of contaminants causing major shutdown time and costly decontamination clean up. The most important recommendation in the clean room protection system is reliable detection, early suppression/extinguishment, and control of contamination in the incipient stages. Also, minimising sources of contamination and ignition sources, including prevention of static electrical discharges, is important. Workstations floors and doors require to be linked to a satisfactory electrical earthing arrangement.

The presence of people contributes to the contamination hazard and in an effort to minimise the hazard full protective clothing and masks are worn to eliminate deposits of dead skin cells or body hair.

17.3.2 **Fire and explosion**

Fires, explosions and related hazards in environments surrounding clean rooms present a serious loss potential because of the stringent control required over air contaminants. Relatively small incidents can contaminate clean rooms and can result in substantial losses.

Clean rooms frequently have a combustible interior finish. The operations in these rooms may also involve the use of flammable and corrosive gases and liquids. Clean rooms may also be exposed by other occupancies within a building. They may sometimes take fresh or make-up air from within a plant building, posing possible contamination problems.

Concealed spaces above the ceiling or below the floor are also common in these rooms. They are frequently used as service spaces or air-handling plenums. Flammable liquid or gas piping, combustible ductwork, cables, etc., may also pass through these spaces. All of these factors contribute to potential losses.

Rapid air movement and high recirculation rates can adversely affect the detection of fires and the actuation of automatic sprinklers. Adjacent clean areas sharing the same air-handling system which have no air locks between them also increase the potential for spread of contaminants in case of fire.

17.3.3   Smoke hazards

The loss potential from smoke damage is very high, even if sprinkler protection is provided. Fire retardant plastic material is often used for fume exhaust ducts. If the duct material poses a major fire hazard it may warrant specific sprinkler protection. However, even a minor fire in these ducts can produce large quantities of smoke, which is often corrosive and very damaging to the room equipment and the product. There are approved ducts available that can be used safely for the removal of smoke.

The increasing use of plastic wall panels in clean rooms actually increases the fuel available to a fire within the room. Therefore, installation of these panels where occupancies are susceptible to damage from smoke or corrosive fumes should be avoided.

Whether filters are combustible or not, they are soon covered with combustible dust and dirt which can be ignited easily and spread flame and smoke rapidly through the room. Special measures should be taken to lessen the potential damage caused by fire in the filtering system.

17.3.4   Gases, vapours and fumes

Contamination may also result from the release of gases, vapours or fumes into the clean room atmosphere, which may affect the final product. The release of corrosive gases or liquids into a clean room may not only affect the product but also corrode the delicate instrumentation in the room. Flammable gases may cause a fire or explosion. Fumes, usually the result of either chemical or thermal decomposition, may produce serious contamination of the product as well as to the processing equipment.

17.3.5   Moisture

Water (or the lack of it) may be a serious problem for some processes used in clean rooms. High humidity conditions can result in corrosion of instrumentation, which then can be accelerated by the presence of corrosive gases, vapours or fumes. Low humidity may increase the fire hazard posed by static electricity.

17.3.6   Temperature

Temperature fluctuations can adversely affect the accuracy of the sensitive instrumentation.

17.3.7   Pressure

Differential positive pressures are maintained between rooms and atmosphere (or adjoining non-clean rooms) to assure outward airflow progressively from the cleanest spaces to the least clean to provide efficient contamination control.

17.3.8 **Vibration**

Vibration may affect ultra-sensitive instrumentation and cause re-suspension of light particle matter, increasing the contamination hazard.

17.3.9 **Biological materials**

In media and pharmaceutical research as well as in pharmaceutical production, contamination from biological materials may produce serious problems. Contamination may bring about the complete shutdown of the facilities as well as the loss of valuable products.

17.3.10 **Radiation**

The release of radioactive materials due to fire, explosion, fracture of shielding, faulty ventilation systems, etc., can seriously affect the operation or process in a clean room.

17.4 Control of clean room hazards

17.4.1 **Fire protection**

A fire in a clean room or a clean workstation can cause extensive smoke and water damage if it is not adequately protected. Providing a water sprinkler system as a first line of protection, however, can lessen smoke and water damage. A VESDA system should be considered within the specification, equipped with appropriate devices, *i.e.* air sampling, particle counter and cloud chamber, that are sufficiently sensitive to detect minute traces of smoke. Water is the preferred extinguishing medium taking full account of the protocol to restrict the use of halons and other chlorofluorocarbons. However, some older rooms will be encountered where Halon 1301 is still the first line of protection and sprinklers used as back-up protection. It is possible that room-flooding Halon 1301 may be ineffective in large clean rooms because the large airflow common in the room will dilute the halon, defeating the protection. This has been overcome by installing local Halon 1301 systems in individual workstations or benches, if it is not practical to protect the entire room.

Sprinkler protection is the most reliable protection against fires. However, at some facilities, such as class 1, 10, 100 and 1000 clean rooms handling radioactive or highly reactive materials, there exists the danger of reactivity with certain materials and contamination by water run-off.

17.4.2 **Clean room environmental control**

Recent developments have produced monitoring devices that detect and indicate directly the amount of contamination deposited on a given surface. The equipment monitors contamination caused by changes in temperature, humidity, pressure, particulate distribution, radiation, noise and vibration, and the presence of gases, vapours, fumes, etc.

Appropriate equipment is selected and monitoring routines established to measure air-cleanliness levels under normal use conditions, so that conformity with the specified air cleanliness class may be determined.

17.4.3 Smoke control

Smoke control is an important factor because clean room occupancies are highly susceptible to smoke damage. Recent losses prove smoke damage to be a substantial portion of the total loss amount.

While air-conditioning systems provide a ready means of spreading smoke and corrosive gases throughout clean rooms, they can be designed to control the smoke movement in a beneficial way. The fume-exhaust system can also be used for smoke removal if adequately designed for such purposes.

Processes in clean rooms sometimes involve the liberation of corrosive fumes, which must be exhausted. Due to the corrosive nature of these fumes, typical metal ductwork cannot be used for the fume exhaust systems. Consequently, plastic ducts are used instead.

Approved plastic ducts may be used for fume removal without sprinklers or with sprinkler protection as specified.

In addition to fume exhaust, it is recommended that a smoke-control system be installed within clean rooms. When smoke exhaust is warranted in addition to fume exhaust, one of the following is needed:

- Plastic duct which is specifically approved for both fume and smoke exhaust. The capacity of this system should be designed specifically for both fume and smoke control.

- Metal duct (such as stainless steel) which can withstand the corrosive environment and which is designed specifically for both fume and smoke control.

- A separate, independent smoke-exhaust system. Typically, this means the plastic duct system will be used for fume removal and a sheet metal duct system (properly designed) will be used for smoke removal.

When an approved plastic duct system or a single metal duct system is used for smoke control, it should be verified that it has been sized and the fan capacity has been properly designed to satisfy the smoke removal criteria. The system designed for fume exhaust only will not be sufficient for smoke exhaust. The smoke removal system will generally require larger diameter ducts and fans with greater capacity. Therefore the system should be designed to maintain the protected area at least 0.20in. water gauge (50 Pa) pressure higher than the fire area.

17.4.4 Air-conditioning and exhaust systems

The ventilation systems are made up of three separate components. These are general air-handling systems for heating, cooling, humidity control and particulate control; exhaust ventilation systems for the capture and removal of unwanted/hazardous materials; and airborne particulate level control systems which provide localised reductions in particulate loads in 'clean room' fabrication areas.

17.4.5 Illustrative losses

Case 1 Lack of smoke control contributed to extensive contamination damage. Sprinklers in the ducts controlled a fire in plastic exhaust ducts in an integrated circuit area, but extensive damage resulted from recirculation of smoke and soot throughout the clean rooms. This was a one-storey computer manufacturing facility with automatic sprinkler protection in the clean rooms and on 20–40ft (6–12m) centres in the fibreglass-reinforced plastic ducts. The facility was divided into several separate rooms (with separate air-circulating systems).

A fire was caused by the ignition of silane (pyrophone in air) and hydrogen in the fibreglass-reinforced plastic duct. Plant personnel unsuccessfully fought the fire with fire extinguishers. A 1–1.5in (38.1mm) hose was used to control the fire, in conjunction with three sprinklers that operated in the ducts and prevented the fire from spreading throughout the duct system.

However, smoke and soot were distributed throughout the clean rooms causing extensive damage to the HEPA filters, equipment, the building and the items being processed.

Case 2 Lack of contamination control resulted in extensive smoke and water damage. Automatic sprinklers controlled a fire of electrical origin in a wash booth in a semiconductor manufacturing facility, preventing a disastrous loss. However, unsprinklered fibreglass-reinforced plastic and aluminium ducts collapsed as a result of heat exposure, allowing considerable smoke and water damage. The direct fire damage was in the immediate area of the wash booths in the die preparation area. Water on the floor in the area of the incident was about 8in (203.2mm) deep and spread to cover about 40% of the floor area on the second floor. It penetrated openings in the floor, dripping on to the diode assembly area, the cafeteria, and the machine shop on the first floor. Smoke was deposited throughout the die preparation area. When the exhaust duct collapsed, smoke was drawn back into the ion implant area, causing extensive damage.

Case 3 Successful operation of the sprinkler protection and smoke control avoided extensive damage. An electrical fire in a clean room resulted in damage to a laminar flow booth, bench and several microscopes. However, due to the adequate sprinkler protection, smoke control system, and quick action taken by all involved plant personnel, damage was confined to the packaging and inspection room. These factors greatly minimised the damage.

Case 4 A good plant emergency organisation prevented a major contamination loss. Malfunction of a valve controlling flow of corrosive fluids allowed the spill of corrosive liquid (silicon tetrachloride) in a semiconductor plant, exposing electronic equipment, process equipment, and piping to the corrosive gas. Plant personnel shut off the return air-conditioning system while leaving the supply and fume exhaust on, which helped prevent spread of fumes to adjacent areas. The liquid spill was neutralised with a solution of ammonium hydroxide and mopped up.

Case 5 Lack of contamination control resulted in extensive damage. A fire of electrical origin started in a polypropylene tank equipped with an electric circulating pump and immersion heater. Two automatic sprinklers controlled this fire, in a semiconductor manufacturing plant. However, smoke and water damage in the clean room area was extensive.

Case 6 Lack of sprinkler protection resulted in a catastrophic loss. A fire originated in a newly built building used for the manufacture of integrated circuits on a large scale. The 76,396sq ft (7,100sq m) reinforced concrete building was divided into several separate rooms for diffusion, masking, photolithography-etching, etc., and was protected with 1.5in (38.1mm) hose but no sprinkler protection.

The fire started at about 8:30am during normal plant operation, when operators smelled something burning and noticed a small column of smoke rising in the vicinity of an exhaust gas duct. The duct was made of polypropylene and was located in the ceiling, just above the burn box of the chemical vapour deposition equipment. The operators immediately attacked the fire with hand-held halon extinguishers. However, they had little success since the fire had spread throughout the duct system in the ceiling.

Thirty-five fire appliances (including chemical appliances) attended the scene, but they did not initially use water because the owner of the plant feared that water would ruin the product. Fire fighters at first used foam extinguishers but finally had to resort to using water from hoses. From the initial stage of fire fighting, a large quantity of smoke and poisonous gas was generated in the ceiling, and the room temperature rose quickly owing to the closed structure of the building. The fire was extinguished by 1:00pm.

As a result of the fire, smoke and soot were distributed in the diffusion room, causing extensive damage to the equipment, the building, and items being processed. The fire was caused by the combustion of unburned silane and ammonia escaping in the exhaust gas duct.

Case 7 Lack of preventative maintenance resulted in extensive contamination damage. A cylinder of carbon tetrachloride ruptured through a mechanical failure, releasing a large corrosive vapour cloud, which was circulated by the air-conditioning system. Damage to work in process was extensive and a large business interruption loss was incurred.

17.5 General protection

Planning means not only designing and supervising the facility for the specific use of the product to be handled but also including the procedures to be followed in the event of an emergency. It should include in the design, control of all known or possible hazards to the clean room. The recommendations should also include a programme of preventative maintenance for the equipment.

17.6 Recommendations

17.6.1 Construction and location

- Operations within the building should be arranged in separate zones according to their clean room classification, and in a manner compatible with operating efficiency. The facility should be located, where possible, in a fire resistive or non-combustible building or area specially designed for the purposes and be well separated or cut off from other areas. The cut-off should have a fire resistant rating commensurate with both the clean room and exposed area hazards and values.

- Clean rooms, ventilating ducts, and equipment should be constructed of non-combustible materials as far as practicable. Where clean rooms adjoin, partitions should have at least a one-hour fire rating.

- Clean rooms should be located to minimise external exposure from fires and other hazards. Locations adjacent to or in storeys below and above anything more severe than ordinary hazard occupancy should be avoided. Floors over clean rooms should be made watertight.

- Fire retardant plastic panels prone to producing large quantities of smoke should not be used in the construction of clean rooms. Non-combustible panels should be used instead.

17.6.2 Occupancy

- Consideration should be given to minimise the size of clean rooms within practical limits of functions. Separation of clean areas is desirable to minimise damage in the event of fire or related hazards.

- Air locks should be provided between adjoining clean areas to minimise damage (contamination) in the event of fire or related hazard. If services must be provided through a concealed space, the services should preferably be run beneath the clean room or in service corridors if provided and the spaces should be protected.

- Ordinary combustibles and flammable liquids should be kept to a minimum within clean rooms. If combustibles must be stored in clean rooms, suitable non-combustible storage cabinets should be provided. Flammable liquids should be stored in approved flammable liquid cabinets. The cabinets should be vented to a flammable vapour exhaust system if available.

- Where flammable gases are used within clean rooms, the cylinder or bulk tanks supply should be located outside the clean area in a non-combustible cut-off area. The control valve for the gases should be readily accessible. Hydrogen may be stored in bulk cryogenic tanks at semiconductor plants. The valves associated with this equipment should be of the fail-safe type — that is, if they are actuated by air pneumatically for example, in the event of failure of the air supply, the valve will naturally move to the closed position. These valves should be connected to the gas detection or fire system and have a provision for remote shut-off from a safe position.

- Where flammable gases are used in process areas, approved combustible gas detectors should be provided at the ceiling above the process and in the sprinklered ventilated cabinets to activate an alarm if a significant concentration is detected; an accessible emergency or automatic gas shut-off should be provided.

- An emergency uninterruptible power or other reliable stand-by power supply should be provided.

- Electrical equipment and wiring should be installed in accordance with the National Electrical Code.

- Bench stations handling different materials which can be flammable, corrosive or can cause other type of contamination, should be arranged as follows:

  - The contaminants' fumes should be exhausted individually, or similar elements should be manifolded together if feasible and exhausted as a group to lessen the probability of contamination to other processes during normal operation or as a result of an accident. Acids and flammable vapours should not be exhausted through a common fume exhaust system.

  - Disposal of used or spilled chemicals should be via separate acid and solvent drainage systems connected to individual pieces of process equipment and workstations. The flammable waste drains should be trapped.

  - The solvents, acids or other contaminants should empty into individual collection tanks remote from the clean room building. The drainage systems should be designed so that no used flammable, corrosive, or other contaminants are allowed to accumulate within the building.

- When a ventilation system handles more than one clean room classification, the system should be arranged to establish an airflow pattern from zones of lower to progressively higher contamination risk.

17.6.3 **Fire protection**

- Sprinklers should be installed throughout all clean rooms regardless of classification, with adequate water supplies. Sprinkler temperature rating should be 130°F (57°C).

- Sprinkler protection should be provided in the building where clean rooms are located if occupancy or construction features are combustible.

- Benches and hoods should preferably be of non-combustible construction or protected with automatic sprinklers.

- Where the ductwork for the air-conditioning and exhaust systems is combustible adequate fire protection must be provided. Sprinkler spacing within the ducts should be no more than 12ft (3.7m) to prevent burn-through of the duct and smoke release into the clean room.

17.6.4 **Vibration prevention**

- The heating, ventilating, and air-conditioning equipment (HVAC) should be isolated from the clean rooms by expansion joins for maximum reduction of vibration, which is critical for the process equipment performance.

- Mechanical equipment should be provided with sound attenuators to eliminate the transmission of vibrations to the clean rooms.

- The noise level in a clean room should be maintained below 65 decibels.

17.6.5 **Environmental control**

- Environmental conditions such as temperature, humidity, pressure differential, and airborne particle count should be controlled and recorded. Records should be reviewed periodically.

- Appropriate equipment should be selected and monitoring routines established to measure air-cleanliness levels under normal use conditions so that conformity with the specified air-cleanliness class may be determined.

- The biological and radioactive concentration of contaminants should be maintained at the allowable level specified by the product requirement.

- If flammable and/or pyrophoric gases from clean room operations are present in the exhaust, it should be purged with nitrogen up to a 'burn box' where the chemicals can be safely oxidised.

17.6.6 **Manual protection**

- Hose stations using 1.5in (38.1mm) hose with combination spray/stream nozzles should be provided near the doors of the clean room so that all points within the room are within reach of a hose stream.

- Portable extinguishers should be provided.

17.6.7 **Smoke control**

In modern, fully sprinklered clean rooms the major losses caused by fire are due to particulate contamination. Thermal damage is generally confined to one or two pieces of equipment or to a single wet bench. Particulate contamination or smoke damage, however, can cause product and equipment loss, decreased product yield, and business interruption. Therefore, exhaust of smoke and toxic products of combustion from a fire area is of primary concern.

● When smoke exhaust is provided in addition to fume exhaust, one of the following is needed:

  ● Plastic duct which is specifically approved for both fume and smoke exhaust. The capacity of this system should be designed specifically for smoke control by designing the system to provide a minimum pressure of at least 0.20in water gauge (50Pa) higher in the exposed areas than fire areas.

  ● Metal duct (such as stainless steel) which can withstand the corrosive environment and which is designed specifically for smoke control.

  ● A separate, independent smoke-exhaust system. Typically, this means a plastic duct system will be used for fume removal and a sheet metal duct system (properly designed) will be used for smoke removal.

● When a property is susceptible to smoke damage, the air-handling system for both environmental and smoke control should be designed and protected specifically.

● When several clean rooms are supplied with a central air-handling system, the system should be designed for the dual purpose of environmental as well as smoke control. Upon the detection of smoke, this operation should automatically put the fire area under 100% exhaust and simultaneously put the areas immediately adjacent to the fire area into 100% supply. The intent of this smoke control concept is to prevent smoke infiltration to the clean rooms adjacent to the one on fire and to purge the fire area of smoke contamination.

● When an independent air-handling system serves each room, it should be designed and arranged to convert to smoke control mode in case of fire in any of the rooms. This conversion involves automatic closing of the supply damper to the room of the fire, and the exhaust dampers of the systems in the adjacent rooms. The exhaust damper in the room of the fire should also open, as well as the supply dampers in the adjacent rooms. (This creates a slight positive pressure in the non involved rooms, thereby resisting smoke infiltration.)

The above systems should be designed to provide at least 0.20in water gauge (50Pa) pressure higher in protected areas than fire areas.

● When fume exhaust systems are also used for smoke removal, the following should be done:

  ● Local operations (bench stations, exhaust hoods, etc.) and other locations susceptible to fire should be designed for the local removal of smoke. The exhaust system should be arranged so that smoke goes directly from the fire to the exhaust inlets without exposing other property.

  ● The smoke control system should be designed to maintain a pressure of at least 0.20in water gauge (50Pa) higher on the adjacent exposed areas than the fire area.

- In older clean rooms where protection with Halon 1301 is provided, the smoke control system should be manually activated only after the fire has been controlled. However, if halon fails to control the fire, the smoke control system should be activated automatically when the sprinkler system activates.

- When Halon 1301 protection is not provided, the smoke control system should be automatically activated by an approved smoke-detection system and if this fails it should be activated by the sprinklers.

- When the air-conditioning system of clean rooms cannot be used for the purpose of smoke control, an independent smoke-control system should be designed and arranged for such a purpose. The smoke-control system should be arranged so as to automatically deactivate the air-conditioning systems of the clean rooms during the smoke control mode. The system should be designed to maintain at least a pressure of 0.20in water gauge (50Pa) higher on the protected areas than fire area.

- The air-handling system in the exposed property should be designed to provide 100% outside fresh air to the areas adjacent to the fire to prevent smoke migration through openings and to pressurise adjacent areas to provide a safe area for fire fighters to combat the fire. The system should be designed to maintain at least a 0.20in water gauge (50Pa) pressure higher on protected areas than fire areas.

- The outside fresh air intakes should be located at floor level and opposite to the exhaust outlets to lessen the possibility of drawing in smoke. A large height difference between the inlet and outlet provides greater reliability. This height difference should preferably be about 20ft (6m).

- The type, location, and spacing of smoke or heat detectors must be adequate.

- Duct materials should be evaluated for their ability to convey smoke and corrosive gases, their ability to withstand additional pressure (both positive and negative) by the supply and exhaust systems, and their ability to maintain structural integrity under fire exposure conditions anticipated in the occupancy. Supply ducts used for control of smoke should be constructed of non-combustible material.

- Where applicable, air-filter systems (laminar flow assemblies) should be used.

- Passing supply and exhaust ducts serving one smoke zone through another smoke zone should be avoided.

- An emergency switch for the air-handling system should be installed at the exit of the clean room. The switch can be used to activate the smoke-control system, if necessary, before the system automatically activates.

17.6.8 Inspection and maintenance

- In addition to the sprinkler system, maintaining other fire-protection systems in good operating condition requires frequent scheduled visual checks and tests at adequate intervals.

- The system-activating devices, such as heat and smoke detectors, and electric thermostats, fire dampers, fire doors, smoke dampers, and sprinklers exposed to corrosive environments should be inspected every six months. Adequately trained personnel should test heat and smoke-detector systems every six months. Manufacturers' recommendations should be followed in maintaining, inspecting, and testing the equipment. The tests should include activation of the fire and smoke-control systems and other related equipment by simulating emergency mode conditions.

- Testing and maintenance manuals for fire protection and other equipment should be provided in accordance with manufacturers' instructions. These should include operating, servicing, testing, and trouble-shooting instructions.

- Air filters should be readily accessible for inspection, maintenance, and fire fighting. Filters and ducts should be inspected frequently, and filters should be cleaned or replaced periodically. HEPA filters should not be patched or plugged to improve their efficiency. This action could adversely affect their fire resistance.

- Detailed emergency procedures should be posted in the clean room. Personnel should be trained in these procedures and practice them periodically.

- The programme should also include preventative maintenance of equipment. There should be a periodic review for checking the efficiency of the entire programme as well as keeping the programme up-to-date with new developments.

- The current NFPA standards for clean rooms, issued in 1995 are:

    - NFPA 318 for VESDA detection systems

    - NFPA 318 for sprinklers inside exhaust ducts

    - NFPA 13 for sprinkler protection

    - NFPA 13 for sprinkler seismic protection

    - NFPA 30 for flammable chemicals, dispense and waste collection.

17.7 General maintenance of machinery

The subject of machinery maintenance is dealt with in more detail in relation to each of the specific key industries elsewhere in this Study Report. All types of machinery will require some form of maintenance during their working life in order to keep them in a safe and reliable condition. The topic is also addressed in Chapter 5, 'Loss prevention' since maintenance is a vital part of risk management through which unexpected or untimely failures can be minimised or avoided.

The purpose of this section is to comment on maintenance in its broadest terms as applicable to most machines and processes.

17.7.1 Manufacturers' recommendations

It is usual practice for manufacturers of machines to recommend the type and frequency at which their machines should be serviced and maintained. The manufacturers are able to make these recommendations because they will have the necessary knowledge about the machine, its design and the materials used in its component parts and this will be partly validated by historical data and pre-production trials.

However in many applications the manufacturer cannot know the exact working conditions and environment in which the machine will operate, especially if it is integrated into a larger process, *e.g.* pumps, motors, gearboxes. In these circumstances the maintenance programme will need to be adapted or tailored to suit the particular application. Through this it may be necessary to increase the intervals at which a machine is taken out of service in order to be receive the desired maintenance work.

17.7.2 Operating staff

The work may be performed by the owner's own staff who may specialise in maintenance works or alternatively by specialist contractors, or a combination of the two. Of course those carrying out the maintenance work must be suitably trained and a good working experience with the particular machine(s) is an essential part of successful maintenance.

The diligence and vigilance of operating staff is an essential part of maintenance. The views of the staff in relation to machinery operation, together with regular and accurate record keeping, will provide maintenance staff with invaluable information that will be useful for the prevention of failures by timely or alternative maintenance procedures.

It is apparent that correct maintenance procedures will lead to fewer failures or sudden stoppages which can have a damaging effect on the business supported by the machines, whose function may prove to be a vital part of the production process.

17.7.3 Forward planning

Maintenance needs advance planning, so that not only can the correct intervals be determined but also the timing can be selected so that the planned outage or shutdown does not unduly interrupt the business. For example, if the business is seasonal (*e.g.* sugar refining) it makes good sense to carry out the maintenance work when the machines are not in high demand. Cooling-down and starting-up times and procedures need to be taken into account, as do difficulties in access that can make maintenance awkward to carry out on some installed machines.

The timely ordering of correct spares from the manufacturer, or its approved suppliers, forms an important element of good maintenance. The fitting of defective parts or the wrong parts has caused failures. Proper maintenance of stored spares is also important, so that strategic spare parts are in good condition when required.

17.7.4 Age and condition factors

The maintenance programme should also take into account the age of machines, as older machines, while remaining serviceable, may require extra maintenance attention in order to remain efficient and reliable. Some spares may be difficult to obtain and this factor should be taken into account in the design of the maintenance programme.

The condition of lubrication oils, coolants, and periodically replaceable parts (filters, belts, seals, linings) is an important part of any maintenance programme and failure to make timely changes can lead to abnormal wear and tear and losses in efficiency.

Aggressive working environments, which may be due to extreme temperatures, high internal pressures, poor air quality, or corrosive chemical elements, will have a bearing on the maintenance programme (*i.e.* filters changed more frequently in dirty air conditions). Various non-destructive testing techniques may be employed to gauge the degree of wear to the machine and the results used in a trend analysis to form the basis of a model preventative maintenance programme.

17.7.5 **Ancillary equipment/systems**

Maintenance should not be confined to the main industrial and process machinery but should extend to include control systems and monitoring equipment. Equally important is the maintenance of fire-detection and protection equipment, including primary and stand-by pumps. It is important to be certain that machinery that is not in continuous use will perform correctly if and when needed, especially in emergency conditions. This approach also applies to security alarm systems.

17.7.6 **Records, trends**

Whatever the prescribed programme, an important aspect of successful maintenance is accurate and accessible record keeping, where all results, readings and observations are registered, and which can be interpreted by those responsible for plant welfare.

It should be noted that maintenance work, with its human interventions, is an area where errors can occur. There have been incidents where parts or supply lines have not been reconnected correctly or even engineers' tools inadvertently left inside a machine during maintenance, which would certainly lead to extensive damage as soon as the machine is restarted. A strict inventory recording system to monitor all parts and tools used in the work should avoid such a mistake.

Increasingly, industry is moving away from unplanned 'failure' maintenance to predictive or 'reliability' based maintenance systems. This change is being driven by financial demand of the business, with condition monitoring of machines becoming more important.

17.8 Control systems

Since the origins of mechanical power there has been a desire to create systems that provide control, none more so than in heavy industry where the forces, power and the speed of reactions are so fast that there is barely sufficient time for human intervention and automated responses are required to help the equipment 'fail-safe'.

The role of controls is to provide a management service to the mechanism and to consolidate the responsibility to one area. Although the controlled mechanism may have great sophistication and may be spread across many hectares it is important that all relevant activities are co-ordinated. The control room is like a hub and if it were to be lost due to a fire then the whole business could be rendered inoperable.

If feedstocks or materials are automatically delivered within a process without reference to quality of the output, great risks to the plant and the accumulated stock may result.

Equally, if the process machinery suffers an emergency it is essential to cut non-safety feeds and 'starve' the emergency while risk management measures are applied. These control systems are integrated in every heavy manufacturing industry, in the form of electronic and hydraulic actuators and and other controls in order to protect even the most complex processes.

Major catastrophic losses often result from a combination of events that individually could be compensated for without serious implications. Control systems should provide an effective defence against such an accumulation of failures in order to minimise its consequences.

The ownership and management of all control systems are of vital importance to all integrated systems. While control systems are complex, they are at the convergence of many connections and form the direct interface between 'man and machine'. As a result they are often exposed to risks of electrical short circuit, fire or human error which could result in direct damage to the control equipment or remote damage to the plant being controlled.

With the presence of workers, the protection systems have to allow for safe evacuation of the working area and at the same time meet the standards of fire protection appropriate to the installation.

In evaluating control systems an allowance for system redundancy should exist. Conversely, some control systems are designed to restrict the operation of high-risk plant and they can become subjected to malpractice that expose the workforce and the equipment to excessive risks for an increase in operational performance and perhaps staff bonus payments.

17.9   Industrial gas turbines

The modern gas turbine is an intricately designed and extensively developed machine, which makes use of many components. These components gain necessary strength or durability by using exotic materials and compounds. Various techniques such as surface coatings bonded to a different base material have been developed to enable performance, efficiency and reliability to be enhanced for a range of demanding applications.

17.9.1   Early developments

From their development in the early 1900s to the first gas turbine compressor construction in 1936, many techniques and designs were tested and evaluated with inevitable failures before acceptable criteria and components were adopted.

By 1936 the Royal Aircraft Establishment recognised the aerojet/turbojet engine potential for powering aeroplanes and built an engine using Sir Frank Whittle's initial design patent granted in 1930.

The initial challenge was to develop a light, efficient and powerful compressor. Two main designs were in contention, *i.e.* the axial or the radial (also known as centrifugal) flow. The early prototypes of the multistage axial-flow design were very disappointing because of low component efficiencies.

Separate philosophies of the gas turbine were developed to meet the criteria of both the oil and aircraft industries. The aircraft industry needed a high power to weight ratio using premium fuel. Conversely, the oil industry's needs were for a low maintenance power unit, capable of burning a wide variety of lower-quality fuels where the weight and size of the machines was of secondary importance. Some development also continued into ship and railway locomotive applications.

The turbojet was notably less reliable than its industrial counterpart. However, with its military potential, research capital was made available and by 1939 and 1941 Germany and Britain respectively had turbojet powered aeroplanes. Both machines were based on the radial compressors due to the higher reliability at this stage of development. This approach was later to be reversed and today axial compressors are almost universally used both in aircraft and industrial applications. This is due to the higher efficiency gained by multistaging and smaller frontal area that are preferable for aircraft applications.

The Brown Boveri Company continued development of the industrial machine with a single large volume 'Silo' combustor giving the fuel flexibility needed for the variety of applications and commercial opportunities. It installed the first gas turbine for power generation for Sun Oil Corporation of Philadelphia USA in 1937.

The early British turbojet engine designs were passed to General Electric of the USA and by 1942 it had a modified engine propelling an aircraft. Further modifications followed and by 1944 mass production started. Material selection in these early days was an inexact science and for this and other reasons, early developments were marred by some spectacular failures. Arising from experience, the terms 'contained' damage and 'uncontained' damage arose, meaning those parts of the machine which, on failure, were contained within the machine or those that were projected or thrown, uncontained, through the casing/casting and had to be retrieved for failure analysis.

Development of the two-shaft machine allowed the gas turbine to rotate at higher speeds. This had the advantage of reducing the length of turbine blades for a given output, but for power generation a constant output speed of rotation is normal and therefore gearboxes are sometimes necessary in the 'power train'.

17.9.2 Operating stresses and forces

Three types of stress work on a turbine blade — centrifugal, from the rotation and mass, torque from the airflow trying to twist the blade during diversion, and bending of the blade caused by axial airflow.

The dynamic forces and temperatures in gas turbines, both aero derivative and industrial are so significant that design features are incorporated solely to control this energy. For example, the combustion flame temperature is so high that if allowed to make contact with the metal wall of the combustion chamber or silo the metal would melt. Accordingly, air is bled from the compressor main flow and directed into the combustion chamber(s) around the flame as an envelope. Additionally, the effectiveness of convectional and impingement cooling was limited, as the trade-off between heat transfer and economical manufacture resulted in many trailing edge failures.

Blades were initially made of solid premium-class material. They are now being re-engineered in new and sometimes exotic materials, with cavities and thermo-efficient geometry to allow cool air to form a 'film' around the outside of the blade or pass through the inside of the blade absorbing heat. Blades operate at trans-sonic speeds and three-dimensional flow analyses ensure the maximum performance of the designs in all conditions.

All designs are a compromise in the essentials of application, thus weight, cost and performance stand alongside reliability, maintainability and manufacturability, and more recently these have been joined by noise and emission considerations.

17.9.3 Exhaust gases, efficiency levels

The exhaust gas emitted from a gas turbine contains substantial energy in the form of heat and whereas this additional energy remains wasted when the turbine is operated in simple (or open) cycle, it is harnessed in a combined cycle application such as a co-generation power plant. This heat is captured in a waste heat recovery boiler to generate steam, used to drive a separate steam turbine, injected into the gas turbine to boost power and/or use in other industrial processes. In a combined heat and power plant residual lower quality heat is also used.

The capacity of gas turbines has progressively increased from the early industrial units with low efficiencies of around 30% to the modern machine producing in excess of 260MW with efficiency in combined cycle mode approaching 60%.

In recent years environmental legislation for both aircraft engines and industrial units has forced further developments. These have addressed concerns over noise and emission levels. To reduce aircraft noise and increase efficiency, larger turbo fans have been developed. To reduce and improve emission levels in industrial units, low NOx burners, water/steam injection or exhaust dosing has been applied. Clearly each of these options will effect the capital cost and may have implications to the maintenance and reliability of the overall plant.

Gas turbines, as stated above, are complex and integrated machines, where design and performance rely on the integrity of many components and every major development has a potential catastrophic impact on the host configuration.

17.9.4 Early failures

Typically, early failures involved blades, nozzles and combustion components. These incidents have never left the industry, yet they are becoming less frequent. With enhanced instrumentation, condition monitoring and limiting operating parameters, machines are normally automatically shut down before major 'uncontained' damage occurs. Further analysis of the results of monitoring and the plotting of trends can identify failing parts before catastrophic damage occurs. Proactive maintenance strategy and the use of predictive and planned maintenance techniques have a beneficial effect on the long-term reliable performance of machines. To this end, many manufacturers operate a 'notices' system to advise users and operators of any identified weakness or early degradation in their plant.

Early failures were relatively low cost. However, as machine values and complexities have increased so the manufacturer has had to address and minimise the risks. With machine output sizes growing ever larger the only 'test' for a new design is in its normal operating location as manufacturers do not have the electrical load facilities to dissipate the electrical or thermal output. Thus the maximum factory test for large machines are low load tests, supplemented by the normal overspeed tests.

It should be understood that the rotor/rotors within the gas turbine rotate at speeds of 20,000rpm and higher and are made of a series of discs/hubs. Each disc can be tested individually both for overspeed and airflow and would be linked during testing and operation to sophisticated instrumentation and strobe analytical devices. Yet, even with these precautions spectacular losses occur, *e.g.* contact between stator and rotor blades (a rub) allow a loosened tie bolt to fracture and this results in an uncontained incident.

Some turbines may accommodate the failure of one blade with a controlled shutdown period, but more than one is likely to cause such imbalance that extensive damage will ensue.

A metal strip (shroud) at the tips and linking segments controls tip-rock in blades and interstage leakage. This can become detached to flail around the turbine damaging other internal parts and causing long outages with consequent high material damage and business interruption costs to insurers.

Not all failures are this graphic and advances in the use of boroscopes and non-destructive examination techniques have improved the effectiveness of preventative maintenance procedures.

17.9.5   Vibration, harmonics

Vibration is endemic in rotating equipment and it is a constantly monitored characteristic in gas turbines. A gas turbine deflects air and hot combustion gases between rotor and stator blades and the vibration, which occurs within the flame itself (pyro-acoustics), can amplify these forces.

The natural frequencies or harmonics of each machine differ and the sequence and operation of the machine as it is driven through its own critical speeds and operational characteristics are vital to the understanding of risk and reduction of damage.

It is interesting to note that the pre-handover testing/commissioning of a gas turbine at the completion of erection, is often the first time the component assembly has ever been run as a complete machine.

Once taken into commercial use, gas turbines are designed to work in a 'steady state'. Each component is vital to performance and efficiency and they are matched to this steady state by a matching study, which investigates the interplay of engine geometry and engine parameters such as pressure ratios, airflow, rotor speed, component efficiencies and mass flow. To achieve the steady state the engine has to be driven through 'transient' speeds. The matching of components is vital to ensure that all parts perform through these 'off-design' conditions.

17.9.6   Fuel, air filtration/intake

The application and installation of each unit is a further component part of the risk factors, for example, a gas turbine working on and receiving fuel from an offshore oil rig could be exposed to residues in the fuel. This may include heavy metals, radioactive particles or tar, all of which have an effect on the long-term operation of the unit. Equally, the air filters have to prevent salt and seawater spray ingestion into the compressor and combustion cycle. Fuel or air contamination is not, however, confined to offshore installations and due to these factors numerous failures have occurred in land-based machines.

The particles carried in either fuel or air (particulates) may cause damage by abrasion on the internal surface, they may block cooling ducts or in some cases react chemically to deposit adhesive compounds on the balanced components. This may cause monitoring equipment to fail or the reparability of the machine to be affected.

To dislodge soot deposit and the products of combustion, gas turbines are 'washed'. This involves injecting a mixture of water and detergent into the air intake and allowing the compressor and turbine to be sprayed with the solution. This exercise is undertaken 'off-line' when the machine is not running under load. Injecting similar quantities of water when the machine was generating would have serious effects.

Air filters are either cleaned by air pulses, when the pressure differential across the filter exceeds a pre-defined limit, or they have disposable filter elements. Replacement of filters exposes the gas turbine to risks of ingestion of foreign bodies. (It should be noted that this risk, for aero engines, is lower as they are designed to accommodate 'bird strike' (ingestion of wild birds) without catastrophic failure.)

Turbine performance is partially a function of the ambient conditions at the site. However, cooling and filtration can improve air quality. Cooling may remove 'condensables' suspended in the air and filters will reduce 'particulates'. The use of gas turbines in inner cities has on some occasions required exhaust gases to be of higher quality than the ambient air. This has a major impact on the filtration plant, which in such cases becomes 100% important for operations.

17.9.7

Operating environment/mode

The roles of the power station chemist and the station laboratory are vital in the control of foreign matter within the system. These experts should check the consistency of the fuel, the quality of lubricating oils and the chemical balance of any water used in NOx control or in combined cycle operations. There is a requirement to protect the 'grid' from the influence of the generator set, not the reverse.

The forces acting on the system from outside may be aggressive and it is necessary to examine the power factors in the grid and any surge voltages that may affect the plant but not trip the breakers and protection devices.

The performance of the machine within parameters will dictate some aspects of operation and give an indication of the stress a machine is put through during transient operations. For example, the 'fired hours' tells of the life of a machine, based on 8000 hours per year of operation together with the maintenance history and intervals so the machine may be evaluated to its risk potential.

However, the machine may have been subjected to a high number of starts including various 'fast starts'; both sequences can have a detrimental effect on component life. Insurers and engineers are often concerned about the 'equivalent' hours being the sum of 'fast starts', multiplied by a formula. Thus a machine which has been installed for two years but has been 'cycled' could have component wear equivalent to a normal operation of a five-year-old machine and be in need of a major outage.

17.9.8

Gas turbine applications

It was always going to be difficult for the 'simple cycle' industrial gas turbine to match the thermal efficiency of the steam turbine. By further comparison the diesel engine has a clear advantage in applications where the speed and load is constantly varying and where there are long periods of idling time, a large proportion of the turbine load is used by the combustion compressor which remains high against varying output.

However, the efficiency of the industrial gas turbine in simple cycle can be improved by achieving higher combustion and turbine temperatures and higher compression ratios.

A gasification process may obtain the gas for the gas turbine. This process converts a fuel, be it coal, tar, wood or production waste into a gas form acceptable to the gas turbine and this is integrated into the overall project philosophy in 'integrated combined cycle power plants'. While the complications of adding this specific dependent process to a gas turbine are obvious, the advantage of utilising waste or low-quality fuel materials in power generation has the double advantage of economy of fuel and consumption of an otherwise waste and unwanted material. From an insurance perspective it should be appreciated that the gasifier brings its own risks, with particular implications when considering business interruption where back-up or alternative forms of fuel supply become highly relevant.

The gas turbine is used for many applications — ship engines, oil field pumps, aircraft engines, gas compressors, power generation, etc. Each application adds its own 'driven' equipment — a gearbox, a pump, a propeller, a generator, or a waste heat recovery boiler. The reliability of all driven plant together with its load characteristics has to be 'matched' within the design configuration. In some single-shaft power generation installations catastrophic failure of the gas turbine will cause additional damage to the equipment mounted upon the same single shaft. This has major implications for the business interruption risk and evaluation.

17.9.9   **Future developments**

Every major gas turbine manufacturer is expending considerable resources in attempting to gain significant improvements in performance and efficiency. A particularly major challenge is the reduction of NOx, CO, CO_2 and UHC (unburned hydrocarbons) emissions. In order to meet increasingly strict environmental emission limits, particularly in the industrialised world, companies are developing dry/low NOx (DLN) burner designs, steam-injection, water-injection and catalytic-conversion systems of emission controls.

The challenge for engineers and designers is to create a machine that meets the environmental demands, having a multi-fuel capability which can constantly perform at the output and efficiency levels demanded, meeting the economic challenge of the installation.

The demand for higher compression ratios and greater firing temperatures is limited by the capability of the machine components to withstand such an aggressive environment. Future generations will find methods of re-firing the hot gases to support higher outputs, within an environment of new materials capable of tolerating these high temperatures and pressures. Finally, the choice of fuel will have to recognise the future cost of premium fuels and machines will need to accept a greater range of fuels with levels of impurities that are not presently acceptable.

17.10   Duty of care, liability to third parties

As already shown, this Study Report focuses on material damage and business interruption risks, or in other words, first party insurance against direct physical damage and its consequences on the machine owner (or operator) and the business. Against this background, a detailed comment on the subject of liability exposures, how they arise and the insurance of those exposures goes beyond the scope of this Study Report. These third party liabilities may arise under the legal system of the country (*i.e.* common law torts, statutory liability, etc.) or under contract or through vicarious liability.

However, in the brief comments that follow, the reader will start to see how and where these third party liabilities might arise.

One of the difficulties in dealing with the subject at an elementary level is the extremely complicated and ever changing legal environment, precedent setting judgments or new laws, all of which have a direct bearing on the exposures. It will be appreciated that there are considerable variations between the laws and legal environment of one country or state and another, which also makes for poor generalised comment.

In some instances insurance against the risks that may arise is compulsory. A good example is employers' liability in the United Kingdom.

Considering the general ownership or operation of machinery, these liabilities may arise under a statutory duty, or a duty to exercise reasonable care or they may arise under a regime of strict, no fault liability, which exists in some countries. The risk may be faced by the general public, specific sectors of the public (*e.g.* product liability) or employees. (*i.e.* those employed to work in the vicinity of the machinery).

These branches of insurance are classified as general or public/product liability and employers' liability respectively, which may be known as casualty or workers' compensation respectively, in some markets (*e.g.* in the USA).

Another branch of liability insurance should be noted, in relation to the particular risks run by 'professionals' and those providing professional services (some of who may also be involved with machinery operations and processes). In the highly specialised areas of professional indemnity and directors' and officers' liability, the exposures are potentially enormous and sometimes difficult to quantify or visualise in advance.

In all cases, the liability will rest upon the individual or group of individuals who are found to be responsible for causing harm or a loss to others. This may take the form of death, bodily injury or disease, including stress and psychological disorders, damage to the property belonging to others, financial loss suffered by others or by causing harm or impairment to the environment through pollution, contamination and the like. The latter illustration is a particularly complex branch of liability insurance coupled with relatively 'young' legislation. Liability for 'damaging' the environment is also an area of particular relevance to machinery uses and there have been many reported cases where watercourses have been polluted by industrial discharge or waste, often following an accident involving machinery. The world at large will be aware of environmental concerns which arise from the widely differing forms of generation and transmission of electrical energy and its effect on the environment. The risk, no matter how small, of a catastrophe, in human terms, is ever present and so is the liability to the public.

In practice, difficulties of definition may arise with regard to 'an event', 'loss date', 'single claim or aggregate claims', 'costs inclusive', 'joint and several liability', whereas, generally, the courts will decided the sum which the responsible party is due to pay by way of an award or compensation. Insurers (subject to the policy limits) may also cover legal expenses and in some circumstances punitive damages may also be covered.

Those engaged in the petrochemical and power industries are required to manage heavy exposures, as are those involved in food or medicines, albeit for different reasons, which should be reasonably obvious to those with an interest in those industries.

18 | Claims

18.1 Introduction

The final chapter of this Study Report contains summarised details of incidents involving industrial or process machinery. These incidents resulted in claims against insurance policies and they are grouped into three categories:

- Major incidents;

- Claims of technical interest;

- Relatively minor, but typical claims.

18.2 Major incidents

18.2.1 Boiler explosion at electrical generating plant

Due to a computer problem a generating unit was operating on manual control. This situation made the automatic shutdown function inoperable.

Two coal mills were simultaneously being brought up to full load. This was the first time that two mills had been run in at the same time.

A severe vibration was felt and the generator output began decaying. A member of staff had observed a black discharge from the stack, and shortly after an explosion occurred.

The turbine was tripped. The explosion damaged the firebox, preheater, economiser, flue gas duct, air heater, water walls, downcomers and ash pit.

There was no damage to an adjacent unit, but the unit tripped off line and was restored to service four days later. This is understood to be the first instance of a pulverised coal boiler exploding while under load.

The explosion occurred as a result of a combination of circumstances that led to a serious disruption in the combustion process. A similar combination of circumstances occurred about a year earlier but at that time the automatic controls shut down the system before an explosion resulted.

The principal factors contributing to the explosion were that

- the oxygen concentration and the furnace pressure sensors were plugged and not operating as designed

- the coal loading was unbalanced due to pulveriser problems.

As a result, some burners were receiving insufficient fuel and this caused an excess of oxygen. Nitrogen oxide emission control procedures requiring a fuel rich at the burners created high levels of potentially explosive carbon monoxide. The fall of a large clinker from the slag hopper caused a serious disturbance in the combustion process, and this disrupted fuel to air mixture controls in the manual mode of operation.

The cost of the loss was £15m.

18.2.2 Mechanical damage at an electrical generating plant

A turbine generator of 415MV capacity was destroyed by an explosion owing to both human error and equipment malfunction. The event occurred during an isolation of the generator from the distribution system.

As a result of a switching error electrical energy flowed back into the generator which had not been isolated from the transmission system. This instantaneously turned the generator into an electric motor and it is reckoned that its speed increased out of control to 3600rpm, far above a safe level, and this created a violent reaction in the generator that lasted nearly two minutes before the system could be shut down.

During this time the shaft between the exciter and the generator twisted off the main shaft through the generator and bent at both the exciter and turbine end causing heavy damage to the bearings and couplings. Fireballs throughout the turbine generator area followed an explosion. The fire was caused by the escape of hydrogen from the generator and oil from the bearings.

The cost of the loss was £13m.

18.2.3 Fire damage to a generator at a paper plant

A hydrogen fire destroyed a combined heat and power plant. Extensive investigations revealed that the fire started in the generating section and was caused by steam escaping via a pin-hole leak and the hydrogen disassociating and igniting. The generator and economiser were totally destroyed.

The cost of the loss was £600,000.

18.2.4 Steam turbine disruption at a power station

A steam turbine generator of 50MW capacity suffered a complete disruption resulting in parts being projected out of the turbine hall. A lubricating oil leak and a subsequent fire brought down the turbine hall roof and caused further damage to the unit.

The cost of the loss was £6m.

18.2.5 Transformer explosion at a power station

Transformers are found in many situations and generally they are uncomplicated and reliable machines. However, when they go wrong they can be expensive and difficult to replace.

A power station had identified a small change in the gases suspended in the transformer oils by a dissolved gas analysis (DGA) test and although this was well within operating limits an inspection was carried out and some adjustments made. The unit was returned to service and after a week in operation there was an explosion inside the transformer. This ruptured the tank and allowed the oils inside the unit to escape. A second explosion occurred as the oil level fell and the oil vapour became exposed to the hot core of the transformer. The deluge system and additional fire teams eventually put the fire out but damage to the unit was irrecoverable.

The insured had investigated suitable replacements and the spare, owned by another company, was purchased and shipped. Co-ordination of the repair was not as simple as was first thought as the replacement was not a simple 'drop-in' solution. The connections and foundation had to be adjusted to take the differing circuits and load of this alternative unit.

Ultimately, the repair cost more than US$10m plus the value of six month's lost production.

18.2.6 Combustion burner failure in gas turbine

Gas turbines are at best complex, and all components have to function together to maintain production.

A recent large loss occurred when a machine experienced a flashback. This happens when the gas entering the burner is able to ignite when the velocity of the fuel through the burner is reduced and allows the flame front to move upstream and burn inside the jets rather than in front of them. The burner material is not designed to withstand temperatures of this level and melts away. The debris from the burner can only travel through the power turbine and will impact on the blades either adding metal splatter deposits to the special thermal surfaces or fracturing the blades when larger pieces strike.

Catastrophic failure will ensue and in the worst case damage is so extensive that the turbine will have to be stripped and rebuilt.

As the machine was among the largest and most advanced of its type, the repair costs were US$20m plus the production lost for six months.

18.2.7 High-cycle fatigue damage in a gas turbine

High-cycle fatigue is a constant concern, as losses only become apparent once the machine has been in production for some time. Fatigue occurs as a result of rapid stressing and de-stressing of components, sometimes following periods of high vibration, or in rotating machines and their components. The consequences are usually catastrophic and recent failures have occurred with the complete gas turbines left in ruins. Long-term repair is required, as the unit needs to be redesigned to prevent recurrence of the problem.

A loss of this type can cost up to $50m to repair and more than a year to put back into service.

18.3 Claims of technical interest

18.3.1 Compressor failure at a nitric acid plant

One of the first stage compressor blades had sheared and passed through the control blades and subsequent stages of fixed and moving blades along the entire length of the compressor. This caused severe damage to the blades.

The cause of the incident was established as fatigue cracking at the edge of the blade and final failure occurred with ensuing catastrophic results. The incident resulted in material damage and business interruption losses. The replacement blades had to be specially manufactured.

The cost of the loss was £1m.

18.3.2 Boiler tube failure at a chemical works

The number one roof tube in boiler at a chemical works failed and caused steam to be released. The failure occurred at a section of the tube that had previously been repaired.

Inspections revealed that the new section of tube was of a lower wall thickness than the original tube, to which it was welded. It had failed because of local overheating due to turbulence created at this discontinuity.

The mistake had arisen because the number one tube required thicker walls than the other tubes in the boiler owing to stresses at certain points. Previously all tubes had been of the same dimensions but several failures of the number one tube in the boiler's early use has led to the change to a thicker walled tube. The incident resulted in both material damage and business interruption losses.

The cost of the loss was £100,000.

18.3.3 **Brewery vessel collapse**

A brewery fermentation vessel collapsed due to vacuum conditions being present in the vessel while emptying the product contents from the vessel.

The vacuum valve jammed and a subsequent revision of procedures was introduced to prevent a recurrence. A new vessel had to be purchased as an initial attempt to blow the vessel back to circularity failed.

The cost of the loss was £60,000.

18.4 Minor but typical claims

18.4.1 **Breakdown of diesel generator**

The mechanical breakdown of an 8MW diesel engine generator leading to connecting rods breaking through the crankcase was caused by piston seizure due to faulty injector maintenance.

The cost of the loss was £150,000.

18.4.2 **Damage to crushing mill due to lubrication failure**

Failure of a lubrication pump and the subsequent loss of lubrication resulted in overheating in the drive end trunnion bearing of the rod mill which was used for crushing ore fines. It cracked in three separate locations.

The cost of the loss was £250,000.

18.4.3 **Damage to printing press**

A locking nut sheared on a five-colour printing press and fell into the gearbox. This caused damage to gears and resulted in distortion of the cut-off cylinder. The machine was temporarily repaired and ran at low speed to mitigate the loss while parts were obtained. It was then taken out of service for two days while permanent repairs were carried out.

The cost of the loss was £200,000.

18.4.4 Transformer failure

A transformer of 400KVA capacity failed due to inadequately tightened bolts in the automatic tap changer mechanism. The fault was traced back to the original manufacture.

The cost of the loss was £1.5m.

18.4.5 Collapse of boiler furnace

A horizontal multi-tubular boiler furnace collapsed due to lack of water. The furnace had to be renewed along with the front tube plate and the boiler required extensive re-tubing.

The cost of the loss was £350,000.

18.4.6 Bursting coils in a fluidised bed boiler

Coils in a fluidised bed boiler burst and caused extensive damage to surroundings. The coil failed where it was eroded to such an extent that it could not withstand internal pressure.

The cost of the loss was £25,000.

Appendix 1: Power generation — risk areas and risk mitigation

The following tables indicate the specific risks/risk areas with suggestions on how these risks might be mitigated. Different forms of power generation are identified together with their specific risks. In some cases the mitigation point shown does not directly correspond to a specific risk but are simply good general practice. In the context of good practice, some of these points will be relevant to other industrial sectors whose machinery exposures are similar to those found in power generation:

Area	Risk	Mitigation
Common areas — fuel handling		
Solid fuels	● Stockpile combustion — spontaneous combustion	The coal stock should be divided into separate piles and there should be monitoring of stockpile temperatures.
	● Conveyor fire — friction or dust accumulation dust explosion	Non-combustible belts, sprinklers, limit switches on lateral movement, housekeeping.
	● pulverised fuel fire (coal) — pulverising mills overheating	CO_2 injection system recommended, temperature recorders on mill bearings, explosion-proof electrics, removal of ferrous material from dust, correct operation and maintenance, proper lubrication, carbon monoxide detectors (indicate spontaneous combustion). Housekeeping.
		Bursting disks.
		Agreed procedure to fight a pulverised fuel fire.
Liquid fuels	● Storage area fire — massive leak due to incorrect handling or unnoticed tank leak.	Tanks located away from generation buildings, tank spill must be contained (bunding) with an adequate volume, nearby hydrants to cool tanks, foam injection systems, rim seal protection of floating roof tanks.
	● Fuel heating skid fire — spray leak	Sprinklers with automatic shutdown interlock, explosion-proof electrical equipment.
Gaseous fuels	● Explosion — fuel leak	Gas detectors with trips, intrinsically safe systems, safety relief valves.
Common areas — control room		
	● General protection	The keyword for prevention and protection of these rooms is isolation. Separation of manned areas from unmanned areas is important to reduce potential loss.
		In all cases, they should be built of non-flammable materials and ideally explosion-proof. Windows can be a weakness and should have a three-hour fire rating.
		Vermin control must be adequate.
		A back-up electricity supply (UPS) is required to ensure safe unit shutdown.

Area	Risk	Mitigation
	● Overriding systems — incorrect operation	Modern control systems are fully sequenced to enable an operator to start up, shut down and control a unit usually with a single instruction. The authority to override such systems, perhaps to avoid a lengthy sequence or an alarm and gain manual control of the units, should be strictly controlled.
	● Fire	Fixed automatic fire protections (although rare in certain territories) can be installed, but care must be taken to ensure that sensitive equipment is not impaired by the protection system; 24-hour manning helps to reduce the dependency on fixed protections but the trend in modern stations towards unmanned control rooms is worthy of note.
		Correct operation of the doors communicating with the process areas; ventilation network without communication with hazardous areas (ideally having an independent ventilation unit), sealing of cable passages.
		Heat load maintained at the minimum level; avoid accumulation of continuous-feed paper or other combustible materials (cardboard, etc.), rooms reduced to a single function; avoid cooking or laboratory experiments.
		Back-up copy of computer data and programs and storage in separate locations.
		Extinguishers for the electrical equipment (halon, CO_2) and water for ordinary fires.
		Smoke detection devices with visual and audible alarms.
		Installation of sprinklers, if the heat load is high, with delayed triggering to allow the installations to be secured.
		Automatic halon or CO_2 extinguishing device in closed areas (or even for a specific part of a piece of equipment), raised floors.
		Interlocked ventilation system. The system should be designed to prevent circulation of smoke from outside. Some control rooms operate at a slight positive pressure.
		Housekeeping — unnecessary paperwork and combustible material should be removed from a control room.
	● Catastrophic breakdown	Redundancy — computer screens and all significant instrumentation (especially safety critical) should have complete redundancy with, in many cases, the spare item on 'hot' stand-by.
		Unitisation — in larger stations with more than one generating unit, it is advantageous for the control system to be unitised, i.e., each unit has its own systems. The level of common equipment

Area	Risk	Mitigation
		should be kept minimal. This unitisation may extend to cable groupings and cable basements with the objective being that a single event cannot shut down multiple units.

Common areas — electrical systems

Area	Risk	Mitigation
Generator	● H_2 explosion/fire leak	Sealed enclosure, CO_2 systems for H_2 alternators, H_2 external storage.
		Bearings should be sprinkler protected. Windings should be fire resistant (class F). Exciters should be well maintained.
	● Motoring	Can cause damage to a turbine and overheating. A reverse power relay will indicate this phenomenon.
	● Electrical failure	Various protective relays to mitigate electrical failure:
	Stator — ground fault (usually caused by deterioration of winding insulation — age or prolonged overheating). Phase to phase fault (usually caused by mechanical deterioration). Field — ground fault Loss of excitation	Stator ground fault (over voltage relay) Phase to phase (differential relay) Negative sequence relay Loss of excitation relay Field ground voltage relay
		Electrical tests should be carried out annually and recorded.
	● Mechanical failure	The generator should be fitted with monitors and alarms; bearing temperature, abnormal lube oil condition, high stator winding temperature, high inlet temperature for cooling air or H_2, low oil seal pressure on H_2 system, low H_2 purity (including moisture), high rotor winding temperature.
	End ring failure Slot wedges movement Fan fracture Bearing failure Overspeed Chemical degradation (increased by ionised air or oxygen).	Certain steel alloys are susceptible to stress corrosion. Careful monitoring and replacement if necessary with upgraded material will help to reduce the problem.
		Fan fracture can be caused by vibration. Monitoring, maintenance and inspection should mitigate losses.
		A contingency plan should be prepared and this should include the sourcing of a replacement unit following a failure.
Transformers	● Electrical breakdown — most failures result from an initial failure in the high voltage windings. The next most common cause of transformer loss is lightning.	They should be protected against lightning, to which they are very vulnerable, by correctly sized lightning arrestors. In addition, transmission and distribution lines may be protected with a shield ground line.
		Protective relays should be located within the transformer. These detect undesirable conditions and alarm or shut down the unit. Various relays are desirable on smaller units and essential on larger (>10MVA); over-pressure (Bucholz), over-current, differential relay.

Area	Risk	Mitigation
		Maintenance: gas in oil testing: various dissolved gases indicate developing problems and can be used to good effect to avoid loss. Gases such as acetylene, ethylene, carbon monoxide, ethane, hydrogen and carbon dioxide should be monitored.
		Oil testing: regular oil testing is an essential component of transformer monitoring. Many measurements can be taken but dielectric strength, pH, interfacial tension (indicates contaminants) and spectrographic analysis are among the most useful.
		With all test results, records and trends should be monitored.
		'Doble' testing to give transformer characteristic.
		Thermographic surveys to see hot spots and potential failure areas.
	● Fire and explosion — usually caused as a result of shorting and oil vaporisation	Separation (refer NFPA 850/851). Blast walls. Containment for oil (especially underground). Fixed protection water spray. Spare unit where justifiable. Age — units more than 20 years old more prone to failure.
		Units should be protected against fire in an adjacent unit, and in particular, the largest units should be placed outside and separated from each other by concrete walls and protected by automatic sprinklers if above 100MVA. Oil releases should be drained to avoid spreading to neighbouring equipment.
	● PCB release	Environmentally damaging and toxic, PCBs are extremely difficult to decontaminate after a fire. All PCBs should be replaced with a modern dielectric. Be aware of the time taken to remove all traces of absorbed PCBs.
Switchgear room	● Elecrical shorting and fire	Maintenance in accordance with manufacturer recommendations, good housekeeping and a clean environment, smoke detectors and, if justified, a gaseous extinguishing system.
Battery room	● Fire and explosion	Ventilation systems in place to remove hydrogen gas, smoke detectors and regular maintenance.
Cables	● Fire	Metal trays should be used. Cables should be manufactured from fire resistant coatings and be bunched tightly together. Intumescent coatings can be put on cables, especially where trays run vertically. Critical cable runs should, where possible, be unitised, *i.e.* a fire will not affect all units. Sprinklers (fire wire), and smoke detectors should be fitted. Access to cable basements should be strictly controlled.
		Cable penetrations through fire separation walls should be packed and sealed to ensure that propagation of fire through the wall is stopped. There

Area	Risk	Mitigation
		are several standards that describe appropriate sealing methods. Ongoing inspection is required to prevent the integrity of such a penetration being destroyed by routine maintenance or the running of an additional cable.

Conventional steam turbine plant

Area	Risk	Mitigation
Boiler	● Fire and explosion — faulty fabrication, defective safety valves, erosion, corrosion, overheating, negligent maintenance or operation, faulty fuel control leading to fuel build up, poor air heater maintenance.	Regular programmed maintenance and testing of boiler parts and safety systems; correct design and operation of fuel control and firing systems; start up interlocks. Good control of water treatment plant. Flame detectors with fuel interlocks. Air heater maintenance and cleanliness.
	● Poor combustion control leading to ash build up on sloping surfaces, walls and tube banks. Draft losses and erosion increase, heat absorption decreases.	Better fuel consistency (particularly waste fuels), *e.g.*, consistent moisture content. Boiler cleaning and maintenance.
	● Cracking — defective materials, poor construction, metal fatigue, improper firing.	Non-destructive testing, correct process controls.
	● Cook dry — no boiler water circulation, no feed water. A large boiler could be dry within 90 seconds.	Flow meters with trips, drum level alarms.
	● Burner front fire — fuel leak.	Sprinklers with interlocks and bunding.
	● Implosion — Forced draft fan after flame out.	Safety vents fitted.
	● Tube failure — hot spot, weld failure, defective materials, corrosion, erosion, creep.	Regular maintenance, non-destructive testing, remnant life assessment.
	● Water chemistry excursion leading to accelerated corrosion and plant problems.	On line monitoring.
FGD	● Fire (usually during shutdown)	Maintenance management and control, permits, etc. Use of non-combustible scaffolding.
Steam turbine	● Lube/hydraulic oil fire — overheating, hot work.	Deluge system on oil tanks and ideally oil lines, directional deluge on turbine bearings, guarded oil supply and return lines.

Area	Risk	Mitigation
	● Mechanical failure: Overspeed Water Induction Cold Stream backflow Shroud and tenon failure Corrosion fatigue in the LP turbine Bearings and lubrication Shaft cracking Stress corrosion Embrittlement Low cycle fatigue	Management and maintenance including condition monitoring, non-destructive testing, boroscopic surveys, etc. Vacuum breaker on condenser. Fixed automatic condition monitoring and protection equipment that will alarm and trip the unit should be fitted. This should include vibration, temperature probes and overspeed protection (regularly tested).
Condenser	● Corrosion and erosion	Regular maintenance, non-destructive testing, dosing of once through cooling water systems with chlorine or sodium hypochlorite to prevent organic growth in the condenser plant.

Gas turbine/CCGT

There are many risks that the CCGT plant share with conventional steam units and this section highlights those unique to gas turbine and CCGT units.

Area	Risk	Mitigation
General	● Technology	Understanding of unique features, appropriate cover and deductibles (including design covers) taking account of any manufacturers warranties and guarantees. All manufacturers notified modifications and upgrades should be implemented as per recommendations.
	● Manning numbers and experience	Experience and training. Levels of manning are being reduced particularly in CCGT plant. The complexities of modern control systems are such that a small number of staff can operate the plant. The optimal use of this reduced number of staff under emergency conditions is however an issue which should be considered.
Turbine hall	● Fuel — volume and pressure	See fuel section, acoustic casing protection on gas turbines and gas sensors.
	● Fire	Key plant areas should be protected in the most appropriate manner. For example, gas turbine enclosures are usually CO_2 protected and lube oil tanks, steam turbine bearings and other main plant items protected with water.
	● Mechanical Breakdown	Access to spares and stock (blades, buckets, etc.) — spares pools and leasing arrangements for components or whole units. Monitoring of the local atmosphere. High levels of dust or corrosive elements can cause obvious erosions and harmful chemical effects.
HRSG	● See steam turbine boiler table (page 225)	See steam turbine boiler table (page 225)

Area	Risk	Mitigation

Hydro electric

Exposures presented by hydroelectric plant include those identified as generic concerns as well as those described for common plant such as generators, transformers and switchgear. This section identifies those exposures unique to hydroelectric plants.

Area	Risk	Mitigation
General	● Location/weather	Access to remote mountainous stations can be problematic. Contingency plans and appropriateness of business interruption waiting periods.
	● Manning	Many stations are unmanned and remote-controlled. Regular visits must be made and emergency plans, fixed systems and communications designed and installed with this mode of operation in mind.
	● Silting	Regular dredging.
Dam — embankment	● Reduced lifetime and integrity	There are a number of aspects of general management and maintenance that help to prolong the life of a dam or indicate a developing problem. Housekeeping — A dam should be kept free of significant vegetation. Riprap — The riprap on the reservoir side of the dam must be kept in good condition to help prevent erosion from water, ice and floating bodies such as logs. Crest movement — This should be monitored at regular intervals to show whether the dam is remaining in position or moving beyond anticipated design specification (a simple vernier scale can be used for this purpose). Dams can lift from their anchors or have their abutments undermined. This is usually as a result of poor construction or a change in operating regime. It should be monitored and remedial action taken before a major fault occurs.
	● Over topping — a major problem for embankment dams. Although less problematic for concrete dams, overtopping must not be a regular occurrence.	Sound flood management and knowledge of the water course characteristics can prevent overtopping. Spillways correctly sized for flood conditions, including the melt waters from higher elevations with snow. Helicopter surveys of snows and melts together with meteorological stations in the catchment areas enable operators to pre-empt high flow rates. All professional operators should have a flood management plan.
	● Seepage	Dams all have some water seepage. It is only when this reaches excessive levels that serious problems can develop. Piping or channelling can form in a dam if operators are not aware of developing problems. Seepage should be continuously monitored and fed to a control centre in the case of larger installations. A well-constructed dam should be self-sealing to prevent this problem occurring. Many significant problems originate from construction defects. The monitoring of the temperature profile in the dam can help to indicate the presence of water movement through

Area	Risk	Mitigation
		the dam. Water resident in the dam will generally be at a higher temperature than the water body it holds back. If internal temperatures start to drop then an investigation should be made.
	● Earthquake	Design standards and monitoring.
Dam — Concrete	● Overtopping	See above.
	● Crest Movement	See above.
	● Earthquake	See above.
Shafts and tunnels	● Collapse	Geology.
		Rock traps to catch debris and avoid damage to the penstock.
Turbine hall	● Flood	Design and operating procedures can help prevent flood of an operating station. In addition inspection of all high-pressure water parts should be formalised and trended. An emergency plan should include all possible flooding events (upsteam, downstream).
	● Fire	This is not a common exposure. On rare occasions, hot oil escaping from a leak has been ignited. High fire resistance hydraulic fluids can be used where hardware is suitable. The main fire risk in a hydro plant is underground electrical equipment such as oil-filled breakers, transformers and oil-filled cables. These items must be separated from main plant areas and ideally be fitted with fixed fire protections. In the case of transformers and large switchgear, explosion venting or containment must be considered.
Turbines	● Overspeed	A fail-safe governor drive mechanism which shuts off water flow in the event of governor drive failure. An overspeed trip device which shuts down the unit. A unit should never exceed 140% of its design speed or a limit designated by the manufacturer.
	● Water hammer	Improved operating procedure to reduce physical shock to the system.
	● Cavitation	Design modifications to change water-flow patterns or change some of the materials affected.
	● Foaming	Improving water quality (may not be under the control of the station operator) by controlling contaminants helps reduce foaming.
	● Erosion/impact damage	Trash racks at the intake gates, rock traps to collect debris especially if open rock headrace tunnels are used. Ice management.

Area	Risk	Mitigation
Diesel		
General	● Mechanical breakdown	The motor and alternator alignment must be done accurately, otherwise large-scale damage can be caused during the trial or guarantee periods.
		Full maintenance following manufacturer's guidelines with suitably trained staff or service contractors (often the manufacturer).
		Bearing clearances should be monitored.
		Ensure that fuel specification meets with the manufacturer's recommendations. Monitor fuel quality especially for landfill, digester, mine and other non-natural gas fuels.
		Lubricating oils should be sampled and monitored for quality and fuel contamination to ensure good performance and prevent crankcase explosions.
	● Fire and explosion	Good servicing, housekeeping and start-up procedures. Explosions have occurred in gas-fired engines as a result of residual fuel being present in the unit on start up.
Wind		
General	● The environment of use — storms, lightning, etc.	Design standards to match actual conditions, lightning protection.
	● Breakdown — fatigue of blades, feathering devices, brake and gearbox failure	Design and material selection adequacy, maintenance, condition monitoring including unit trips.
	● Type faults	This concern is particularly relevant to wind turbines since a significant number of units are generally grouped together. Operators and insurers must be aware of a fault which might be common to all units. Design and build standards, type testing.
Solar		
General	● Apart from the problems linked to the construction and testing of all proto types, consideration must be given to the number, surface area and fragility of the directional mirrors that have considerable wind resistance and other natural perils.	Control and operational procedures. For example, in winds in excess of 50kmh, heliostats should be moved into a horizontal position with mirrors facing towards the ground. There is ultimately no way to protect a site from the natural elements but operating procedures can significantly reduce the likelihood of a major loss.

Area	Risk	Mitigation

Geothermal

The risks presented by a geothermal plant are basically identical to those of a conventional steam turbine generator with some additional unique exposures. This table concentrates on those more specific to geothermal applications.

Area	Risk	Mitigation
General	● Technology — as new geothermal plants are constructed so the more hostile conditions are encountered. Most ideal sites have already been developed leaving those predisposed to higher levels of corrosion, wetter steam, etc.	Monitoring and inspection of plant and steam conditions.

Appendix 2: Member's profiles

Stephen Coward

Stephen is an Underwriting Manager at Copenhagen Reinsurance Company, based in London. He has almost 30 years experience as an underwriter of engineering and industrial risks. He spent the formative part of his career at British Engine where he received technical insurance and underwriter training before taking up appointments with Assurances Générales de France and SCOR, where he spent a total of 16 years.

During his insurance and reinsurance career, he has gained considerable first-hand experience in operational risk underwriting and claims handling, involving the exposures from most industrial sectors around the world, including those associated with construction sites. Stephen is a past Chairman of the London Engineering Group and was a member of the Institute's ASG 230 'Insurance Against Inherent Defects in Buildings'.

Pat Beckett BA, CEng, MIMechE, MInstNDT

Pat is a Chartered Mechanical Engineer with a Bachelors Degree in Material Science and is a Director of the insurance technical services company of Beckett Whelan. He has been closely involved in the international insurance technical field since 1970. Pat specialises in leading programmes to mitigate loss, managing investigations into major losses and failures, and is a practitioner and presenter in loss prevention and physical risk management.

Ann Foss

Ann is the Insurance Manager at Sunley Turriff Holdings Ltd. She joined insurance broker Bland Welch in 1957 and moved to Leslie & Godwin in 1969, remaining in the group, which subsequently became Aon, until 1997. She spent the majority of her time in the Construction Division and one of the last projects in which she became involved before retiring from the Group in 1998 was the Bluewater Development in Kent. She was also a member of the Institute's ASG 230 'Insurance Against Inherent Defects in Buildings'.

Robert Glynn BSc Hons (Chem.Eng), ACII., Chartered Insurance Practitioner, MCIArb, Accredited Mediator

After qualifying from the University of Exeter, Robert has spent more than 18 years in the insurance industry, working mainly in the energy sector. He is a Senior Vice President of Marsh Limited and he advises major energy clients of their insurance needs and is responsible for negotiating the placement of construction, machinery breakdown and operational property insurance programmes for them. Additionally, he advises financial institutions on the types of insurance that should be purchased by their borrowers. Robert has been involved in resolving many extremely large and complex claims and policy disputes. He has also successfully acted as mediator in several cases including the first Lloyd's dispute that was resolved by mediation.

John Hanson MA (Oxon)

John is a graduate of Lincoln College, Oxford, and was admitted as a solicitor in 1977. For several years he was a partner in a law firm in Australia and joined Barlow Lyde & Gilbert in 1986, becoming a partner in 1987. He specialises in policy coverage and recoveries work and is particularly interested in global insurance programmes involving facultative reinsurance issues.

John is a prolific author, having been a previous co-editor of *Reinsurance Practice and the Law*, and a continuing contributing author. He is also co-author of *All Risks Property Insurance*, a book which won the British Insurance Law Association book prize 1996 and it has now been published in its second edition. This year he has also contributed two chapters to *Insurance Disputes*. He frequently writes for the insurance press and lectures at conferences and seminars.

Jason Harris BSc

Jason is the Engineering Department Manager at Chubb Insurance in London. Having graduated as a geologist, he worked in the oil exploration business in both the North Sea and in the USA prior to moving into the insurance discipline. His insurance career started as a freelance risk control engineer working within a small independent consultancy. He then moved to Gan Insurance as an underwriter within its large risk property department in London. In 1997 Jason moved to Chubb Insurance where he has progressed from Underwriter to his present post, in which he concentrates on technical engineering lines with a strong personal focus on the power generation sector.

Peter Kelly

Peter is Deputy Underwriting Manager for the Engineering and Construction Division of AXA Global Risks UK. He started his career with National Vulcan in 1970 and was based in its Head Office in Manchester before moving to London in 1992 as Head of Underwriting. In 1996 he moved to the French insurance company UAP, before it became part of the AXA organisation. He has 30 years experience in the Engineering and Construction market dealing with UK and Overseas risks and is well known as a lecturer at various insurance institutes throughout the UK.

Michael Quy

Mike is an Executive Director, Reinsurance at Willis Limited, specialising in engineering reinsurance. His current role is to arrange underwriting capacity, mainly through treaties, and to find other reinsurance solutions for international underwriters who specialise in engineering classes.

For the majority of his career Mike has been involved in the underwriting of machinery risks, beginning with British Engine in 1967 and transferring to Royal Reinsurance following the Group's integration in 1982. During that time he gained considerable experience through leading international industrial risks. In 1992 he joined French insurer Gan in London as City Engineering Underwriter and was closely involved in establishing its market position in this field. He took up his present position in July 1997.

Joe Telford CEng, FIMarE

Joe is an Engineering Director with Crawford & Company. His career commenced in engineering in Northern England, later moving into the mercantile marine industry. In 1974 he joined a Process Engineering Group as Project Manager, from where he was persuaded to join Toplis & Harding Technical, working internationally and on overseas posting. With the demise of Toplis, he joined Brocklehursts as Engineering Director, remaining in a similar role through various mergers. His knowledge of rotating machinery and failures, including diesel engines and gas turbines, covers most industries and he is a firm advocate of loss prevention.

Philip Veale

Philip is a director of Aon Group's Energy, Construction & Engineering Division and he has 30 years experience in the construction and engineering insurance industry. Initially working in the engineering industry, he came to the insurance in 1971 with Leslie & Godwin International, moving to the Insurance Company of North America as an underwriter in 1973. Philip then spent several years in Hong Kong with Jardine Matheson, returning to the UK to join Sedgwick in 1983. He then joined Alexander & Alexander (which later became part of Aon Group) as a Director of Power and Construction.

Philip is a past Chairman of the Combined Heat & Power Association's London Branch and was also a member of the Institute's ASG 230 'Insurance Against Inherent Defects in Buildings'.